THE MAKAH INDIANS

A Study of an Indian Tribe in Modern American Society

THE
MAKAH INDIANS

A STUDY OF AN INDIAN TRIBE
IN MODERN AMERICAN SOCIETY

by

ELIZABETH COLSON

Senior Lecturer in Social Anthropology in the University of Manchester

MANCHESTER UNIVERSITY PRESS

Published 1953

by

THE UNIVERSITY OF MANCHESTER

at the

UNIVERSITY PRESS

316–324, Oxford Road

Manchester, 13

PREFACE

I GATHERED the material on which this book is based ten years ago, when I lived from November 1941 to November 1942 among the Makah Indians on their reservation at Neah Bay, Washington. The original draft of the book was submitted to Radcliffe College in December 1944 as a doctoral dissertation. Before I could revise it for publication, I became a research officer of the Rhodes-Livingstone Institute and my time was fully committed to a field investigation in Central Africa. In 1951, I became a Simon Research Fellow at the University of Manchester, and under the gentle prodding of Professor M. Gluckman began the revision of the manuscript for publication. In the main, I have followed my original plan and have made no attempt to expand the treatment or to change the argument. I knew the Makah better in 1944 than I do now, and it seems unwise to tamper with the evidence. The chief changes are therefore the addition of information on Indian Service policies unnecessary for an American audience but useful to my British colleagues who are unfamiliar with American material, and a general rewriting to clarify and tighten the original argument. I have also rechristened all Makah who appear in the book, and changed a few minor details in an attempt to protect them from identification by those who know the area.

If I were to do the field work today, this book would be rather different. When I originally went to Neah Bay, I was under the influence of an interest in culture and personality studies, which have occupied the attention of many American anthropologists during the last two decades. I hoped to collect a series of life histories from people of different generations but of the same family lines as a means of testing the hypothesis that basic orientations are resistant to change while cultural content changes much more rapidly. The struggle to understand the heterogeneous community at Neah Bay led to the formulation of quite other problems which had to be solved by an approach more comparable to that developed by British social anthropologists who have also been concerned to under-

stand communities rather than cultures. My original presupposi-
tions and field programme made it difficult to clarify the new
formulations, and the original manuscript is therefore marked
throughout by the struggle. It is my hope that the rewriting
has eliminated the marks of struggle, and that this book will
stand as a picture of a modern American Indian group faced
with the problem of understanding its position within American
society.

Field Work

My original introduction to the people of Neah Bay was
informal, for I arrived in the village without introductions and
knowing no one. Since the village was crowded, and the hotel
filled past capacity, a friendly bus driver found me lodgings for
the night with the Customs Officer and his wife. The following day, in my search for both informants and a more permanent
home, I began my acquaintance with the Makah, who proved
friendly and hospitable. One woman encountered during this
first day's search devoted much of her time during the next week
to introducing me to her older relatives. Another stopped me
on the street to offer her services as an interpreter. Another
found me a room with her stepdaughter.

I announced my purpose in coming to Neah Bay to be that
of obtaining material for a history of the Makah, with special
emphasis upon the past. This seemed as good an explanation
as any, despite the general reaction that either everything to
be known was already written or those who knew anything
worth recording were dead. My position was summed up by
the description soon applied to me as ' that white lady who gets
stories on the old times '. I went about collecting information
in two quite different ways. I used the formal ethnographer-
informant relationship with various elderly people who were
regarded as possibly knowing more about the old life and
Makah history than the rest of the people. I also attempted
to observe what was happening and to meet and talk with as
many people from all age groups as possible.

At one time or another during the year, I used twenty-one
paid informants. They received the fee of twenty-five cents
an hour, which was said by anthropologists at the University
of Washington to be standard in the area, to the extent that

they would pay no more and people would work for no less. These informants numbered eleven men and ten women. Their ages ranged from over eighty to about thirty-eight. Thirteen were over sixty. Twelve were used consistently over many months ; others were formally interviewed only once or twice. Most of them spoke English, but six preferred to speak through interpreters because they felt unable to express themselves adequately in English. Seven interpreters, all women, were used. Three were over fifty, one was in the middle thirties, three were younger. The latter proved unsatisfactory because of their limited knowledge of Makah and were used only a few times. The interpreters also acted as informants, since they volunteered information or expressed ignorance of various customs and thus helped to indicate which groups of people were cognizant of different types of information.

I also attempted to establish myself in a position to observe as much of the life of the community as possible. During the first week I arranged to stay with an Indian family, which was, however, not a typical family since it consisted of a young Makah woman and her Filipino husband. This was not the drawback that it might have been, since the woman's parents and siblings spent much of their time at the house, and kinship ties linked her with most of the Makah in the village. Through her I was introduced to many other households. At the end of eight months, I moved to stay with a white family, belonging to a transient group brought by the war to Neah Bay, who were on friendly terms with many of the Indians.

During the first few months, I used paid informants extensively, and by this means found an entrée into different households which I later followed up by informal interview techniques. During the last few months, I did only enough formal work to maintain the fiction that I was interested in the old times, though by that time most people were aware that I was also interested in the present life of the group. Throughout the year, much of my time was spent in informal visits. I visited forty-three out of the ninety-six Makah households, and in eight I was a frequent visitor. With their members, a relationship of intimacy gradually developed which led to long rambling conversations where I frequently made no attempt to guide the conversation. A few of the older people who refused to become paid informants were especially pleased by this type of approach, and they were willing and eager to explain customs, to talk about their life, and to retail the gossip of the village if I were content to sit with them without pencil and paper.

Besides these visits, there were informal contacts with people on the beach, in the streets, or in the stores and restaurants. I went on a number of fishing trips in the waters off Cape Flattery, and accompanied women on berry-picking excursions. I accompanied the family with which I stayed on trips to near-by cities and also went with them to visit relatives on another reservation. I was invited to birthday parties and on picnics. I also attended everything of community nature that I could : church services, funerals, wedding parties, the Christmas party, the Makah Day celebrations, and the cinema. In these informal contacts, I met people of all ages and saw many in a wide variety of situations. Nevertheless, I do not believe that I was ever in the complete confidence of any member of the group. They told me what they wanted me to hear at any particular time, and I found myself adapting to their behaviour and understanding perfectly why they frequently answered my questions with, ' I don't know. I never asked.' After a few months of living surrounded by the complexities of Makah social life, I learned that this was the best and only protection against the love of gossip, probably common to most small villages where news and comment upon it quickly travels the length of the village and back again. The quickest way to create a lack of response was to seem to be prying into someone's personal affairs. So I learned to wait patiently and talk of ordinary matters until someone felt inclined to grow more confidential.

During formal interviews, I made a verbatim shorthand record, which included what informants said, remarks of others present, incidents during the interview period, and the setting of the interviews. Other notes were written down from memory as soon as possible.

It is difficult to enumerate or even to indicate what recompense people received, for much of the work was so informal that no question of payment or return seems to have been raised. In ordinary contacts, I received more than I ever returned, for not only did people give me information, but they invited me to their houses, loaned me a bed when my landlords were away, and took me about in their cars. At wedding and birthday parties, I followed local custom by presenting a gift to those in whose honour the affairs were held. When I visited Seattle and Victoria, I brought presents back to one and another. Others I invited to the restaurants for snacks, and while we sat we talked lazily of this and that. I was called upon to write letters and to help with draft papers and other matters. I carried messages to friends and relatives in Seattle, and did some investigating about old age pensions. With some, I exchanged books and magazines. For a few others, I acted as baby-sitter so that they could go out for the evening.

By the end of the year, I think I was generally accepted by the Makah as someone fairly harmless, though there were those who still had considerable reservations about the value of what I was presumably doing. In the fall when wedding parties were given by families with whom I had had very little contact, I was included in the list of people to whom the messenger with invitations came. I also suspected that I was beginning to be accepted when those who were drinking sat on with their bottles when I appeared, or when a baby was left in my care though it was never entrusted to any Makah who was not related to the parents. This, however, was a gradual development, and with most members of the group I never came to such intimacy. In the beginning, I had to overcome certain difficulties. I had arrived a month before the attack upon Pearl Harbour at a most exposed part of the coast in an area where there were frequent submarine scares and rumours of expected Japanese raids. Members of the tribe were not immune from arrest by suspicious soldiers who could not distinguish them from Japanese. For a few months, a number of people suspected me of being a Nazi spy and referred to me as 'the Spy Lady'. They used this to attack people with whom I worked. Some of the latter intimated strongly that the tale was believed only because the believers were not being used as informants at the moment and felt insulted at the slight. Some people were also afraid to talk about Makah customs or the past because they were certain that it would expose them to ridicule from other members of the group. The claim was constantly made that no living person knew enough about the old life to discuss it intelligently and that all who did talk were distorting facts so that the history of the tribe reflected the glory of their own family lines. Some people said that whenever anything had been published on the Makah and people learned about it, those who had supplied the information were scorned as liars and braggarts. Moreover, some explained that while they themselves did not believe some of the published statements they were afraid to attempt to give a correct version for fear that matters would only be confused further. Often someone would say, 'We will explain this to you, but because other people tell about this differently we don't want you to write down what we tell you.' On the whole, however, people were generous with their information and time. They put up with what they regarded as stupid questions about commonplaces with only an occasional demur.

There is much information which I did not obtain. I was never able to be sure whether or not men have obtained guardian spirits in recent years. I know little about what happens immediately after death in a family. I failed to investigate the political organization of the tribe sufficiently to give a clear account of its workings. I was able to attend one council meeting, but not the tribal meeting. I never attended a court session, though I talked with the judges, the man employed as policeman, and many of those who received sentences from the court. For the study of the community, I also failed to do enough work with the whites living in the village. I realized the importance of such work, but was never able to rid myself of the feeling that it was a dull job which could be pushed aside for more interesting ones. As a result, I know the interaction of the Makah with the whites chiefly from the Makah side. However, I had considerable contact with one of the school teachers, and talked with various others. I also had informal conversations with the Customs Officer and his wife, with the Presbyterian minister and his wife, with the white woman in charge of the Sewing Room, and with a few of the other permanent white residents. I lived for several months with a white family belonging to the transient group and met such of their friends as visited their house. Through Makah, I met a few other transient families.

Certain inadequacies in the data are due to the limitations placed on a young woman. The people I knew best were women. The old men I knew because they were informants. The young and middle-aged men I knew little about save from village gossip. It was impossible for a woman to join the groups of men as they sat watching the beach and the boats in the bay.

I made no attempt to learn the Makah language. Since most people spoke in English, there was little opportunity to acquire the language in ordinary contacts. Even in a community such as Neah Bay where English is rapidly becoming the only medium of communication, it was a mistake to give so little attention to language. By the end of my stay, I knew a few words which occasionally gave me the drift of a conversation or allowed me to check upon the thoroughness of an interpreter, but I could not frame a sentence in Makah nor understand any extended conversation.

ACKNOWLEDGMENTS

I am indebted to Radcliffe College and to the American Association of University Women whose grants of travelling fellowships made it possible for me to do the field work at Neah Bay and to prepare the original manuscript on which this work is based, and to the University of Manchester for the Simon Research Fellowship which permitted me to spend time in revising the manuscript for publication.

Indirectly responsible for the initiation and carrying out of the study are Drs. Wilson D. and Ruth Sawtell Wallis, who led me into anthropology and saw to it that I stayed there, and Drs. B. W. and Ethel G. Aginsky, who trained me in field work. Dr. Clyde Kluckhohn acted as counsellor and supervisor while I was collecting the field data, and he and Dr. William Kelly supervised the writing of my original thesis. Members of the staff at the University of Washington also gave assistance. Dr. Erna Gunther was most kind in outlining the difficulties to be expected in working among the Makah, and made available to me the resources of the University of Washington Library. Dr. Melville Jacobs was most gracious in placing at my disposal his extensive knowledge of the ethnography of the Washington Area. Mr. and Mrs. Raymond G. Day of Seattle gave hospitality and encouragement. More recently my former colleagues of the Rhodes-Livingstone Institute and present colleagues of the Department of Social Anthropology at the University of Manchester—Professor M. Gluckman, Dr. J. A. Barnes, and Dr. I. Cunnison—have patiently criticized the revised draft, and wherever possible I have bowed to their dicta on English usage. However, despite their urging I have maintained the right of the anthropologist to use a few native terms in his text, and thus fishing boats have remained fishing boats and have not become smacks, although built with small cabins and holds, in which a number of men can sleep. I have regretfully accepted their stand that docks are jetties, though neither I nor the people of Neah Bay would recognize the familiar structures under that name. But they, and especially Professor Gluckman, are responsible for a general tightening of style and presentation. I, of course, am responsible for the material and for the analysis, and must accept the blame for any lack of clarity or gaps in the information supplied.

Finally, I must thank the Makah. Their magnificent vitality and zest for life, their outrageous humour, their independence and courage, are not reflected in these pages. A novelist and poet is needed to give the full flavour of the turmoil of their life. Some of those who helped me are now dead. The rest I have sought to protect by such disguise as I could give them. Knowing the quarrels which have arisen in the past over whatever has been written about their customs, I cannot expect them to like this book if they should ever chance to see it. But it is written out of a great respect and affection for them.

Various aspects of the old Makah culture have been dealt with by ethnographers who have worked with the tribe. Since I have been dealing with present Makah life, I have not attempted to summarize this material in the text. I have given, however, as full a bibliography as possible. Thanks to the assistance of the staffs of the University of Washington Library, and the Library of the Peabody Museum of Harvard University, I was able to go through the material which had appeared up to the end of 1944. American publications are not always obtainable in Central Africa or in Great Britain, and I may therefore have missed items which appeared since then. I have also made some comparisons with the situation of other American Indian groups, but again I have not been able to see all the relevant reports that have appeared in recent years. As I began to write this preface, after completing the final draft for the press, I discovered the very excellent report by George A. Pettitt on the Quileute of La Push, which shows a situation so similar to that of the Makah that my text should be studded with cross-references to it. I regret that it is too late to make the detailed comparisons with the Quileute whom Mr. Pettitt has described so well and so appositely for my purposes.

ORTHOGRAPHY

Though only a few Makah words appear in the body of the text, I give below an orthography, which is based on that used by Sapir and Swadesh in their work on the Nootka.[1] The phonemic system of the Makah language has never been worked out. My own phonetic recording is hazardous as I am neither a trained linguist nor am I blessed with an ear for phonetic subtleties. However, material published by Waterman corroborates my findings.[2]

TABLE OF CONSONANTS

| | STOPS | | | SPIRANTS | | | AFFRICATIVES | | |
	Voiced	Voiceless	Glottal	Voiced	Voiceless		Voiced	Voiceless	Glottal
LABIALS	b	p	p'						
DENTALS	d	t	t'		s			c	c'
ALVEOLARS					š			č	č'
PALATALS	g	ĸ	ĸ'		x				
VELARS		ꞯ	ꞯ'		x̣				
LATERALS				l	ł			ƛ'	ƛ'
GLOTTAL		ʔ			h				

[1] Sapir and Swadesh, 1939, pp. 12–13.   [2] Waterman, 1920, 5–8.

Both palatal and velar voiceless and glottalized stops may be palatalized. Palatalization is indicated by the letter ^w placed above the sound palatalized.

TABLE OF VOWELS

	Front	Middle	Back	Back Rounded
High	i I			u
Mid-wide . .	e E	A		o
Low			a ɑ	ɔ

i as in mach*i*ne	a as in bar
I as in p*i*n	ɑ as in hat
e as in g*a*te	u as in r*u*le
E as in m*e*t	o as in note
A as in ide*a*	ɔ as in ought

There are also the diphthongs a̰ as in a̰isle ; and o̰i as in bo̰il. The semivowels w and y are substantially as in English. Where vowels are lengthened this is indicated by a following dot.

Manchester, 1951.

CONTENTS

xv

LIST OF TABLES AND CHARTS

LIST OF MAPS

CHAPTER I

INTRODUCTION

A STUDY OF ASSIMILATION

AMERICAN Indians who live upon the reservations scattered about the United States find themselves in a unique position in relation to the greater American society. They are a part of this society, but neither they nor the whites with whom they come in contact have been able to rid themselves of the belief that Indians, as Indians, do not belong in the same way as do other Americans, including those who have come to the country in recent years. Generation after generation, large numbers of immigrants have been absorbed into the body of American society, and their descendants live together as holders of a common culture, with few signs of their divergent origins. Their assimilation has been brought about without any direct pressure by the Government to produce this end. The American Indians have been subject to systematic attempts to hasten their assimilation. The United States Indian Service was for many years the agent of a policy which was expected to lead to the extinction of the American Indians as a people and to their absorption into the general society of the nation. Today American Indian tribes continue to exist. They are deviant groups within American society. But we have few studies which seek to define the extent and manner of the deviation. The anthropologists have concerned themselves chiefly with the problem of describing the manner of life of the different tribes in the last days of their independence, or have attempted to deal with particular problems of culture change in a somewhat reified fashion. The result is that we know more about how American Indians lived a hundred years ago than we do about how they are living today.

This book is an attempt to describe a particular Indian group, the Makah of Neah Bay, Washington, as it exists at the present time. Or rather, though I write throughout in the present tense, as it existed in 1941-2, at the period when my field study was made. I shall be particularly concerned with the problem

B

of assimilation, and the definition of the factors which lead to the continued existence of the Makah as a people. To do this, it will also be necessary to consider the nature of the differences which distinguished them from other Americans.

Since this is a study of assimilation rather than acculturation, I have seen no reason to produce a detailed reconstruction of the culture of the Makah of the pre-reservation period.[1] One of the factors distinguishing the Makah at the present time is the possession of a body of tradition about their former life, but I believe that this can be most satisfactorily studied as an element in their present situation. It gives them the assurance that they are a unique people with a common past. It defines the terms upon which they interact with one another in certain situations. To this extent, the tradition, though not the cultural reality to which it refers, is of importance to the Makah and therefore to this study. It will also be relevant to ask why the tradition appears to be less important to the Makah than it is in the present life of certain other Indian groups. This I shall attempt to relate to favourable economic conditions which have permitted the Makah to develop along new lines, with the result that they have had little need to obtain a nebulous security through dwelling upon a romanticized group past. I shall also attempt to relate their failure to live in accordance with their tradition and their general adoption of much of American culture to the efforts of the Indian Service during the long rule of the Neah Bay agency when the Makah were encouraged to break with their past and to transform themselves into American citizens. That the Indian Service has been more successful here than elsewhere appears to be due to the small size of the group, to their accessibility in villages close to the agency, and to the economic factors which simplified the work of the Indian Service.

Other factors which distinguish the Makah from white Americans are their political organization in the tribe, their joint owner-

---

[1] I define *acculturation* to mean the changes which take place within the culture of a given group through contact with people or peoples of a different culture. *Assimilation* I define as the amalgamation of people derived from different groups into one social body whose members appear in the same social organizations and where the group to which the different individuals originally belonged is not instrumental in defining their rôles within these organizations. Essentially, complete assimilation implies the disappearance of the cultural differences originally characterizing the two groups.

ship of the reservation, and their status as wards of the government. These are direct developments of the work of the Indian Service, and are probably more conducive to the perpetuation of the Makah as a group than is the influence of their traditions. Finally, the Makah feel that they and other Indians do not find complete acceptance from the whites, whom they in turn castigate as exploiters and snobs. This feeling has developed in response to incidents which have occurred throughout the immediate past, and today it is used by the Makah as a justification for any advantages they derive from their peculiar status within American society.

Finally, it will be seen that individual Makah are able to take their places within American society, and many leave the reservation for a time to live among whites. On the reservation, the Makah approximate more and more to the whites in custom, and govern less and less of their lives by reference to their traditions. They associate freely with whites in many situations. Despite this, their group persists, buttressed by the development of a particular legal status and rights in property and by prejudices maintained by both Makahs and whites, which seem to assume differences in culture which in fact do not exist. If the present trend continues, in another generation the Makah will differ from the whites only in their status as wards of the government and members of a tribal political organization in which vests the ownership of the reservation. It will then be easily seen that their sense of local tradition and their pride in their common past are equivalent to those held by the members of many small long-settled communities in other parts of the nation.

The Makah and their History

The Makah in 1860

The Makah first appear in recorded history at the end of the eighteenth century when they were already settled in their present home about Cape Flattery, just to the south of Vancouver Island. Their territory included an area extending some fifteen miles on either side of the Cape, southward along the Pacific Coast and eastward along the coast of the Strait of Juan de Fuca. They had no tradition of any previous home and must have been long established in this area.

They spoke a dialect of the Nootka language, like their neighbours to the north along the western coast of Vancouver Island, and their culture was very similar to that of other Nootka groups. With them, the Makah shared traits characteristic of the peoples of the Northwest Coast. Political organization was on the basis of villages and lineages, the latter unnamed patrilineal groups. There was no clan system. The Makah lived in five winter villages, each an independent entity. In the summer the people from these villages moved to three summer villages nearer to the Cape and to the halibut fisheries. In the fall, they camped in smaller groups along the rivers running into ocean and strait to exploit the salmon fisheries. The return of the bad weather of the winter months brought them back to the winter villages for a round of feasts and ceremonials.

Within each village, the population was divided into three classes : ' chiefs ', commoners, and slaves. The latter were captured in warfare, or they were purchased from other tribes who had acquired them by capture. Only members of the first two classes were regarded as true members of the village communities. To some extent class position was hereditary, and slave blood was a stigma to any member of the free classes. Property in fishing grounds, berry patches, and coastal strips, as well as in ceremonial privileges, was vested in the lineages and controlled by the lineage heads.

Three secret societies existed which had both religious and curative functions. The ceremonies of the societies formed a prominent part of the winter life of each village. All three societies accepted both men and women as members. Into one every member of the community was initiated in childhood. The other two were more limited in membership, although they also received child initiates. Men and women were also expected to have individual religious experiences. Young boys spent periods away from the villages when they fasted and sought to obtain guardian spirits which would give them power for specific types of success. Girls did so very rarely, but were not absolutely debarred from seeking spirit guardians. Since boys sought guardians to give them power for particular occupations, there was some degree of specialization, into whale hunters, seal hunters, doctors, gamblers, warriors, and fishermen.

The Makah were primarily a seafaring people who spent their

lives either on the water or close to the shore, seldom venturing more than a few miles inland. Most of their subsistence came from the sea, where they fished for salmon, halibut, and other fish, and hunted for whale and seal. The excess over what they needed for consumption within the village was traded to other tribes in return for many of the raw materials and some of the finished articles used in the daily and ceremonial life of the village. There was little in their material culture therefore to differentiate them from other tribes about them. They were the middlemen in an extensive coastwise trade which ran from the Columbia River north to Nootka Sound, and they also had extensive trade contacts with the peoples of Puget Sound.

Whale hunting for which they had elaborate techniques and ritual played a central rôle in their culture. The whale hunter, since he obtained large stocks of whale oil and meat, was able to gather the other material possessions available to members of the group and to take his place in the system of potlatching in which he showed his greatness by distributing great quantities of property to his guests.[1] Since they were expected to return these gifts at some future date with some increase in value, he became a wealthier man, and his prestige was great. His success was regarded as proof that he had acquired a powerful guardian spirit, or several such, and he was therefore endowed with supernatural power as well as material possessions. For their own subsistence and for a trade article, the Makah were equally or even more dependent upon their halibut fishing, but this fishing played a secondary rôle in the activities and prestige system of the group. Every man fished for halibut ; only a few rose to the heights of becoming a successful harpooner of whales.

The Makah were an aggressive warlike people who made frequent raids against neighbouring tribes from which they

[1] Potlatching appeared throughout the Northwest Coast area, though it varied considerably from group to group. In its broadest definition, the potlatch is ' a congregation of people, ceremoniously and often individually invited to witness a demonstration of family prerogative ' (Barnett, 1938, pp. 349–58). More specifically, the host summons guests to whom he distributes large quantities of goods and before whom he expounds the claims of his family to particular property in economic rights and in titles, songs, and other ceremonial prerogatives. This confirms his position and that of his family. His guests must at some future date hold an equivalent affair, or they lose prestige.

returned with captives and the heads of victims. The warrior, however, acquired no special status or honours, and warfare was of secondary importance to a people engrossed in whaling and potlatching, and for whom the potlatch afforded an alternative method to that of warfare for the humbling of rivals and the enhancing of the prestige of the leaders of the community.[1]

Prior to about 1863, when the Indian Service established an agent at Neah Bay to control the Makah and supervise their affairs, there was little in the nature of the contacts with the whites to make the Makah change their habitual activities in any detail. It is not to be assumed, however, that at this period the Makah had a static culture which operated within a closed orbit into which no new influences entered. Actually, I believe, few groups in aboriginal days were more open to varied influences from outside than were the Makah. Very probably there was a constant influx of new ideas and customs. Situated as they were on the trade route between Nootka Sound and the Columbia River and on the route which led eastward to Puget Sound and thence to the interior, they were in a position to meet numerous different groups practising different customs. Their accessibility to new influences was increased by customs such as slavery, intermarriage with other tribes, distant trips for trade or attendance at potlatches, and ceremonies. During a part of the year, family groups often left the villages with which they were primarily affiliated to live with relatives in other localities.

There was thus a constant interchange of ideas between the Makah and members of surrounding tribes, though the influence of those living to the north was particularly strong ; for in this direction there was no language barrier to make communication difficult.

Contacts with the Whites

The earliest contacts between the Makah and whites began in 1788 with the appearance of exploring expeditions and fur traders in the first assault upon the Northwest Coast. The chief effect of this contact was the development of trade with the whites, which resulted in the adoption of many new goods by

[1] The above sketch is based on Swan, 1869. For a generalized description of Northwest Coast culture, see Forde, 1948, Chapter VI. For the Nootka, see Drucker, 1951.

the Makah and the creation of a greater market for such goods
as the Makah themselves produced and which they had previously
traded with other Indian groups. There were also devastating
epidemics which broke out in the wake of the trading vessels.
Throughout this early period, however, the Makah were not
disturbed in the possession of their land nor did whites settle
among them. Within reach of their canoes there were only a
few small settlements of whites even in the last years of their
independence.

After the creation of the Indian agency at Neah Bay, the
Makah found themselves exposed to two different sets of influences stemming from the whites. One involved the highly
conscious administration of their affairs by employees of the
Indian Service. The other sprang from the continued presence
of whites for other than administrative and educational purposes.
The latter was of less importance than it was for many groups
of Indians. Living as the Makah did at the tip of the Olympic
Peninsula, surrounded on the landward side by great stands of
almost impenetrable forests which only now are being attacked
by lumber companies and settlers, they were not exposed to the
full onslaught of American colonization. Before there was any
question of settlement within their territory, the United States
Government made treaties with the Makah in which their
reservation was created. Later attempts by whites to settle
within the borders of the reservation were successfully combated
by Indian Service employees and by the Makah themselves,
though on one occasion the presence of troops was required
before the whites were evicted. The Makah were never subjected to successive despoilment of their land. Instead, at one
period, the boundaries of the reservation were extended, and
between its borders and the nearest settlements of whites were
the protecting forests which acted as a barrier against the onrush
of ' civilized ' men.

The Makah, however, were free to leave their reservation for
trading expeditions to the settlements in the Sound area or on
Vancouver Island, or to work in the hop fields, the berry farms,
and the lumber camps that grew up in the settled areas to the
east. Some accompanied sealing boats on the long trip to Alaska
and the Bering Sea, where they poached on the seal rookeries.
During the summer months, boats touched at Neah Bay.

Later, Neah Bay became a rendezvous for the fishing boats which discovered the great fishing banks in the Flattery waters. On the reservation, however, the whites were subject to the authority of the Indian agent who could prevent those whites whom he regarded as inimical to the welfare of his Indian wards from landing in their territory. He also had some veto power over the importation of new activities learned by the Makah on their visits to the settled areas.

Within their own territory, the Makah were not faced with any drastic readjustment in their lives due to the presence of whites who had no government authority. Throughout the period that the agency existed, there were no cataclysmic changes in their subsistence resources. The resources of the land and sea upon which they had always depended remained available to them. The entrance of the whites into the fishing grounds eventually depleted the fishing banks, but it was not until the agency had been established for over fifty years that the effect of indiscriminate fishing was felt.[1] Even then it was still possible to derive an adequate living from fishing the Flattery waters. Throughout their contact with the whites, the Makah remained self-supporting and never became dependent upon the issue of government rations, though during the depression of the 1930's some of them required government relief.

This economic independence is an important element in the situation of the Makah. Probably of equal importance is their continued protection from the encroachment of white settlers. In both, they differed from most of the other Indian groups in the United States and Canada, though not from other tribes along the north Pacific Coast. Within the reservation, the most important element affecting their behaviour was the presence and the demands of the Indian agents. The government itself by its creation of the reservation and the institution of the agency ensured that the Makah would not be faced within their home area with any need to adjust to constant demands from other white groups. At the same time, the Makah, as individuals, lost all right to retain their own customs if these clashed with standards approved by the Indian Service.

[1] By 1934, according to one estimate, the fishing banks off Cape Flattery had been depleted to about one-fourth their former size. Since then measures of conservation may have changed the trend. Cf. Gregory and Barnes, 1939.

The Indian Agency

In 1855, the Makah by treaty with the United States Government ceded the territory which they claimed to control and received in return a small reservation occupying a portion of this area. By the terms of their treaty, they were to be given an Indian agent to supervise their interests, tools, and equipment for use in cultivating their land, and teachers and artisans to train them in civilized pursuits. The terms of the treaty were not enforced until 1863, when the agency was first established. From then until the abolition of the Neah Bay agency in the 1930's, after the tribe accepted the Indian Reorganization Act, the group was under the continuous domination of one Indian agent after another.

Because of the isolation of the reservation, the agents received little attention from their superiors who were generally ignorant of the specific happenings in this remote area. An old Makah who lived through the agency period told me once : ' We weren't allowed to have any of our Indian things because the agents didn't believe in it. I don't know if the Indian Service was against it, or whether it was just the agents. I always think of it as though we were just a bunch of wild animals penned in here with the agent who could do anything he liked to us. The agent was just like a king, and he could do as he pleased.'

The Makah had little opportunity to escape from such measures as the agent wished to use. They lived in small villages close to the shore. The village farthest from the agency headquarters was only fifteen miles away and like all the villages it was located at a spot easily accessible from the sea. The Makah were shore-dwellers, who lived upon the products of the sea. The forests pressing close at their backs had few attractions for them. They could not retire from the supervision of their agents into any mountain or desert fastnesses where the difficulty of pursuit would leave them some measure of freedom. Their only escape lay in crossing the Strait to join other Indian communities on Vancouver Island ; but in doing so, they left behind their own people and lost contact with their own culture. The agent, as the representative of a government which had troops stationed less than a day's journey away, was in a position to enforce his orders. In the early days, there were a few attempts to stand against his authority. Makah warriors raided up the Strait to take Clallam heads when the government failed to act quickly enough in punishing the Clallam Indians for killing some Makah. Makah parents refused to place their children in the government school. But after the prompt appearance of American soldiers who arrested the warriors and took them off to prison in the one case, and the arrest of the recalcitrant parents by agency police in the other, the Makah seem to have accepted the agent's authority as something which might be evaded but not successfully opposed.

A situation such as this would seem to be an ideal one for implementing a programme of social change. The situation included a small group of people, never more than six hundred strong during the agency period, who were concentrated at a few spots along the coastline, and a number of representatives of a government which had laid down a policy for the control of the group and was prepared to back its representatives by force of arms if necessary. The agents were in a position to force a good deal of personal supervision upon their charges, if they wished to do so. The people themselves were regarded as having no recognizable right to manage their own affairs or to decide whether or not they would accept the terms, or the aims, of the programme laid down for them. Legally they were wards of the government and might be treated as though they were irresponsible children. Implicit in the situation was the assumption that the Indians were children who must be trained to become members of American society. The first agent sent to the Makah made this explicit when he said : ' Force is what we need, not only to carry out the wise regulations of the department, but to make them receive the benefits we desire to bestow upon them.' [1] The present-day culture of the Makah may therefore be regarded as partly the result of the impact of the agency upon successive generations of the tribe.

Indian Service Policies

So far, no discussion of the programme developed by the Indian Service for its wards has been attempted. In the span of eighty years, there were shifts in detail and in emphasis. In this sense, it is impossible to speak of ' a programme '. But

[1] *Report of the Commissioner of Indian Affairs,* 1866, p. 67.

through the reports of the Indian Commissioners for the first seventy years of the period, there is a remarkable consistency with regard to the ultimate goal towards which the policies of the Service were oriented. This goal, towards which all the early government employees paid at least lip service, was the complete assimilation of the Indians, and therefore the Makah, into American society in as short a period as possible. The Indians were to be 'civilized', and the programme would fail in so far as they emerged from the moulding process one jot different from the ideal average American. This was enunciated by the Commissioners, and echoed in the reports issued by the agents on the reservation.

In 1863, the Commissioner speaks of his policy as one 'designed to civilize and reclaim the Indians within our borders, and induce them to adopt the customs of civilization. . . .' [1] In 1887, the Commissioner reports that the Indians have made great progress which is shown 'in increased knowledge and experience as to the arts of agriculture, in enlarged facilities for stock-growing, in better buildings and better home appointments, and in the adoption of the dress and customs of the white man'.[2] Later in his report, he insists that Indian children must be taught in English on the ground that

To teach Indian school children in their native tongue is practically to exclude English, and to prevent them from acquiring it. This language, which is good enough for a white man and a black man, ought to be good enough for the red man. It is also believed that teaching an Indian youth in his own barbarous dialect is a positive detriment to him. The first step to be taken toward civilization, toward teaching the Indian the mischief and folly of continuing in their barbarous practices, is to teach them the English language. . . . If we expect to infuse into the rising generation the leaven of American citizenship, we must remove the stumbling-blocks of hereditary customs and manners, and of these language is one of the most important elements.[3]

In 1903, the Commissioner is still insistent that the work of the Indian Service is the civilizing of the Indian and the obliteration of cultural differences between Indians and whites.

[1] *Report of the Commissioner of Indian Affairs*, 1863, p. 6.
[2] *Report of the Commissioner of Indian Affairs*, 1887, p. iii.
[3] *Report of the Commissioner of Indian Affairs*, 1887, p. xxiii.

There are only two phases of the Indian question : One, that the American Indian shall remain in the country as a survival of the aboriginal inhabitants, a study for the ethnologist, a toy for the tourist, a vagrant at the mercy of the State, and a continual pensioner upon the bounty of the people ; the other, that he shall be educated to work, live, and act as a reputable, moral citizen, and thus become a self-supporting, useful member of society. The latter is the policy of the present administration of Indian Affairs, and if carried to its legitimate conclusion will settle for all time the 'Indian question'. Such a settlement will be an honor to the Government and a credit to the Indian. He will then pass out of our national life as a painted, feather-crowned hero of the novelist to add the current of his free, original American blood to the heart of this great nation. . . . To educate the Indian is to prepare him for the abolishment of tribal relations, to take his land in severalty, and in the sweat of his brow and by the toil of his hands to carve out, as his white brother has done, a home for himself and his family.[1]

The policy, as enunciated from the central offices of the Indian Service and echoed by the agents on the reservation, was not a selective one, of eradicating certain activities of the Indians while desired traits from white American culture were introduced. The policy was one of wholesale transformation, or the substitution of one entire way of life for an alien one. Into the 1920's,

The cumulated and inherited official policy . . . was moving ahead impersonally, and with a ruthless benevolence or a benevolent ruthlessness. That policy was one of extinguishing the Indianhood of all Indians through all the devices within the control of a government whose power over Indians was absolute ; it included a continuing expropriation of the Indian land.[2]

During the 1920's, there are signs that a new approach to the Indian problem was developing, but it is not until 1931, a time when the Makah had been under the Indian Service for seventy years, that a Commissioner speaks of his purpose as one of helping Indians 'to adapt themselves successfully to modern life with as little cultural loss as possible . . .'[3]

The Indian Service and its employees throughout this period

[1] *Report of the Commissioner of Indian Affairs*, 1903, pp. 2–3.
[2] *Report of the Commissioner of Indian Affairs*, 1940, p. 357.
[3] *Report of the Commissioner of Indian Affairs*, 1931, pp. 6–7.

gave implicit acceptance to the concept of culture. It was assumed that the behaviour of the Indians was not biologically determined, but that by careful training they could be induced to acquire the culture of the white Americans with whom they were in contact. The race of their charges was taken as given, but race was not regarded as a barrier to the acquisition of American culture.

The temper of the reports of the Commissioners is reflected in the published reports of the agents on the reservation, which in terms of an ultimate goal remain remarkably uniform. Agents varied in assessing the period of years necessary for attaining the goal of complete Americanization, and with reference to the means whereby it was to be achieved, but never with regard to the desirability of the goal or the necessity of attaining it. The actual implementation of the policy varied, however, with the particular personality of the agent who at any one time was in charge of the reservation. The station was too isolated for the superior officials of the Indian Service to have much opportunity of keeping check upon the activities of the workers on the reservation to see how thoroughly the official programme was being carried out or by what measures. The only check upon an agent's work seems to have been the visits of an inspector, who appeared perhaps three times a year for a visit of a few hours and then departed to make his report. Some of the agents, according to their own account, were repressive and prohibited the practice of any activities which they considered to be Indian. Others were less stringent. They allowed the older people to live much as they pleased, so long as their activities outraged no particular standards of humanity or legal principle, while they concentrated their efforts on isolating the children from contact with tribal life and on indoctrinating them with American culture. Others still were accused by their successors of accomplishing nothing while in charge of the reservation save to pocket the money allotted for the running of the agency and the school.[1]

Despite the variation in the intensity of the programme and the stringency with which it was carried out, it is safe to say that certain general trends appeared consistently over long periods

[1] See the reports of the agents for Neah Bay published in the *Annual Reports of the Commissioner of Indian Affairs*, 1862–1906. After this date, the agents' reports are not published.

of time. Activities of a ceremonial or ritual nature were discouraged or prohibited. Any occasion which drew crowds of people for some purpose other than that immediately obvious to and approved by the observer from another society seem to have fallen under suspicion. Potlatches, gambling games, the performance of Indian dances were usually forbidden. The ceremonies of the secret religious and curing societies were first expurgated of features regarded as particularly obnoxious and then banned altogether. Those who insisted on holding the performances or on participating in them ran the risk of punishment by the agent. The use of native curing methods was first ridiculed and then forbidden, while the agency doctor was sent to treat the sick. Makah doctors who continued to practise were called before the agent and ordered to cease under penalty of a jail sentence.

These were obvious foci for attack, but the daily life of the people was not exempt from interference. The agents encouraged men to build houses of their own on the American pattern, and in some cases helped them with the building, and urged them to abandon the old ' smokehouses ' which housed a number of families under one roof. Eventually, the few remaining large houses were torn down at the agent's orders. The agents or their subordinates at times instituted a weekly check-up of the households. One reported :

I have made it a part of my duties to visit each separate lodge once a week and examine their daily mode of living, correct irregularities, reprimand any cases of misdemeanors, and impress on their minds the importance of a higher standard of morality, which, added to their expanding ideas of civilization, is having the desired effect on the Indian mind.[1]

Sometimes the agent inspected the housekeeping of the women, and according to older Makah informants, one made it a practice to give women who failed to meet his standards of cleanliness a few days' imprisonment in the agency jail in which to meditate upon the desirability of better housekeeping. The beaches in front of the villages were inspected, and the men required or persuaded to keep them clean and free from refuse. The dress to which the Makah were accustomed was regarded as indecent,

[1] *Report of the Commissioner of Indian Affairs*, 1891, p. 162.

and 'civilized' clothing was substituted. Among the signs of progress faithfully recorded in the reports year after year was the increase in the number of people wearing 'citizen's dress'.

The sexual life of the Makah also received the careful attention of their guardians, who, administration after administration, wrote of their measures for keeping the people to a rigid monogamy. In 1879, an agent wrote : 'It is a pleasure to state that although the morality of these people is not of a very high order . . . I have, by punishment and otherwise, greatly reduced crime in this direction, and cases of infidelity are comparatively rare now.' [1] Twenty years later, one of his successors seems equally jubilant about his success in this direction, having solved the problem of infidelity to his satisfaction by ordering that couples who formed liaisons should be punished unless they first went through the formalities of divorce and remarriage and then refusing to permit them to obtain divorces. Men and women who lived together without some sanctioned form of marriage ceremony were given their choice of immediate marriage or a jail sentence. If an unmarried girl conceived, she was forced to name the father of her child, who was then tried before the agent, and if found guilty required to marry her unless he already had a wife.

Warfare and feuds were forbidden. The class system of the Makah, with its recognition of 'chiefs', commoners, and slaves, met with disapproval. Slavery was abolished, and the social status of the former slaves was ignored by agents who attempted to treat all Makah as though they were on the same social level. Discrimination along the lines of status institutionalized in Makah society was theoretically forbidden. Where leadership from the tribe was necessary, the agents attempted to set up men of their own choice rather than accept leaders recognized by the Makah. These were ignored, as far as possible, because they were regarded as upholders of tribal tradition and opponents of the government programme of change. American legal procedure, with police, courts, and definite sentences, was instituted to replace the controls formerly recognized by the Makah. The offences as well as the procedure were determined by the decision of the agent and those behind him in the Indian Service rather than by the people themselves. An attempt was made to supersede Makah concepts

[1] *Report of the Commissioner of Indian Affairs,* 1879, p. 146.

of property and of labour by those derived from American systems of values. The potlatch was frowned upon and then forbidden because it mobilized the economic resources of the Makah in a manner alien to the comprehension of the agents who saw in it only a custom which first led people to hoard their wealth and then to give it away without profit to themselves. Makah land-holding was revolutionized. Under the old system each extended family had rights over certain stretches of the coast and to fishing sites. These were now considered to be the common property of the tribe. Later an attempt was made to introduce a system of individual land-holding. The reservation was surveyed, and each member of the tribe received an allotment of a certain number of acres as his private property. For a period the land was to be held in trust for him by the Indian Service. When the trust period should expire, the land was to pass into his control, and he would be free to rent, sell, or use it as he pleased. The unallotted portion of the reservation would then be sold and the money divided among the tribe. The Trust period for the Makah Reservation had not expired at the time of the passing of the Indian Reorganization Act, and the land was reconverted into a tribal trust safe from alienation. Members of the tribe say that one of their reasons for accepting the Reorganization Act was the fear that when the trust period expired, individual members of the tribe would sell their holdings to the whites who were hovering on their borders ready for the chance to acquire the valuable timber holdings and fishing sites.

More extreme measures against the group were meditated and could have been carried through. At the time the Indian Service was engaged in a war of extermination, not against individual Indians but against social groups, and any measure which hastened the victory might be regarded as justified and useful. The Makah were in a position where they did not know and could not know when some new ruling would be made that would further disrupt their life. One of the agents seriously put forward the suggestion that the Makah be divided and segregated on generation lines.

The greatest drawback we have to contend with is that after the girls and boys who have attended school for from five to ten years settle down among their tribes, they are soon overcome by the ridicule and jeerings of the old Indians at any attempts they may make to live like white people—sitting at the table to eat their meals with china plates and dishes, and knives and forks—at any unusual care in keeping their houses nice and clean, or at the least attempt to act as Christians should. The influence exerted by these older savages over them is very deleterious. As is the case with all Indians, they can not stand being laughed at. Some of these young Indians, if they marry and go to housekeeping by themselves, do overcome and withstand this, and do live quite nicely ; but if they go to live in the lodges with the older ones they soon succumb, and in a few years can scarcely be distinguished from those who have not attended school. As a remedy for this, it has struck me that it would advance these people many years toward civilization could a reservation be set apart for all old Indians, say all that are over fifty-five years of age. Let them live and die together, having no intercourse with the younger ones except at long and rare intervals. By the time the old ones die, my belief is that the others would be living in as civilized a manner as the same class of white people ; indeed, perhaps better. I have never seen this idea advanced, but hope some abler hand will take hold of and develop it. It certainly would, I think, be an economical solution of the Indian question.[1]

When such drastic measures could be proposed by one who was in authority over them, nothing that was theirs could be considered to be safe from interference or suppression. Agents did not bother to investigate a particular custom before they acted to ban it. One wrote : ' All heathenish and barbarous practices I have endeavoured to stop, and where possible prohibit altogether, such as the " cloqually dance ". This dance, from what I have heard of it, must be a cross between the devil's dance and the can-can.' [2]

The Makah did not tamely accept the numerous attacks upon their own customs. They showed considerable ingenuity in adapting their customs to suit the agent's whims while still retaining the essential elements. After potlatches were forbidden, one member of the tribe who had some acquaintance with European customs succeeded in giving a potlatch with the agent's approval by quietly waiting until Christmas time, when he put up a spruce tree, hung his goods upon this and then gave them away as Christmas presents with the blessings of the agent and the missionary. For some years after this, the Makah spent

[1] *Report of the Commissioner of Indian Affairs*, 1887, p. 211.
[2] *Report of the Commissioner of Indian Affairs*, 1890, p. 224.

much of the profits from their various enterprises in seeing who could give the biggest Christmas parties. Later, they adapted birthday parties with equal enthusiasm. During the most repressive periods, they also evaded their agents by going off in their canoes or boats and landing just beyond the reservation boundaries. There they proceeded to have their parties with full enjoyment of their agent's helplessness in the territory beyond his jurisdiction. Older members of the tribe still snicker reminiscently when they recall how the agent used to sit glowering on his porch while they came paddling home after a glorious day spent in defiance of his orders. Nevertheless, the attempts at adaptation and evasion were rearguard actions, with little effect in the long run.

In the meantime, accompanying the prohibition and attempt to exterminate the practices regarded as 'Indian' and 'uncivilized', a positive programme for indoctrinating the people and especially the young with the culture of the whites was instituted. Government employees were sent to the reservation to train children and adults in what were regarded as civilized pursuits : farming, carpentry, and blacksmithing. It is noteworthy that although the Makah were fishermen, seal hunters, and whalers who from the resources of ocean and strait received a high return for their labours, no particular attempt was made to further these activities. Instead, the agents were told to turn them into agriculturalists, though they knew nothing about farming and it was admitted by all who knew the area that the soil of the reservation was not fertile enough to warrant extensive cultivation. Farming was a civilized occupation and therefore to be encouraged. Agents frequently protested against this aspect of the policy, and some of them on their own intiative encouraged boat building and new methods of fishing and hunting, but since their protests continued for generations it must be assumed that their superiors paid no heed.

The principal tool for the inculcation of 'civilized' habits into the Makah, however, was the school. After an initial experiment with a day school at Neah Bay, it was decided that this was not sufficient since it left the children exposed to two educational experiences : that of the school and that which they received from daily contacts with older relatives who were passing on to them the culture of the group. Since the school was not conceived as a medium for training the child in a limited number of skills, but as a learning situation which would supersede all other influences, the day school was replaced by a boarding school where the children could be segregated from intimate daily contacts with their parents and other relatives. In this school, founded in 1874 about a mile from the nearest Makah village, the children were under the exclusive supervision of whites, and save for the presence of their fellow-students, isolated from influences stemming from Makah culture. The founder of the boarding school said that his policy was to take Makah children

entirely out of barbarous surroundings and put them in the midst of a civilized Christian home. It will be my endeavor to reject from my own mind and from their minds the notion that the clay of which Indians are made is of a coarser grit than the clay of which other people are made, and act upon the hypothesis that they have souls and bodies just like other people, and the same precious interests for time and eternity. I shall insist, first of all, upon cleanliness of person ; shall clothe them as comfortably as I clothe my own children ; shall give them good clean beds to sleep in ; shall seat them at the same table with my own family, kneel them at the same altar, and require of them the same good behavior. In connection with all this, I shall make it my first endeavor to teach them to speak the English language, not by the slow process of letters and books, but by the usage of common parlance. The Indian tongue must be put to silence and nothing but English allowed in all social intercourse. Meanwhile, habits of industry must be cultivated. The girls must be practised in all domestic duty, in cooking, sweeping, scrubbing, sewing, and knitting, and the boys must be practised in gardening and all kinds of useful work. Suitable amusements must be devised for them, more attractive than any they have ever known before, and such as will tend to good morals, health, and happiness.[1]

After a generation, this school was discontinued in 1895, and thereafter children were taught in a day school located at Neah Bay village, and older children who could be induced to leave home were sent to large boarding schools serving the children of many different tribes. Many children then went to Chemawa and Cushman, at that time an Indian boarding school, where they were completely cut off from contacts with Makah culture. In the schools, both boarding and day, the programme was adapted to fit the children into the life of an American

[1] *Report of the Commissioner of Indian Affairs*, 1874, p. 333.

community rather than to enable them to take their places in the group to which they belonged as it then existed. The parents, when they were required to place their children in the early boarding school, 'were made to understand that the school develops a relationship which is to result in such a change in the child's tastes and habits that he will never return to Indian life, but will seek new social alliances and a better form of life'.[1] And generation after generation, this policy was made the core of the school system both in the boarding school and its successors. Girls were taught domestic duties, useful in American households. Boys were taught crafts to fit them to earn their living away from the reservation, though the lack of skilled teachers often hindered their acquiring the requisite degree of skill. Indeed, at some periods, parents complained bitterly that the only vocational training given to boys was the chopping of the agent's wood pile and that they would be better employed chopping firewood for their parents. English was the only language permitted not only in the classrooms but also in the dormitories and about the school. The children were kept to American standards of dress and cleanliness, and trained in American customs of eating, posture, and sleeping. No one, apparently, was forced to accept Christianity, but all those in the school were exposed to Christian teachings through required attendance at church services and at daily prayers. Often the agents, or the superintendents of the school, were qualified missionaries who combined religious instruction with their other duties. Such recreation as the children were allowed was predominantly of American games supervised by instructors from the school. At the same time as they were receiving this training, those in charge of the school attempted to wean them from any lingering belief in the customs of their ancestors by a policy of ridicule. They were taught to regard their own elders as ignorant and superstitious barbarians whose advice should be ignored.

Attendance at the school was compulsory. Parents who refused to send their children to school were imprisoned until they saw the uselessness of refusal. At certain periods of the boarding school's existence, the children were kept in the school twelve months of the year, and were allowed to visit their homes for only a few hours each week. At other times, they attended

[1] *Report of the Commissioner of Indian Affairs*, 1875, p. 363.

for only ten months and spent a long weekend in the Makah village each week. As a rule, the school age was from seven years to fourteen, though some children remained longer, and a few managed to escape any schooling whatsoever by a judicious policy of inconspicuousness when the agent or the school employees appeared combined with the payment of the proper bribe to Indian employees of the agency. In the day school period, there was apparently no attempt on the part of the parents to prevent the attendance of their children, though some objected successfully to the sending of their children to boarding schools away from the reservation. It is safe to say that in every generation the overwhelming majority of children were processed through the Indian Service schools. The school equipment was usually poor. The teachers were frequently unqualified, to say the least. Nevertheless, the school had a profound influence on most of the students.

It is thus obvious that for a number of generations, the Makah were exposed to continuous pressure to accept American customs and to abandon their own ways. Where possible, they were prevented from acquiring the culture of their elders. Where this was impossible, they were punished for continuing to practise those forms which could be observed by those in authority. It is eighty years since this programme was first instituted, and for seventy years there was no major change in emphasis or any hope held out to the Makah that the Indian Service would ever recognize their own customs as worthy of survival. This length of time, the period that the Makah have been reservation Indians, should be an adequate testing period for determining the efficacy of a programme of enforced change, for the programme acted upon all those who participated in Makah culture and thus upon the only medium for the transmittal of Makah culture to new generations. In the 1930's, the policy of the Indian Service changed, but the people who are now Makah are the products of the situations of the previous seventy years.

In 1934, the United States Congress passed the Indian Reorganization Act, which has the following provisions :

(1) It prohibits the further individual allotment of lands now owned by the tribes, or to be acquired for the tribes.

(2) It returns to tribal use lands withdrawn for homestead purposes but not settled.

(3) It authorizes an annual appropriation of funds for land purchase.

(4) It makes mandatory the practice of conservation in the administration of Indian lands.

(5) It establishes a revolving credit fund out of which loans may be made to the tribe and the individual for productive farming and industrial operations.

(6) It encourages the organization and incorporation of the tribes for self-government and self-management of economic resources.

(7) It provides funds out of which loans may be made to Indian students seeking higher academic or vocational education.

(8) It gives Indians a preference basis under Civil Service rules for employment in the Indian Service.[1]

Inherent in the act is the recognition that

Each tribe should have the right to exercise all its inherent powers— the right to adopt a constitution, the power to operate its own machinery of government, to determine rights of membership (citizenship in the tribe), to regulate domestic relations within the tribe, to levy taxes upon members, to regulate tribal property, including the right to prescribe rules of inheritance, and to administer law and order within the tribal jurisdiction. The possibilities are unlimited. The way is open for an Indian tribe to assume a political and economic control over its internal affairs, as complete as that of any incorporated municipality.[2]

A further provision of the Act limited its application to those tribes which agreed to accept its terms ; it was not to be forced upon them against their wills. Each tribe was permitted to decide for itself whether or not it would accept the terms of the Act. The Makah voted to accept it, and obtained a Tribal Constitution in 1936 and a Tribal Charter in 1937. With this, members of the tribe again achieved a fair degree of autonomy in the management of their own affairs after a period of some seventy years spent as a subject people. The new policy of the Indian Service was to encourage Indians to improve their economic position and to learn new techniques and goals, but there was to be no further indiscriminate outlawing of customs simply because they were different from those known to the

---

[1] *Report of the Commissioner for Indian Affairs*, 1940, p. 359.

[2] *Report of the Commissioner for Indian Affairs*, 1940, p. 364. For a description of the organization of one group of Indians under this Act, see Aberle, 1948.

whites. The Indians were also given a voice in their own affairs and were consulted on matters involving them.

On paper, the plan seems to give Indian tribes considerable freedom. It might be assumed, therefore, that the Makah even though still subject to a degree of supervision are now in a position to express their own preferred ways of behaviour. However, the Makah are not fully convinced that this is so. Although they no longer have a resident agent and the tribe has become a political body with a governing council elected from its own members, they were still suspicious of the future. The change in policy had come after decades of repressive measures aimed at overthrowing everything ' Indian '. Many Makah gave me the impression that they regarded the new policy as very possibly a temporary relaxation or interval in the policy of repression. They had known somewhat similar relaxations in the past, which were followed by renewed repressive regulations against ' Indian ' culture. Many of them thought that they might be placed under an agent again within a few years, and they argued that even as matters stood they had only traded an immediate dictator for a long-distance one ; for they claimed that the officials of the Indian Service still controlled their affairs.[1] They said that the officials now sent papers for the council to sign instead of giving orders directly to the people, but that otherwise there was little difference. Their attitude to the Indian Service was coloured by their failure to gain control of the tribal trust funds which may have made them magnify the influence of the Indian Service officials over their lives.

Nevertheless, they admitted that they were now free to carry on many of their old customs if they so wished. They were also free to continue the practices which they had learned under the direction of the agency. Since they were in a position to make a choice, it can be assumed that the life of the Makah today is a fairly accurate index of the measure to which members of the tribe have accepted the goals and standards of their mentors, the whites. If their associations and their systems of thought and behaviour are such that they still retain their identity as a distinct community, then they are not assimilated no matter how much their culture has changed. In this measure, the programme of

[1] The Indian Service office at Hoquium in Southern Washington supervises the work of the local tribal authorities.

assimilation will have failed in its goal ; for the aim was not the change of Makah culture so much as the complete acceptance of American goals and behaviour by members of the group so that they could take their place as ordinary members of American society.

CHAPTER II

THE LAND OF THE MAKAH

The Reservation

THE life of the Makah is largely centred within their reservation which occupies the northwestern tip of the Olympic Peninsula, jutting out into the Pacific Ocean. Cape Flattery itself, and the islands lying immediately offshore, are reserved to the United States War Department, but starting a short distance south and east of the Cape, the reservation extends six miles in both directions. On the north it is bounded by the Strait of Juan de Fuca ; on the west, by the Pacific Ocean. The eastern boundary is a small river, Sail River, which empties into the Strait. Owing to military restrictions on travel along the Pacific beaches enforced in 1941-2, I was never able to visit the southern boundary or to learn how it is marked. No one seemed to know or care, since few Makah venture into the southern portion of the reservation.[1]

The reservation has been surveyed, and a portion of the area has been allotted to individual Makah, but most of the thirty-six square miles included in the reservation is left unused and unvisited. No one lives inland. Men row or motor up the streams for fishing and trapping ; sometimes small groups of men and women go into the forests to gather cedar bark or other wild produce. But for the most part, few go far from the beaches. Nevertheless, unvisited though most of the reservation may be, the Makah value it highly because of the value of the timber.

Topography

A highway running parallel to the coast of the Strait penetrates the reservation to reach the village of Neah Bay. It connects the reservation with Port Angeles and ultimately with the cities of the Puget Sound area, as well as with other small settle-

[1] The boundaries of the present reservation are given in the *Report of the Commissioner of Indian Affairs*, 1886, p. 372.

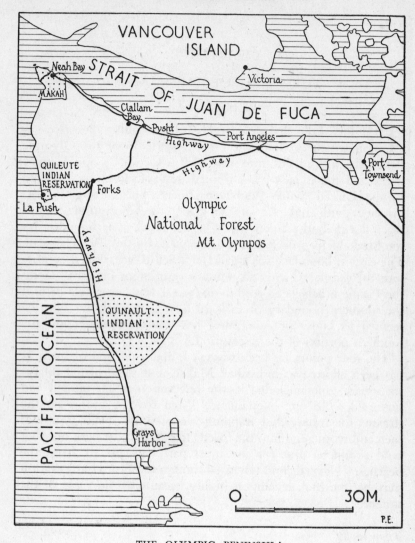

THE OLYMPIC PENINSULA

ments on the Olympic Peninsula. Another road, maintained by reservation officials, connects Neah Bay with the Pacific Coast near the mouth of the Sues River. Those who wish to go further down the coast must go on foot along the beach, or by boat, for no road enters the reservation from the south. A few

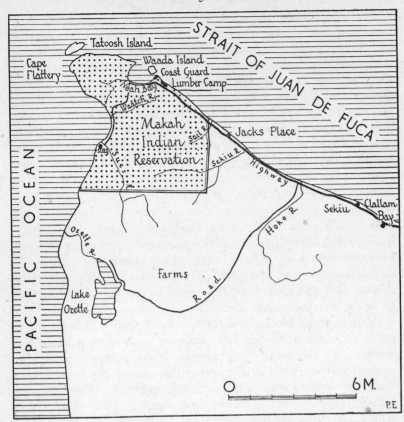

THE MAKAH RESERVATION

paths lead into the hills away from the coast, and these are usually covered with logs to make them passable during rainy weather. Even so, an incautious step sends one ankle deep into the muck. If they are neglected for a few years, the paths become almost impassable, as fresh growths of salmonberry bushes twine together into a thorny barrier. The Lumber Company which is cutting the reservation timber has built a small railway spur for transporting logs from the inland tracts to the Strait. As the timber is cut, the track is moved to give access to new stands, and the roadbed of the old track remains as convenient trails for berry pickers or for boys on some of their mysterious expeditions.

At two spots near the coast, the land is low, level, and clear of forest. These are the prairies near the mouths of the Waatch and Sues Rivers, where a few Makah keep a small number of cattle and cut wild hay for winter feeding. The rest of the reservation is rugged and covered with forests. It is a continuation of the Olympic Range, though by the time the Olympics reach the Cape Flattery Coast they have sunk to low rolling hills five or six hundred feet high, covered with masses of vegetation to their very crests. Berry bushes, ferns, alder, crab apple, hemlock, and cedar struggle for a place in the soggy soil composed of the decaying vegetation of centuries. On the eastern portion of the reservation, the hemlock and cedar stands have been cut, and logging operations are now well inland in the higher hills some miles from the coast. Where the loggers have passed, berry bushes, alder, crab apple, and other saplings have sprung up again. At some places, young plantations of fir are being set out under the direction of a Forestry agent, but despite the rapid growth of vegetation in this area they have yet to reach an appreciable size.

Springs, small creeks, and tiny pools abound. In level spots, pools of water collect which disappear only during the driest seasons. In the swampy lowlands, standing water is a permanent feature ; and in the spring the swamp pools are bright with the yellow flags of the skunk cabbage. Even on the hillsides, the ground is moist and soggy. Two small rivers which run through the reservation to empty into the Pacific are deep enough for canoes or small motor boats. One is used as a winter anchorage for small fishing boats, and during the summer its upper waters become a swimming pool for the children and young people of Neah Bay. In the fall, men set their nets in both rivers to catch a few salmon, but the runs are never large. A few small creeks have been dammed to make reservoirs from which water is piped to the village and lumber camp, but the reservoirs are back in the hills where they are rarely visited except by boys who are fishing for trout. The other creeks and the two small lakes are of little importance save as boundary marks or the foci for stories and legends. All, even the most insignificant bear Makah names, now known only to the older people, and a few have also received English names.

At Neah Bay and again about the mouths of the Waatch

and Sues Rivers, the rocky cliffs give way to white sandy beaches which extend for several miles. Along most of the coast, the hills run almost to the shore and then end with a precipitous drop to either beach or water. There are few indentations of the coast sufficient to provide safe anchorage or protection from winds and surf in bad weather, though at many places canoes can land and small boats venture close to shore when the sea is calm. Only at Neah Bay does a harbour exist, and as this is exposed during winter months to winds from several quarters it is unsafe for boats to winter in the bay. Along the rest of the coast, rough surf makes landing and launching dangerous except in the best weather and for those who know the landing places. The coast is known as a treacherous one with dangerous currents and tide-rips, and hidden rocks submerged at high tide which may rip the bottom from ships which edge too close. Today the danger is less, since the coastline is well marked with lights and buoys, and there is a great lighthouse at Tatoosh Island, but wrecks still occur.

A few hills or peaks inland which stand out above the general hilly terrain are used as landmarks by the fishermen who fish beyond the Cape in the Pacific for locating the fishing banks and for finding their way back to the harbour, but only the older men who fished in the days before the introduction of the compass and the placing of the marking buoys made navigation simple pay much attention to the hills or bother to know their names.

Bordering the shores of the reservation are numerous fishing banks which lie in both the ocean and the strait. These are close to the coastline, and are marked by objects on the adjacent shore. The most distant bank frequently visited by Makah fishermen is in the Pacific, fifteen miles from the Cape. Although the banks are public property in which all may fish, the Makah feel a proprietary interest in them since they claim that the banks belonged to their ancestors. They are as much a part of the environment of the Makah as is the land area of the reservation. Although not all Makah, especially the women, have visited the distant fishing banks, they have all heard about the banks and benefited from their existence ; and probably more members of the tribe have been out to the banks than have visited distant interior parts of the reservation.

The Climate

The climate at Neah Bay is probably one of the wettest in the continental United States. The average annual rainfall is in the neighbourhood of 110 inches.[1]   Most of the rainfall comes in the seven months from the beginning of October to the end of April.   A little rain falls in May and September.   The rest of the year is usually dry.   During the summer months, dust gathers thick upon the vegetation and the brilliance of the spring green is dulled and greyed by the heavy covering of dust.   Pools and creeks run low, until in some years the creeks are only trickles of water discoloured by the hemlock bark which lies rotting in the creek beds.   But throughout the summer, thick fogs roll in from the Pacific fog bank which lies a few miles off the coast, and the boom of the fog horn is a familiar sound. When the fog recedes, a slight haze in the air still obscures or blurs distant objects.   Only on fine winter days is the atmosphere clear.

The usual variation in temperature is between a low of 28 degrees and a high of 60 or 61 degrees.   Occasionally, it drops to 18 degrees or rises to 72 degrees.   At 72, the day is oppressively hot, and people complain of heat and a lack of energy. During most of the winter, it is warm enough so that those accustomed to the region need only a jacket thrown over their ordinary garments.   Late into the year, children play about the beach without coats, and in November they are still running barefoot.   Raincoats and boots are more necessary than overcoats, and even tiny children are provided with rubber boots for wading through the puddles and along the beach.   Wild roses may bloom as late as the middle of December, and the daffodils are in flower in February.   Still, many days during the winter are cold, and fires are necessary to warm the houses which are pervaded by a chill damp which strikes to the bone. Occasionally snow falls.   At Neah Bay, which has an altitude of 10 feet, this is rare, but the men cutting timber back in the hills sometimes find their work impeded by the snow.   For a short period during the coldest months, the waters in the swamp may freeze over.   But during most of the winter there is only the monotonous heavy rain which continues day in and day out

[1] Information provided by the official weather recorder at Neah Bay.

until the board-walks in the village begin to float, and the ditches along the roadways are filled with small torrents. With the rain come squalls of wind, hitting through the gap in the mountains behind the village. As these burst across the opening and out into the bay, the houses rock back and forth upon their posts as though in danger of being torn from their foundations and hurled into the bay. These are commonplaces of life in the village, and people are out and about with little attention to the weather. Occasionally during the winter, storms may strike which fill the bay with great breakers. These start at the entrance of the little harbour and come thundering in upon the shore wrecking the fishing boats wintering in the bay and snapping the pilings of the jetty.

The long rainy spell of the winter is usually broken by a short period in February when the weather clears for a week or so, and the sea is calm. During this period, fishermen go out, and men seize the opportunity to replenish depleted stores of firewood, going out to search the shore of the Strait for driftwood. This is about the time of the migration of the fur seals, and men go out to hunt these animals which they are allowed to spear from their canoes.[1] Then the bad weather shuts in again. The worst storms are expected about the time of the equinoxes. After the great winds and rains of April, the weather clears rapidly, and the fishing season begins in earnest. Most men leave whatever employment they have found for the winter months and begin fishing. When the rains start again in October the fishing season ends for most men, and many turn to the lumber camp for jobs which will keep them from the ocean during the stormy weather.

Economic Resources of the Reservation

The Makah are fortunate in the resources of their reservation. Without doubt, the most important single product is the timber. Though this is of an inferior type, suitable principally as pulp wood, its presence is of the greatest economic importance to the Makah. The original sale of the reservation timber increased the size of the fund held in trust for the tribe by the Indian Service to be used for the benefit of the Makah as a group.

[1] It is illegal to shoot seals, or to hunt them with motor boats or with large boats. Only Indians are allowed to spear from canoes.

Moreover, part of the reservation had been allotted to individual Makah, and the timber on these allotments was sold by the owners who received the money realized. The Makah draw further advantages since the lumber company which bought the rights to the reservation timber agreed as a part of the transaction to give Makah preference when it came to employing labour. Many Makah are employed at good wages in cutting the reservation timber. Most of the adult males of the tribe have worked at some time or other for the lumber company.

Other vegetation is of less importance. Berry bushes are plentiful, especially the salmonberry and blackberry. From the salmonberry the women gather sprouts in the spring, and both produce fruit which are welcome additions to the family diet. Sallal, thimbleberry, and huckleberry bushes and elder trees also produce wild fruit which is gathered and eaten, and near the Pacific a small cranberry patch still produces a few small berries though the patch is neglected. A few other plants produce sprouts which are eaten in the spring, but most people feel that they no longer make full use of all the edible plants provided by their land. They say that in former days the Makah used roots and plants which they can no longer recognize. Such fruit and roots as they do gather, they use only for home consumption. They make no attempt to commercialize their abundance.

For other purposes today, they make little use of the abundance available to them. Some people collect plants for medicines. They collect a small amount of cedar bark for making baskets, although they import most of it from Canada. They gathered some long grasses with which the basket makers experimented as raffia grew scarce with the development of the war. They use a white seaweed for some types of baskets. This is all. Despite the stands of timber everywhere, these are not cut for building or for firewood.[1]

They show little more interest in the animals still to be found on the reservation. Deer are fairly common and occasionally hunted. Elk are said to exist, but none were seen in 1942. Bear inhabit the hills and sometimes wander down to the prairie. They may be killed for their skins, although the meat is not eaten. Some fur-bearing animals occur, and a few men trap

[1] See Gunther, 1945.

for beaver or raccoon when funds are low or they have nothing else they prefer to do. The only dangerous animals are the cougar which are said to live back in the hills, although they are rarely seen and as seldom heard. Ducks and geese are found along the shore and in the prairie, and occasionally a few are shot for the table, although usually they are undisturbed.

During the low tides of winter, people occasionally go out with bucket and shovel to dig for clams in the beds along the shore, or to gather the mussels and barnacles which cover the rocks at a few sites on the Pacific Coast. The Makah also eat sea urchins, china slippers, and several other small shellfish, and they take octopuses for both food and bait.

But the real wealth of the Makah lies not so much in the resources of the reservation as in its proximity to the fishing grounds. Some of the biggest halibut fisheries of the Pacific Coast lie a few miles from Cape Flattery. During the late spring and early summer, these are fished commercially. After the official season closes and white fishermen turn to other occupations, the Makah are allowed to continue fishing for their private supply. They then catch halibut for immediate use or to dry or to preserve for winter. The other important commercial fish is the salmon, which occurs in several varieties. In spring and early summer, they are caught in the waters of ocean and strait. In the fall, when the fish start up the rivers, they are caught with nets. Sharks are caught for their livers, which sell for high prices, and throughout the year men fish for what are known as scrap fish : red snapper, ling cod, sea bass. These bring small prices, but they can be caught in large numbers if the fisherman is skilled and fortunate. Close to the shore, small boys fish for kelp fish, with lines dropped from the jetty, and thus help with the family food supply. For those who venture further out into the Pacific there are smelts, herring, and tuna fish. Only a small portion of the fish is consumed locally, and the Makah today are primarily commercial fishermen supplying the markets of the Sound area.

Sea mammals are still found in the waters near the reservation, though they play only a small part in Makah economy. Hair seals breed in the caves near the Cape, and are occasionally killed. The meat is eaten, the oil is used as a seasoning, and the hide is used in various ways. The government also pays a small

D

bounty for each seal killed because the seals are destructive to the more valuable fish. But only a few are killed each year. When the fur seals pass the Cape in their migrations, a few are usually speared and the furs brought to Neah Bay and sold. Porpoises and whales are occasionally seen, but despite the remembrance of the former glory of the Makah as whale hunters, these are allowed to escape without pursuit.[1]

Other possible resources of the reservation are not exploited by the Makah. They live upon the surface of the area, and are not concerned with what lies beneath their feet. In 1942, the tribe sold the right to quarry rock from one of the hillsides to the company building a breakwater at Neah Bay. The money was placed in the Tribal Trust Fund, and Makah were employed in blasting and carting away the rock. At one place a gravel pit has been opened, and its contents used for covering the road leading from Neah Bay to the ocean. Otherwise, the mineral resources, if present, are unexploited. The soil itself is not considered to be suitable for extensive farming, and the Makah make no effort to adapt it to this purpose. Only a few gardens are planted and a few hayfields harvested. Potentialities for dairy farming and stock raising are greater, but only a small proportion of the reservation is used for grazing. In 1939, the total land area of the reservation was 20,539 acres. Ten acres were cultivated ; 400 acres were used for grazing ; 129 acres were devoted to unspecified purposes ; and the remaining 20,000 acres were described as used for timber operations.[2]

As the reservation exists at the moment then, it is little more than a habitation site for the people, who depend not so much upon its resources as they do upon their own skill in exploiting the fishing opportunities of the public domain. Over this they have no control, and they compete with whites who also have free access to the Flattery waters. The timber resources of the reservation are sold to outside interests, and the owners of the reservation work as employees of the lumber company. Once the timber is cut, they will be left without the supplementary wages upon which most families in the tribe depend for their living throughout the winter months. An attempt is being

[1] See, Gunther, 1936.
[2] *Statistical Supplement to the Annual Report of the Commissioner of Indian Affairs for 1939.* This is the last year for which I have information.

made by the Indian Service to conserve the timber through the replanting with seedlings of the land where the trees have been cut. For this members of the tribe are hired. The replanting, however, is done under the direction of a white employee of the Indian Service, and members of the tribe take little interest in the procedure. No Makah has attempted to replant his own allotment in order to be assured of a further income from his own acreage.

The two industries upon which the economic life of the tribe depends are thus completely at the mercy of the whites, and the tribe at present lives upon its capital. No attempt has been made to find or develop other resources which may exist upon the reservation. Instead, over a period of years there has been a continuous decline in interest in products which were formerly used. Up to the present, moreover, there has been an exploitation and exhaustion of one resource after another. Originally the Makah lived upon whaling and fishing with the addition of supplementary resources such as game, shellfish, and wild plants. With the appearance of the whites and an enlarged market for furs, the strategic position of the Makah gave them an advantage in the sealing industry. When this was closed because of the quick depletion of the fur seal herds, the tribe turned to the exploitation of the fishing banks for commercial fishing. Soon the whites entered the field, and each year there were fewer fish, until fishing became a considerable gamble. But about the time that the returns from fishing became too small to support the people throughout the year, the timber was sold and there were jobs at the lumber camp. At the same time, the Makah became more and more dependent upon a cash economy ; for there was a rising standard of living with a desire for goods produced by whites and obtainable only through trading channels. Those products which could not be sold for a money return were increasingly ignored, as the people concentrated upon obtaining a cash return for their efforts.

In the late 'thirties, after the building of the highway made the area accessible to tourists, some of the Makah began to consider the feasibility of exploiting the scenic advantages of their reservation to obtain a new source of income. Three men built tourist cabins ; two families opened restaurants ; one man put up a garage and filling station. Presumably, the tourist trade will become of increasing importance in balancing Makah budgets. However, most members of the tribe have not thought so far ahead. Instead, they deplore the failure of the fishing banks, and fear the poverty which may descend upon them if the lumber camp closes. Memories of the depression of the 1930's, when lumber-camp jobs were scarce and fish prices were low, are vivid enough to make this prospect a nightmare to the most thoughtful.

SETTLEMENTS

Temporary Camps

A number of small settlements are scattered about the reservation. Near its eastern boundary cluster a few houses, survivors from a lumber camp which stood on the site when logging operations first started on the reservation. At the present time no Makah lives at the site nor does it figure in the life of the Neah Bay people, save as a source of income for one Makah who owns the land on which the houses are built. Between this spot and Neah Bay, is the lumber-camp settlement at Bahaada Point, where some hundreds of whites live. The camp is a company town with white bungalows for the officials of the lumber company and long rows of barracks for the lumberjacks who come in from ' outside ' to work at the camp. Also at Bahaada Point, its buildings intermingled with those of the lumber camp, is all that remains of the Neah Bay Agency : the office, the agency guest house, and the house where lives the man who guards the timber interests of the Makah and serves as their unofficial agent. Adjoining the lumber camp, with its buildings facing Neah Bay, is the Coast Guard Station. During 1942, this grew from a few buildings, housing coast guard personnel and life-saving equipment, to a naval station with jetties for small craft and barracks for navy personnel.

On the Pacific Coast, a temporary camp was built in 1942 to house construction workers who were building the breakwater which is to transform Neah Bay into a permanent harbour to guard the opening of the Straits. As soon as the breakwater should be completed, the buildings were to be torn down, and the site revert to its natural state, according to the agreement with the tribe.

These settlements are inhabited only by whites. With the

exception of the Coast Guard Station, all are regarded as temporary dwelling-places which will ultimately revert to the Makah tribe when the operations on which their occupants are engaged have ended. Between the people who live in them and the people of Neah Bay, there is little social contact, save that the children from the camps come to the Neah Bay school, and the men of Neah Bay go to the camps to work. Their working days during the winter are apt to be spent among the men who live in the camps, but during leisure hours there is little mixing.

Permanent Settlements

A few Makah have houses on the Pacific at the mouth of the Sues River, about two hours by foot from Neah Bay. Here they spend a part of the year in what is called ' the country '. Rarely are more than three houses occupied at the same time. Their owners, though they may have spent much of their lives at Sues and be descendants of the inhabitants of the Makah village which once stood near by, are still regarded as residents of Neah Bay where they also own houses and spend much of their time. Sues is not even a hamlet. Its few houses, strung at wide intervals along the beach, are unobtrusive. Looking eastward from the beach, you see the weathered boards of the wooden buildings, the blue smoke of wood fires, and the hayfields extending back towards the river. Facing the ocean, there is only the empty stretch of the long beach covered with driftwood, then the ocean broken by small reefs and standing rocks, and the distant smudge of smoke from some steamer passing on the far horizon. In the summer, the quiet of Sues is broken by parties of Indians and whites picnicking upon the beach or swimming where the Sues River empties into the Pacific. In the fall, men come for salmon fishing. During the rest of the year the beach is deserted save for sporadic parties gathering driftwood or shellfish.

For the Makah the real centre of the reservation is the village of Neah Bay. This is the only settlement upon the reservation dignified with the name of ' village '. All the rest are called ' camps ', emphasizing their temporary nature. Neah Bay is permanent, and while most of its inhabitants are either descended from inhabitants of other Makah villages now abandoned or come from outside the area entirely, there are people living at Neah Bay whose ancestors lived there since time immemorial.

Some of the buildings in the village are said to be more than fifty years old and have stood there since before most of the inhabitants can remember. Now the village is greatly grown in population and in area, and the nature of its organization has changed. Still the tradition of its earlier form is preserved and explained to anyone who will listen to the history of the Makah.

The village lies facing the bay which bears the same name. Its houses run for half a mile or more along the water front, following the contour of the bay. The principal street, only a continuation of the highway which connects the reservation with the outside world, separates the first row of houses from the beach. In width the village is no match for its length ; for at its widest point there are only four shallow blocks before salmon-berry and blackberry bushes grow unhindered into a dense tangle around the swampy lowlands of the prairie which lies directly behind the village. Low hills rise on either side. On the east, the village dwindles imperceptibly, until it narrows to a single string of houses fronting the highway. On the west, the houses end abruptly where a spur of hillside runs directly down to the water. Forests encircle the town on three sides, but the people forget the forests and orient themselves to the beach and the harbour in the bay.

The Village and the Harbour

Back and forth through the opening of the Strait pass great steamers, tramp vessels, and naval craft on their way up the Strait to the harbours of Puget Sound or outward bound to San Francisco or the Orient. These ships pass quietly along the horizon and are gone. No steamer stops at tiny Neah Bay since the road was built and the tri-weekly steamer to Seattle became only another village tradition. Now only fishing boats, and an occasional oil tanker bringing oil to the fish jetty disturb the quiet of its waters.[1] In the winter the harbour lies deserted save for some dozen boats owned by Makah fishermen. When good weather seems assured, quietly the harbour fills with fishing vessels of all descriptions come to anchor close to the great

[1] During 1942, equipment for building the breakwater was carried to the bay on rafts towed by small tugs. Larger naval craft were stationed at the bay, but they anchored near the naval station and the expanse in front of the village was little affected by this increase in water traffic.

fishing banks off Cape Flattery. Each day a few more boats enter the harbour, until the bay is crowded and vessels coming in at night thread their way through lines of small craft to their anchorages. In the grey haze of the early morning, the sputter of their engines mingles with the shrieks of scavenging gulls quarrelling over the early morning deposits of garbage, and then the boats and men are off to patrol the waters of the Cape with lines and nets. At night they return to the harbour to sell their fish at the fish houses in the village and to replenish their supplies of gasolene and oil. In the darkness the lights shining from the boats outnumber those shining from the land. The people of the village then say that there is another village upon the waters. Early in the summer a co-operative fishing scow is towed into the harbour by a busy tug, and for some months it lies anchored a short distance from the shore until it seems as much a permanent feature of the bay as the rocky tip of Koitlah point which juts out into the Strait on the west, hiding the Cape and Tatoosh Island from sight. When autumn approaches, the boats leave the harbour one by one, until one day only the vessels owned by members of the village are left, and the bay looks strangely quiet and empty with but ten or twelve craft to occupy the space once filled by hundreds.

Features of the Village

The link between the bay and its activities and the village and the life of the shore is the long jetty of the fish house, with its superstructures of sheds and buildings of greying wood, which seems to carry the village itself out upon the bay. It is so old that the planks are badly rotted, and in many places an open space where a plank has disappeared gives a sudden glimpse of the grey water below. Yet it is sturdy enough to bear the weight of lorries which drive out to the fish house at the far end of the dock where fish are packed in ice for shipment to the markets of Seattle and Tacoma. The landward end of the jetty rests upon the beach amidst a number of buildings owned by the same company. In one it manufactures ice in which the fish are packed. Another houses the power plant which provides electricity for the village when its machinery is functioning properly, though it would be foolhardy in Neah Bay to dispose of lamps and candles because a house is wired for electricity.

Further along the beach stands a small shack with the imposing legend, Makah Cooperative Fish House. This has no jetty. Boats sending their catch here must anchor at their regular places and the fish are brought ashore in dories, to be weighed, cleaned, packed in ice, and shipped off to the cities for market.

The rest of the village lies separated from the beach by the highway. It is laid out in blocks and streets, and has a few cement-topped sidewalks. Stop signs mark the intersections along the street leading to the school. The buildings are all simple wooden structures except for the brick school house. Some of the buildings are painted white, or green, or yellow. Others have been weathered by winds and rains and mists to a silvery grey that shines softly in the sunlight. In the yards behind most houses are sheds or smokehouses which have never been painted but are covered with thick slabs or shingles of cedar, and these shine with an almost platinum hue. Behind almost every house is a small privy, indicating that plumbing is still primitive for most of the village. Old houses and new are found side by side. All are raised upon low posts to protect them from the winter damp and floods. The space between house and ground makes a convenient storage place for old nets and canoes amongst which the dogs take refuge. Houses near the beach are built close together, with little space separating each from its neighbours. Further from the beach, houses are surrounded by sufficient space for gardens and berry patches. But no matter where a house is set within the village, it usually faces the beach. Life in Neah Bay is directed towards the beach and the street that edges it.

There are few reasons for one who lives upon the front street to go to ' the back ' of the village unless he has friends there or wishes to attend a church service, but almost everyone in the village is found upon the front street at some time during the day or evening hours. Early in the morning, some member of the family goes to the beach to deposit the collection of garbage to be washed away by the tide. On the beach are drawn up the canoes and dories in which the men go out to the fishing boats anchored in the bay. Logs are brought there for sawing and splitting into firewood. Fishing boats are drawn up for repair or painting. While men work cutting wood or repairing a boat, their friends gather to gossip or offer advice while they lean against a boat or uncut log. The beach is the playground of the children. In the summer small children spend their time swimming in the water close to shore, or rowing about in canoes or dories, or playing house with rooms built of sand and furnished with bits of kelp. Unless the rain is lashing across the village, the beach is rarely vacant of groups of men and playing children until late at night. During the summer, when most men are engaged in fishing, the beach is a scene of great activity and gaiety, with fishermen cleaning their catch at the water's edge and white gulls flashing down to grab the red offal that is flung to them. As the catch is brought in, the men make friendly bets about the weight of the catch and compare notes on their luck with much joking back and forth. Women may come down to the fish house, either to sit nearby and watch for their men or to beg those who have already returned for fish heads to cook for dinner. Others go out to the jetty where they sit leaning against the shed, watching the boats and gossiping.

Others settle themselves on the doorsteps and porches of the buildings along the first street. During the summer evenings when the whole village seems to migrate to the front every door-step is crowded, but the older men have their favourite porches where they sit talking in all save the worst weather. Along this same street are most of the business places of the village, set in amidst the dwelling-houses. The business premises, other than those connected with the fish jetties, are : large trading store with a post office, smaller store, hotel, barber's shop, carpenter's shop, two restaurants, two filling stations, garage, and two halls. The last are used for wedding parties and other large gatherings, and before one rises the flag pole from which the American flag belonging to the Makah Tribe is flown on great occasions. A quarter of a mile east of the village stands another hall where once a week a white man brings film and sound track for the weekly cinema showing. During the rest of the week the place is deserted except for an occasional Sunday, when a priest appears to hold mass for the few Roman Catholics in the village.

Towards the back of the village are set three churches, and a few government buildings : the house of the Customs Officer who has his office in the house, the school and the houses occupied by school teachers, the Sewing Room, the jail, and some buildings to house government equipment. The only other public building is the Tribal Office where the Council meets, court is held, and the tribal books are kept, and this is located on the front street. The rest of the village consists of dwelling-houses, inhabited by whites and Indians. These are not segregated into different sections but are interspersed amongst each other.

Within or near the village are several graveyards. On the far west end, a small graveyard dates from the period when the Makah were first persuaded by the whites to bury their dead instead of placing them above ground in canoes or trees. Near the centre of the village, on the beach itself, a small area enclosed by an inconspicuous fence is said to be another graveyard. Close to the Presbyterian church and manse is a still more recent graveyard, also surrounded with a fence, and so modern that a few graves are marked with tombstones with family names engraved upon them. This is no longer used, and the tribal dead are now taken to a plot along the highway two miles east of the village and buried on a hillside overlooking the Strait.

BEYOND THE RESERVATION

To the people of Neah Bay, lands beyond their reservation are familiar parts of their lives.

From the village they look across the Strait to the coastline of Vancouver Island bending off towards the northwest. On clear days, the separate trees of its forested mountains seem visible to the watcher in the village, and the white speck that is a lighthouse on its shore can be picked out. When the air is blurred with haze, the island is only a dim outline looming to the north. Then the swift descent of fog blots it out altogether. Dwellers in the village say that Vancouver is only an hour or so away with one of the fishing boats and fishermen often go close to its shores, ignoring the existence of the International Boundary which runs through the Strait. Many Makah have close relatives among the Indians on the southern coast of the island, with whom they correspond and visit, aided by the fact that as Indians and hereditary owners of the Straits they need not enter and leave the country through a port of entry as all whites must do. The mountains of Vancouver Island are used by fishermen as landmarks for locating the fishing grounds, and they bear Makah names known to the older men. Yet close as the island is, it seems remote and legendary. Even those who have lived their lives at Neah Bay and visited the island on many occasions feel this to be true. They speak of it as a place remote from foreign contacts where the old life, similar to that of their own past, continues with little interruption in a country unchanged by lumbering and road building.

Of more immediate interest to them is the land adjacent to the reservation which their forefathers formerly claimed as their own. To this they are attached by tradition and by the use which they still make of it.[1] They pay least attention to the former Makah territories lying to the south of the reservation, for the only approach is by boat or by foot along the beach and no-one lives along the shore. Within this area, however, lies Lake Ozette about whose shores Makah used to fish for salmon. One of the Makah villages was on the ocean south of the mouth of Ozette River, and many Makah legends refer to this village, where some still living were born. Near Ozette are fishing grounds which men seek during the summer, and some occasionally camp at the old village site in the winter to be near the migration route of the fur seals.

Inland, about Lake Ozette, are farms owned by whites, who once came in numbers to homestead the area. Now only a few remain. Some, however, have built cottages along the shores of the lake to attract summer visitors, and some Makah go there for

[1] In the 1855 treaty between the Makah and the United States Government, the total territory claimed by the Makah is given as follows : ' within the following boundaries : Commencing at the mouth of the Okeho (Hoko) river, on the Straits of Fuca ; thence westwardly with said straits to Cape Classet or Flattery ; thence southwardly along the coast to Osett or the Lower Cape Flattery ; thence eastwardly along the line of lands occupied by the Kwe-deh-tut or Kwill-eh-yute tribe to the summit of the Coast Range mountains ; thence northwardly along the line of lands ceded to the U.S by the S'Klallam tribe to the place of beginning, including all islands lying off the same on the straits and coast.' See ' Indian Land Cessions in the United States ', *Report of the Bureau of American Ethnology*, 18 : 800, 1896–7, Washington : Government Printing Office (1899). The Makah, through their Council, claim that before the treaty, Makah territory extended from Cape Johnson on the Pacific to Eagle Point on the Straits, rather a larger area than reported in the treaty. The matter is of more than historical interest to the tribe today because involved in it is the legal right to fish at certain rivers outside the reservation. In the fall of 1941, the Council held a meeting with all the older men of the tribe in which a formal list of the landmarks along the coastline claimed by the Makah in pre-treaty days was drawn up.

weekends, following a road which runs to the lake from the coast of the Strait. Along this road are lumber camps and sawmills and further inland are cranberry farms. Makah work on the farms during the berry season, and they visit the sawmills to buy lumber for building. The area itself, lying inland as it does, has few traditional associations for the Makah, though older men say that when they were boys Makah hunters ranged this far in hunting elk and bear. A few young men have set their traps about Lake Ozette in more recent years, and others have visited the lake to fish.

Makah have more frequent contacts with places along the coast of the Strait. In this area, settlement is advancing rapidly, pushing almost to the white sign near Sail River which marks the boundary of the reservation. Here and there clearings along the road have been hollowed out and cabins built by modern pioneers. These are still few and inconspicuous and seem overshadowed by the massive forests. The beaches along the Strait stretch long and untouched, save for parties in search of firewood and sea food. In the nearby bush, women gather berries and sprouts, while their men search the beaches. As a group, the Makah feel that they have a particular right to what they find along this stretch of land, though they admit that whites also may gather driftwood or shellfish ; for they claim that their lands extended in this direction as far as Hoko River, and possibly to Lyre River near Port Angeles. At the mouth of the Hoko, many gather in the fall to set their nets for the salmon that run up the Hoko in large numbers. It is an important economic asset to the tribe : the Hoko fishing often supplies a family with money to last the winter. The tribe claims the right to unrestricted fishing in the river on the ground that it is an old traditional fishing site of the Makah and therefore by the terms of their treaty they are entitled to fish here without hindrance. The State of Washington denied this claim and sought to restrict their right to fish at Hoko so that they might be controlled by the State Fisheries Department which would enjoin upon them the same regulations that apply to Indians of other tribes and to the whites who fish there.[1]

Ordinary daily activities take few Makah much beyond Hoko. But many buy supplies from a small store owned by a white man

[1] This case was being contested in the courts in 1941–2.

who has built a few miles east of the reservation. Others go beyond to the small villages built along the road between Neah Bay and the nearest large town, Port Angeles.

THE LAND OF THE MAKAH

The Makah Reservation is an area with legally defined boundaries. It has certain natural features which can be described without appealing to traditional associations. For the whites who live in the area, indeed, the land has few associations beyond those of the immediate present. A few may know something of the early historic explorations of the coast when American, English, and Spanish, vessels visited the area, and they may realize that the first European settlement in the State of Washington was the short-lived settlement founded by Spaniards at Neah Bay. But for the majority of whites the land has not even these associations, and they tend to think of it, and to compare it with other areas, in terms of productivity and land values.

Since the Makah themselves make little use of most of their reservation save for the village lots upon which they live, it might be assumed that the reservation as such is of little importance to them and that they could easily adjust to a change in location. During 1942, the suggestion was heard several times that the Makah should be moved from this particularly exposed coastline which could then be turned into a military reservation and in exchange they should receive land in some other coastal portion of Washington. Economically they might not suffer from such an exchange, though they might have difficulty in learning to fish successfully in unfamiliar waters. In other ways, they would face a great loss ; for to the Makah the Cape Flattery area is the centre of countless associations which distinguish it from all other areas no matter how similar the two may seem to the outsider. Failure to understand this would lead to a complete misconception of the relationship of the Makah to their land.

Their own history as a group is almost entirely bound up with the natural features of this region, about which are associated the events of their myths and folk stories, the events which they regard as their own history, and many of the happenings of their own lives. It is as though we lived in a small country within which were to be found the sites of the Garden of Eden, the landing-place of the Ark, the field of Marathon, King Arthur's castle, the battle grounds of Hastings, Lexington, Waterloo, and Gettysburg, the ports from which explorers sailed and to which they returned, the home of the New Bedford whalers and fishermen, the places where the mystics had their visions of deity. If, moreover, when we heard the tales of these events the speakers had been careful to point out where each one had occurred, if we ourselves had roamed the area as children and lived through some of the events referred to in the tales, we would be in a better position to understand the attitude of the Makah to their reservation and the nearby lands which their ancestors claimed.

The Makah learn something of European and American history in school, but they know that they also have a history which has nothing to do with this learning from books and which took place within the Cape Flattery area. Even the accounts which they say are not history but ' fairy stories such as you tell to children ' are set firmly within the framework of the natural features of the Makah land, and those telling the stories distinguish them from tales learned from other tribes on the assumption that if a story mentions places within the region then it belongs to the Makah. Stories which mention places beyond their borders are regarded as importations.

Though not necessarily accepted as true, the folk tales are still told. Older people recite them at small parties as part of the evening's entertainment. Grandparents and parents repeat them to small children. Older men who sit watching the harbour have their fund of stories. Women as they pick berries repeat them to each other. In at least a few families, husband and wife murmur the stories to each other as they lie waiting for sleep. For older people, the tales have an added emotional connotation because they bring back memories of the old smoke-houses and childhood days when they sat nestling close to some older person beside the fire listening to the story-teller until they fell asleep and were stowed away in their sleeping-places.

In the beginning, say the Makah legends, the land already existed. On it lived people who were the ancestors of the present animals. Among them was Kwáɪti, a dwarf-like man whose strange speech came whistling through his teeth. Although he did great deeds which changed the face of the earth and the character of the sky above, most of his life was spent in playing practical jokes such that people dismissed him with,

' Oh ! It's only Kwạ́lti ! ' The people of that far-off time lived about Cape Flattery, but the land was then not as it is now. Most of the cycle of tales in which Kwạ́lti appears are accounts of how he made the land into its present shape. Kwạ́lti also stole the day from its owner and arranged the tides so that the people would be able to gather shellfish along the shore. Throughout Makah territory are rocks and springs and beaches which are the scenes of incidents in the Kwạ́lti cycle. As they pass these spots, the people laugh as they recall what Kwạ́lti did there to trick people. Finally, after many years, a being known as the Transformer came through the land changing all whom he met into animals. Some say that Kwạ́lti was changed into a mink. Others say that Kwạ́lti still lives on a rocky reef near Waatch and that if you go near and call his name, he answers, ' Here I am, down here eating shellfish.'

These things happened before history, or before the Makah themselves existed. They distinguish a historic time of events through which they believe their own ancestors lived. These too are localized within the Cape region. Some say that the Makah have always lived here, created in the region by the Transformer when he came. Others think that an ancient flood, whose traces they still find in the shells and sand dug up away from the beaches, brought them drifting down from Vancouver Island. The folktales which they regard as accounts of their earliest history are of a time when their ancestors were already settled in the villages about the Cape. Throughout this history, they have defended the land against invaders who wished to drive them out and take the fishing grounds. The old people end their stories of these struggles with the words, ' Neah Bay is our land because we spilt our blood for it.' The waters of the Strait and ocean are not merely fishing grounds. They are the pathways along which the war canoes of Quileutes, Clallams, Nitinats, Clayoquets, and Cowichans came to attack Makah villages, and upon which the Makah in turn set forth to raid the villages of other groups. They are the scene of great whale hunts which are still described in detail. Through them great flotillas of canoes came bearing guests to potlatches which made Makah names renowned among the surrounding tribes. The beaches are associated with the ancient winter villages and with the summer villages to which the Makah migrated annually to be near the halibut fisheries off the Cape. Though the ancient houses of the old villages have vanished, and no trace of their planks and posts remain, the villages still figure in the stories and in the memory of the older people who once lived within them. Upon the beach were fought great fist fights between different sections of a village over affairs involving family honour. Upon the beach, Makah hosts stood to receive their potlatch guests. Here the children played, kept close to the beach by threats that if they wandered into the forest they would be found by a huge woman who would throw them into her basket woven of snakes and take them off to the mountains where they would either be eaten or be made to work much harder than they did for indulgent parents. Along the vacant beaches far from the villages, and in the forests behind, the boys and men went to seek for guardian spirits to assist them throughout their lives. Each man usually had his private spot to which he retired to bathe and pray, and the appearance of his ' power ' or spirit guardian gave special meaning to the spot. Other places are said to be the spots where the spirits of the dead appeared to relatives who had slighted the mourning ritual. Still others are regarded as the haunts of supernatural beings who will harm those who see them or who approach too near.

The stories dealing with the first appearance of the whites are localized at Neah Bay. Here the Spaniards attempted to found a fort. In the prairie near by, Spanish sailors attempted to rape two Makah women, and their avengers came through the woods on the west to attack the Spaniards who were washing clothes in the creek and drive them back to their boats. Later other ships came, including one which brought clothing which infected the Makah with smallpox. Some say that the whites landed and poisoned the waters of the creek so that the people who drank this water might take the disease. As the smallpox spread through the villages, the Makah died rapidly and the beach along Neah Bay was covered with their dead bodies deserted by the survivors who fled to Vancouver Island or into the forests or to distant beaches. On the eastern side of the bay, the people gathered to hear Governor Stevens who made with them a treaty in which they agreed to cede to the United States much of their land and to receive in return the benefits of a reservation and agency. Here stood the buildings of the agency, and the old boarding school where so many of them had first to adapt themselves to the strange ways of the whites.

Most of the whites who come to Neah Bay have never heard these tales which deal with the area and give a symbolic value to so many of its natural features. If they have heard some of the tales, they think of them only as the queer stories of an alien group which have nothing to do with their own background. But to the Makah, they relate the deeds of their own ancestors within their own traditional land. Old Louis Keller told me that he had seen whale bones and the remains of clam and mussel shells found when a house was built near Sues. To him they were 'the remains of feasts my grandfathers ate'. His ancestors' spirits live underneath the ground of the reservation, and at times they return to walk the places where they used to live. Even the weather phenomena are to him fraught with particular meaning because he was taught to observe them by his old relatives who sat each day to watch the weather.

For Makah and whites, the features of the landscape may seem to be the same ; but so long as these traditions are repeated and known, the two do not live in the same land ; for they do not share a common background of symbolism and each reacts to the land in a different way.

E

CHAPTER III

THE MAKAH TRIBE

THE 357 Makah who live on the reservation do not form a local group or community, for the community to which they belong is that of Neah Bay which is composed of Makah, Indians from other tribes, and whites.[1] Many Makah live in households which include one or more members of foreign derivation.

THE 'VISIBILITY' OF THE MAKAH

It would be difficult for the newcomer to Neah Bay to distinguish members of the Makah tribe from other inhabitants of the village. Indeed, save for the physical features of some of the inhabitants, he would have little reason to suspect that he was in an Indian village on an Indian reservation. Neah Bay has little about its external appearance to distinguish it from other villages along the coast. Only the stocks of woven baskets and garishly painted wooden totem poles at the trading store, the few rotting canoes on the beach, the features of a few of the people about the streets, and perhaps the explosive glottals of the Makah language caught from the conversation of a group of older men or women, or the sound of a Makah song hummed by an old man as he goes back and forth upon the beach, indicate a background different from that of other American villages.

The visitor might think that the yards and houses were shabbier and more disordered than is usual elsewhere, but the houses are frame buildings, similar to those found in many other small coast towns.[2] Beside one house stand two weatherbeaten boards on which the owner once painted a design which he regards as

---

[1] In 1939 there were 411 Makah, but only 354 were living on the reservation. See *Statistical Supplement to the Annual Report of the Commissioner of Indian Affairs for 1939*, p. 14. This is the last date for which figures were available at the time of my study. In 1942, I found 357 living on the reservation.

[2] Many houses are of a standard lower than is common in a middle-class neighbourhood in most American towns. Most of them have been built by their owners rather than by professional builders, and the majority are twenty to thirty years old.

aboriginal Makah art. When he points it out and traces the faded lines, the design can still be seen ; otherwise it does not attract attention. Cows roam the streets of the village or pace along the beach, pausing now and then to gaze out to sea, and dogs sleep peacefully amidst the ruts in the streets despite the dangers of increased traffic. But dogs in equal numbers and with quite comparable placidity sleep in the streets of the neighbouring village twenty miles east where the population is overwhelmingly white and the only inhabitants with Indian blood seek to deny it by snubbing their Indian relatives when they appear from Neah Bay.

The people as they pass in the streets seem equally commonplace. Small babies go abroad in perambulators or carried in the arms of some relative. Most Indian babies are tightly swaddled cocoons in their wrappings of blankets, but you would look in vain for the cradle boards or baskets in which Makah babies were carried long ago. Men and women walk the streets side by side. No lofty male stalks ahead while his women follow carrying the family burdens. Children ride past on bicycles or scooters, and boys play baseball or football through the streets. The language ordinarily heard is English, and from the houses come the strains of cowboy music or jazz rather than the sound of an Indian drum or song. In the restaurants, young people, both Indian and white, sit over bottles of pop or concoctions of ice cream and watch others dancing to the music of the jukebox. In the stocks of goods carried in the stores, there is nothing that seems aimed at tastes alien to those one might expect to find in any other coastal village, except for objects carried for the tourist trade.

Dress

The people of Neah Bay wear ordinary clothing. That of the men is determined by their work. Fishermen go about in raincoats and rubber hip boots rolled down about the knees. Men working at the lumber camp stalk through the village with great calked boots. Both fishermen and lumberjacks wear overalls and heavy shirts, and in the winter, the clothes-lines on wash day bear witness to the fact that they wear heavy winter underwear as well. Most of them, whites and Indians alike, own suits for dress occasions.

The women dress in much the same fashion as do women throughout the nearby areas. Most of the time they go about in cotton house-dresses, which are either purchased at cheap department stores in nearby cities or ordered from the big mail order houses or made by the wearers from standard patterns. Most women also own silk or rayon or woollen dresses for important occasions, and a few own formal evening gowns. Young women also wear woollen suits and whatever coats are in fashion at the moment. Sweaters and skirts are the common garb for high-school students, although after school many young girls wear slack suits. Children have cotton dresses, slack suits, and overalls. Small children play about during the summer in sun suits or bathing suits. Babies wear dresses or knitted suits, and the lines behind the houses where they live are usually filled with long displays of white napkins.

The Makah are not distinguishable by their dress from the others in the village. A few very old women wear kerchiefs tied about their heads [1] and shawls over their shoulders. Some women have graceful gold earrings hanging from pierced ears. A few of these ornaments were made by an old Makah who learned the art when he was blacksmith's apprentice at the Indian boarding school. Others came from jewellery stores in the cities. Makah women have no distinguishing hair style. Some wear their hair long. Young girls may let their hair drop straight and loose about the shoulders. Others have their hair cut short and curled with the aid of a permanent wave. Some Indians, but no whites, wear capes or coats of khaki cloth made from old army uniforms donated by the government during the depression to assist those too poor to buy materials of their own. But it is not common enough to be considered a distinctive Indian garb. Some of the older men wear clothing which looks as though it has been acquired second-hand without too much regard for fit, but cut and material are similar to those of clothing worn by whites. Indian men, however, have one custom with

[1] These are worn in a manner popular among university women in the late 1930's and still in some vogue in 1942. Although most fashions are adopted quickly by younger Makah women, this one was rejected. White tourists who wore kerchiefs were laughed at for adopting an 'Indian' custom. I suspect this is why the younger Makah refused to accept it. It has too many 'Indian' associations for them, and they are trying to dress like white women.

regard to dress which distinguishes them from whites. Invariably all wear hats when out-of-doors. This is so much the rule that if a man is seen without his hat it arouses speculations as to whether he may be drunk. These items exhaust the distinctive features of dress, and all together do not distinguish the Makah or the Indians from the other residents.

Spatial Segregation

Whites and Indians do not live in separate sections of the village. They are scattered throughout the length and breadth of the village and live as neighbours. Some whites are members of Indian households ; others rent rooms from Makah landlords ; others have houses of their own. Most of these, however, are owned by Makah landlords, who themselves built the houses. A few whites have rented land from Makah owners on long leases and built their own houses to their own tastes, but these do not differ obviously from the newer houses in which some Makah families live. Some Makah, it is true, live in old shacks which look as though a sudden puff of wind might send them clattering down about the heads of the inhabitants. In 1942, white families were living in no better places ; for such was the pressure for housing at this period that they rented anything they could find so long as it had a roof.

Language

Language is not a barrier cutting off the Makah from the whites. Most whites, it is true, speak only English or possibly English and some other European language. A few who have been long resident on the reservation speak Makah as well as do members of the Makah tribe. Most Makah are either bilingual or speak only English.[1]

Only five Makah know so little English that I needed an interpreter for ordinary conversations with them, and two of these are perfectly capable of carrying on a conversation in English if they care to do so. The rest use English at least as commonly as they do Makah. Young people habitually speak in English,

[1] Some of the older men also speak the Chinook jargon, although Chinook is little used today since English has replaced it as a common medium in dealing with members of other tribes. Some Makah also speak other Indian languages : various dialects of Nootka, Clallam, Quileute, and Quinault.

and many know so little Makah that they can neither understand nor carry on an extended conversation with the few old people who know no English. In only two families are small children learning anything of the language. Both households contain an old person who uses no English, and so they hear discussion in Makah. In all other households, children and adolescents are addressed in English as this is the language they understand. When people in their twenties attempt to speak Makah, they are usually understood only by older members of their own families who are accustomed to their distortion of the language. Although probably all over forty speak a Makah adequate for ordinary conversational purposes, the older people laugh at them for corrupting Makah to bring it closer to English in pronunciation and grammar. But even some of the old people admit that they do not speak Makah correctly.

Despite this, the old language is still important to the Makah, though its importance is waning and those who speak it realize it is a dying language. For most of them it is an alternative, and a less useful, language than English. When people come together, either language may be used, though where all age grades are represented, English is usually spoken. In smaller gatherings where only the older people who are still interested in Makah dances and songs come together, they use Makah. Children are said to use Makah only for cursing which they do not wish their teachers or their white schoolmates to understand.

Some of the old, and a few of the middle aged, speak an English which betrays the influence of another language upon it. Genders and tenses shift uncertainly, and the vocabulary is not extensive. Most people, however, do not give the impression that in speaking English they are using a foreign language, though those with better ears for nuances of accent are able to discern peculiarities that escaped me. The teacher of the high-school speech class said that most Indian children have difficulties in enunciation, such as a tendency to gutteralize sounds, which distinguish them from their white schoolmates. I do not believe, however, that most people would be conscious of these minute variations.

This shift towards a general English-speaking population is an important development, because of the implications of such a shift for ease of social intercourse with the whites and also because it implies the sharing of the basic assumptions which a language fosters.

Names

Sometimes the surnames and Christian names borne by individuals in a heterogeneous population show the varied origins clearly and make it possible to assign with some accuracy families and individuals to one of the original elements composing the community. This is not true at Neah Bay. Of the forty-six surnames borne by members of the Makah tribe, only ten are said to be derived from Indian names, and even these are not ostentatiously different from names borne by whites. These ' Indian ' names are said to be derived from a personal name borne by some immediate ancestor, which the agency officials converted into family names when members of the tribe were given surnames for registration purposes. In all cases, the original name has been changed slightly in its phonetic character to make it easier for whites to pronounce. This meets with no objection from the Makah, who recognize that some of the names had been inherited from ancestors belonging to other tribes and that they had already been altered to fit the phonetics of the Makah language. A few bear the surnames of white ancestors. Surnames borne by the rest of the Makah were arbitrarily given to them or to their immediate ancestors by agency officials or by ship crews with which they served and are drawn from common stock of American names. Under ordinary conditions they would warrant the assumption that the bearers were of English, Scotch, or Irish descent. Only one or two of these surnames are also borne by white residents of Neah Bay, but the two lists are of much the same character.

Personal names in common use are no more enlightening as to background, though Makah may have a slightly greater tendency than whites to use an abbreviated form of a Christian name rather than the full name for which it stands. Only two personal names borne by Makah are peculiar to the Neah Bay community. One Makah child is named for the village, or perhaps for an older white child who bears this name. An old man has a peculiar name whose derivation I never learned.

These names are the ones by which individuals are identified both by whites and by other Makah. However, most Makah also have another name known as an 'Indian' name, which is usually so little used that its bearer may not remember what it is. Children rarely know their own 'Indian' names. Even their parents may have to consult some older person with a good memory to discover what names have been bestowed upon their children. But in a few cases people are known even to whites by their Indian names.

Whites, with a very few exceptions, do not have 'Indian' names though all those who have lived in the village for many years know something about the system of giving these names and they would probably feel flattered if they were given an 'Indian' name. The whites who have Makah names are those married to Makah. The only other white who has ever received a Makah name is an Indian Service doctor who was given his name as a final compliment on his transfer to another reservation.

Physical Type

Physical appearance is not a good basis for classification, for within the Indian group there is a great variation of physical type. Many Makah cannot be distinguished from those who have only white ancestors. Some are identifiable as of Indian blood only because they are on a reservation where one watches for Indian features. Elsewhere they would probably be assumed to be of European stock. A blond young man driving a truck for the construction company would unhesitatingly be identified as white although he is a member of the Makah tribe. A small blond boy playing in the streets with other children resembles his playmates whose ancestors came from Sweden, though again he is a member of the Makah tribe.

'Racially' the members of the Neah Bay community are thus a heterogeneous mixture, with no clear dividing-line separating the different groups in the village. At one end of the scale are those who have only white ancestors, so far as anyone knows, and who would repudiate the suggestion of any foreign strain. At the other end are a few people who can be presumed to be of pure Indian descent, though some of those who claim to be 'pure-bloods' undoubtedly have ancestors of another race. Even those who look most Indian may claim that one of their ancestors had light skin, blue eyes, and curly hair, and they offer this as proof that Indians and whites are really members of the same race. Those with European features may claim a pure Indian descent, though further acquaintance with the ancient gossip may cast doubt upon the claim. In between the two groups of ' pure whites ' and ' pure Indians ' are many who have so little Indian blood that to call them Indian deprives the term of any implication of racial affinity. Yet they maintain their Indian status because of the benefits the status confers. On the reservation, they call themselves Indians. Away from the reservation, they pass as whites. Although most of those with any claim to Indian blood thus appropriate the name of Indian while they live at Neah Bay, a few people living there who have acknowledged Indian ancestry are known as whites. They live as whites and are accepted as such by other whites in the village, though they may have more Indian ancestors than do some who are referred to as Indians.

The Makah are thus a racially heterogeneous group, and they themselves are unaware of quite how complex their background may be ; for intermarriages with other Indian groups may have introduced an increment of white blood about which the Makah themselves have no knowledge. Many of the tribes with which they intermarry have been even more exposed to white contacts than they themselves.[1]

[1] The intermixture has been going on for 150 years, since the earliest contacts with the whites. According to early reports, Makah prostituted their slave women to ships crews from the beginning of contact with Europeans in 1790. See *A Spanish Voyage to Vancouver and the Northwest Coast of America being the Narrative of the Voyage Made in the Year 1792 by the Schooners 'Sutil' and 'Mexicana' to Explore the Strait of Fuca*, p. 28 (translated by Cecil Jane). London : Argonaut Press, 1930. Later there were numerous wrecks upon the coast, and some of the survivors lived for some months in Makah villages and probably added new strains to the Makah population. Gibbs, who was at Neah Bay in 1855, reported that many showed signs of European ancestry. This was true of Makah leaders as well as of the lower classes. Cf. Swan, 1866, footnote on p. 3.

The Makah today ignore this earlier admixture, and the white ancestors they remember are those who began to come to the area after the creation of the reservation. Only one line traces its white ancestry to an earlier period, and this descends from Yallakub, a Makah leader who died in 1852 or 1853, who is said to have been a half-breed.

It is possible that other racial strains are also represented in the Makah population. In the late eighteenth century, Chinese were imported as labourers to Vancouver Island, and they are said to have intermarried with the Nootka Indians. Doubtless intermarriages have spread this strain along the coast. In

In the following table I have attempted to show the racial diversity of the Makah by classifying them according to their ancestry. But I have had to rely upon the Makah themselves for the information, and have accepted their statements about their ancestry. Those for whom no white ancestors could be traced are classified as ' pure-blood ' Indians, even though some have features which make it fairly certain that some degree of white admixture is present.[1]

TABLE I

' RACIAL ' MIXTURE OF THE MAKAH

	Number	% of Total
' Pure-blood ' Indians	210	58·8
' Mixed-bloods ' with less than half white ancestry	103	28·8
' Mixed-bloods ' with half or more white ancestry	44	12·3
Total	357	

I was not able to obtain enough information about Makah who are not resident on the reservation to make it worth while including them in the above table, which covers only residents at Neah Bay. The numbers involved are too small to make it worth while to break the data down into age grades. Half-breeds are about equally distributed throughout the age range, but most of those who are less than half-white are found in the younger group. This indicates that half-breeds are marrying back into the tribe.

The intermixture is continuing at the present time. In 1941–2, there were ten whites and 34 Indians of other tribes married to

the early years of the twentieth century, there was a canning factory at Neah Bay which employed Chinese, Japanese, Filipino, and Mexican workers. Makah have been in contact with these people also when they have visited other places on the West Coast. The Makah, however, do not accept an oriental strain in any member of the tribe, nor do they consider that any member is of negro descent.

[1] Dr. F. Hulse, who has been investigating blood types among Indians in the state of Washington, has informed me that the distribution of blood types found among the Makah suggests that there has actually been much less admixture with whites than one would expect from their history. [Personal communication, August 1952.]

members of the tribe. I could not classify the foreign Indians for admixture, as many of the Makah knew little about their ancestry. It is probable that most of them had some degree of white ancestry. A few were known to be less than a quarter Indian.

In the following table, I have classified pairs of spouses to show whether their unions represent in intermarriages between ' pure-bloods ', ' pure-bloods ' and ' mixed-bloods ', ' pure-bloods ' and whites, or ' mixed-bloods ' and whites.

TABLE II

' RACIAL ' MIXTURE IN PRESENT MARITAL UNIONS

Type of Marriage	No. Unions	% of Total Unions
Both spouses ' pure-blood '	39	41·4
Both spouses ' mixed-blood '	17	18·0
One spouse ' mixed-blood ', one spouse ' pure-blood '	11	11·7
One spouse ' pure-blood ', one spouse white . .	2	2·1
One spouse ' mixed-blood ', one spouse white . .	8	8·5
One spouse ' pure-blood ', one spouse either Mexican or Filipino	2	2·1
Marriages in which classification of one spouse unknown . . . . (Represent marriage with an Indian of another tribe.)	15	15·9
Total	94	

Five Makah women who had married white men were living away from the reservation. Two of these were ' pure-bloods '; three were ' mixed-bloods '.

There is thus a slightly greater tendency for mixed-bloods to marry whites than for ' pure-bloods ', but both types of marriage take place. It can be presumed that future generations of Makah will be more homogeneous, and that all will be of mixed-blood, since even today the ' pure-bloods ' may be of a mixed ancestry.[1]

[1] In this the Makah show the same trend as appears on other reservations. The Office of Indian Affairs made an analysis of data of the degree of Indian blood on a few selected reservations. ' These analyses corroborate the belief that the full-bloods are declining at an accelerating rate, and that the rate of decline is the highest where the per cent of full-bloods in an Indian community is the smallest. These studies, however, brought to light another trend which

Even those who claim to be 'pure-blood' do not claim that all their ancestors have been Makah. The Makah have always intermarried freely with members of other tribes, and they accept the fact that their ancestors come from many different tribes. This intermixture continues at the present time. Of the 94 marital unions in which at least one spouse is Makah, 34 or 36·1 per cent are with Indians of other tribes. In only 51 per cent of the unions are both spouses Makah. Presumably the number of intermarriages with other tribes has always been high, though the Makah themselves think that it is higher today than in former times. Some say that the young people must marry strangers from other tribes since within the village all are interrelated and marriage with even distant relatives is strongly condemned. In 1942, only one marriage of the six that took place was between two Makah. In the period immediately preceding 1942, seven marriages had taken place, and in only one were both spouses Makah. The trend thus seems to be towards more marriages with members of other groups, Indian or white, and a breaking away from the inbreeding which has interrelated all the people in the village. This involves an increase in the foreign element living at Neah Bay.

The tribes from which the alien Indians living at Neah Bay are drawn is shown in Table III opposite. The list includes only those who are or have been married to Makah and does not include all those of alien origin living in the village.

Most of the intermarriages are with people from tribes living on the Olympic Peninsula or the immediately adjacent area about Puget Sound, or with people on Vancouver Island. This is to

is extremely significant; namely, that assimilation of the Indian population into the white race is now being retarded at least on certain reservations.

'On all of the reservations studied, the decline in the percentage of full-bloods and the increase in the percentage of mixed-bloods was marked, but on the Pine Ridge, Lower Brule, Sacramento, and part of the Uintah and Ouray jurisdictions, the quantum of Indian blood among the mixed-bloods is increasing, indicating not only that intermarriage between mixed-bloods and full-bloods is fairly common but also that mixed-bloods are now tending to marry back into the Indian group rather than to marry whites.

'This trend arises from the fact that most Indian communities are no longer parts of frontier or pioneer white communities where the number of white men greatly exceeds the number of white women. As the sex ratio among whites becomes more and more normal, the chief reason for intermarriage is removed.'—*Report of the Commissioner of Indian Affairs*, 1939, p. 67.

TABLE III
TRIBAL ORIGIN OF SPOUSES

Tribe	Total	Number Males	Number Females
Quileute	5	1	4
Clallam	11	3	8
Quinault	4	—	4
Clayoquet	1	—	1
Nitinat	3	3	—
Lummi	3	1	2
Cowichan	2	—	2
Other Salish	7	—	7
Other tribal	5	4	1
Total	41 *	12	29

* This differs from the figure given for alien spouses living in extant unions since it includes those whose marriages have been terminated by death or divorce if the alien continued to live at Neah Bay.

be expected, since these are the nearest neighbours and are most accessible. Most Makah have ancestors drawn from these same groups.

DEFINITION OF MAKAH

From the previous section it is apparent that the Makah are not distinguished from other peoples by their physical appearance. They are not distinguished as a group by the possession of a common language or a common culture. They are not people descended from a common group of ancestors. They are not a segregated group, isolated from social contacts with those who are not considered to be members of the tribe. Nevertheless, the Makah themselves are perfectly certain about who are to be considered members of their group. Throughout this book, I am using Makah as defined by the people who bear that title, and not with reference to any idea of physical, cultural, or linguistic homogeneity.[1]

The Makah conception of the common ties which bind them, a heterogeneous assemblage of people, into one common body

[1] Few anthropologists have concerned themselves with this problem. But see Noon, 1949, pp. 75–84.

is not based on culture, or on the strength of social interaction between individuals, or on heredity, or on residence on the reservation. The people regarded as Makah, by themselves and by those who are not of their group, are such by a political definition framed to organize a group of people with political rights as members of the Makah Tribe. It is a concept similar to that of American citizenship rather than to that of membership in a community ; for those who have long since left the reservation and lost all contact with other members of the group may still retain their membership within it. It differs from American citizenship since naturalization is impossible unless the one seeking entrance is an actual descendant of a former member of the group.

The definition is embodied in the tribal constitution, in which membership in the tribe is restricted to :

(*a*) All persons of Indian blood whose names appear on the official census rôle of the tribe as of April 1, 1935.

(*b*) All children born to any member of the Makah Indian Tribe who is a resident of the reservation at the time of the birth of said child.

(*c*) Persons of Makah Indian blood who may hereafter be adopted as tribal members by order of the tribe.[1]

The minimum definition of the Makah then becomes : that group composed of individuals who are descendants of free [2] inhabitants of the villages of the Cape Flattery area and whose claims to membership are not in conflict with enrolment in some other tribal group.

An Inherited Status

Without this blood link to the past, there can be no membership in the group. This does not mean that those who have ancestors from other tribal groups are excluded from membership. There are none of pure Makah ancestry among them, and this is explicitly recognized by the Makah themselves. Every Makah can trace his ancestors into other villages located up and

[1] *Constitution and By-Laws of the Makah Indian Tribe of the Makah Indian Reservation Washington*, p. 1. Washington : Government Printing Office, 1936.

[2] Slaves were not regarded as members of the village communities and their descendants are not Makah.

down the Pacific Coast and inland to the Puget Sound area, and many have whites among their immediate forbears. An individual who has only one Makah grandparent is still eligible for membership in the tribe and his claims are as acceptable as those of one who has four Makah grandparents, if there is such a person among the present-day members of the group. The right to membership can be acquired through either maternal or paternal lines, though paternal claims are commoner and seem to be regarded as somewhat stronger than those derived from maternal ancestors.

Yet descent from Makah ancestors does not necessarily ensure acceptance as a Makah. Louise Armstrong who lives at Neah Bay is denied all privileges restricted to members of the Makah Tribe and is regarded as an alien although her mother was Makah and she herself was reared by Makah relatives upon the reservation. She has spent most of her life at Neah Bay except when away at Indian boarding schools. But her father was a member of another tribe and she was enrolled as a member of his tribe before her parents separated. Makah ancestry, a knowledge of the Makah language, residence on the reservation, inheritance of land on the reservation from her Makah grandfather, and finally marriage with a member of the tribe, did not affect her alien status. Members of the tribe insist that she is not a Makah. Before her marriage, and after her divorce, they resented her presence on the reservation. Her own relatives are powerless to alter her status, but they are attempting to obtain a house for her on the reservation so that she may remain in the village permanently and they are trying to persuade her to register a child by a previous marriage as a Makah. They argue that this is possible since the child is a descendant of the Makah and has never been enrolled as a member of another tribe, though both her parents officially belong to other tribes.

Another woman is a Makah, though to the outsider her claim to the status looks much weaker than that of Louise Armstrong. This is Dorcas Halvorson, who first moved to the village about 1939. She speaks no Makah, and knows little about Makah traditions. Her Makah grandmother married a white man and with him moved from the reservation. Their children were reared away from the reservation, and the daughters in their turn married white men and ignored their Indian heritage. One was the mother of Mrs. Halvorson. In 1939, her husband found work on the reservation, and the family came to live at Neah Bay. When Mrs. Halvorson decided to open a business, she discovered that she would have to pay a fee and obtain a licence as she was not a member of the tribe. She arranged to be adopted into the tribe. She is therefore a Makah though she considers herself a white woman and has little concern with the other Makah. Members of the tribe complain of her attitude towards them, but they do not deny that she is a Makah and by virtue of that fact is entitled to live upon the reservation, receive an assignment of land, and share in the proceeds of the tribal property. Her children, though their father is a white man and they have but an eighth Makah blood, are equally accepted.

Residence at Neah Bay, and even birth in that community combined with a life lived in close association with those regarded as Makah, does not entitle one to claim membership in the tribe. In a city on the Sound I met an old woman who was brought to Neah Bay as a slave when she was a small girl. She grew up at Neah Bay and continued to live there after slavery was abolished. When her relatives sought her out and asked her to return to her own tribe, she refused on the ground that Neah Bay was the only home she knew. She married a Makah. She was initiated into Makah ceremonial societies which existed when she was a young woman and was active in the winter festivities where she was in much demand as a performer because of her fine voice and knowledge of many songs. She was respected and liked by other members of the community. When land was allotted to members of the tribe, the allotting agent attempted to discover which of the people on the reservation were Makah and had a right to receive allotments. The members of the tribe refused to allow her to receive land on the ground that she was not a Makah. The daughter whom she had borne to a member of another tribe was also refused an allotment on the same ground, although she was born at Neah Bay and lived there until she was a young woman. The people of Neah Bay refused to admit that either woman was a Makah, though they maintained friendly relations with them after they left the reservation. I found only one Makah who thought that the old woman should receive an allotment and be treated as a member of the tribe. This was Maud Foote, a woman of over seventy. Her father was a Makah ; her mother came from a Nootka tribe on Vancouver Island. Mrs. Foote spoke her mother's dialect as a child and spent much of her girlhood amongst her mother's people. Later she lived away from Neah Bay when she worked in the Sound area as a young woman. When she married it was to a man of another tribe. For a long time she lived with him amongst his people. In middle age she returned to Neah Bay with her children. She is accepted as a Makah, though some members of the tribe object because her children have been registered as Makah rather than as members of their father's tribe.

A Clayoquet woman who married into the tribe as a young girl died in the winter of 1940. She had lived at Neah Bay for over sixty years, part of the time as a widow. Members of the tribe refused to give her a pension from the tribal funds, although she was helpless and had no means of support, for they considered her an alien. They suggested that she either return to her own home on Vancouver Island or that the Canadian Government should provide for her.

Many similar cases reflect the attitude of the Makah, that there must be an acknowledged blood tie, however slight, and that residence itself is unimportant in establishing membership in the group. Many years ago a Quinault woman, now dead, married Manny Day, a member of the Makah tribe. She had been married previously to a member of her own tribe by whom she had two children. When she came to Neah Bay her children accompanied her. They grew up at Neah Bay in the household of their Makah stepfather. Their mother's children by this man are accepted as Makah. They themselves remained alien. The daughter married a Makah and continues to live at Neah Bay. Her closest friends are amongst Makah women. She speaks the language as well as they do, and knows as much about Makah traditions. She appears at most gatherings where Makah appear. The Makah, however, regard her as a member of the Quinault tribe. Her brother also grew up at Neah Bay, and at one time was married to a Makah wife. After their divorce, he married a Quinault woman with whom he lives at Neah Bay. He is always referred to as an alien who has no right to be on the reservation. Makah object if he fishes in rivers reserved to the tribe. He said that, when he took a job with a construction

F

company which had agreed to give preference in employment to members of the Makah tribe for work being done upon the reservation, Makah men complained to the company and said he had no right to the job.

A few genealogies of people accepted as members of the tribe, will show more clearly the heterogeneous ancestry of the Makah. I have for this purpose chosen four children, who are probably a representative sample of the types of descent found in the group. Triangles represent males, circles females. Blackened triangles and circles represent individuals regarded as Makah ; open ones, individuals regarded as aliens. The genealogies are set out on pages 68 and 69.

Divergent though their ancestry is, all four children are considered to have good claims to be considered as Makah and thus as members of the tribe. Some objected to the enrolment of Child C who has a white father, but her claim has been recognized. The genealogy of Child D has a further interest, because of the status of his paternal grandmother. Her Quileute father moved to Neah Bay when he married a Makah woman. She herself grew up at Neah Bay and then married a Makah man. The Makah still referred to her as a Quileute. If her mother was actually a Makah, Makah ancestry seems to have been ineffective in this instance in securing her acceptance by the group. It is likely, however, that her mother had been a slave or the child of slave parents.

A few people cannot claim membership in the tribe by virtue of consanguineal descent, but have the status by virtue of a legal descent. These are people whose alien mothers bore adulterine children to men of other stocks while living in wedlock with a member of the Makah tribe. Where the husband acknowledges the child as his own, the child becomes a member of the tribe, though all may know that it has no physical claim to Makah ancestry.

Summarizing the material shown in the genealogies, it is clear that the status of Makah descends through either males or females. From the definition of membership given in the tribal constitution, it is clear that a woman may legally pass the right to membership down to her children no less than a man. Actually, other members of the tribe may object. A sentiment exists, sometimes openly expressed, that the children of a man from another group should belong to his group. If he is an Indian, they should be enrolled on his reservation. If he is a white, they should be reared as ' whites '. The sentiment cannot crystallize into a guiding principle, however, for most Makah have some immediate relatives for whom they would wish an exception to be made, and they will urge their claims to Makah status at the same time that they complain about the usurpation of the status by others who are less closely related but have exactly the same claims to the status. Thus Charles Reader, a Quileute, is married to a Makah woman and they have registered their children as Makah, with the support of the wife's family. Reader himself has Makah ancestors, but is not considered a possible member of the tribe. Makah other than his close affinal kin object to his children being enrolled as Makah and say they should have no right to claim the benefit of the tribal funds. Reader says that the Makah have attempted to drive him from the reservation, and that they object whenever he finds work on projects which they think should be reserved to tribal members.

This discrimination between the rights given by paternal and maternal descent seems based on the feeling that a marriage should be patrilocal. Sally Grove, a Makah woman of over sixty, who was explaining the complexity of the background of different individuals at Neah Bay said : ' Of course, we're all mixed up in here because the men marry into different tribes and bring their wives here and that way we have women from all over. But a funny thing is that when the girls marry, they don't seem to move away. Instead their husbands come here, so we have men from all over too.' When this happens, however, the position of the husband remains anomalous. Members of the tribe may work against him to try and force him to leave the village. If he refuses to do so, and if his children are enrolled as Makah, people will remember the alien origin of the paternal line, but will be forced to admit the Makah status of the children.

If the paternal line is Makah, there is no question about the status of the children, though an alien woman's status is not changed by her marriage to a Makah. If the woman seems to be infringing upon the prerogatives of the group, there may be protests ; for the feeling is strong that anything that belongs to the Makah should not be used for the benefit of anyone outside the group. The feeling came out strongly in connection with

CHILD A

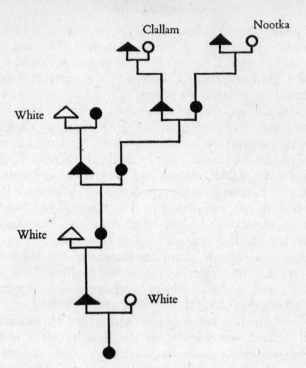

CHILD B

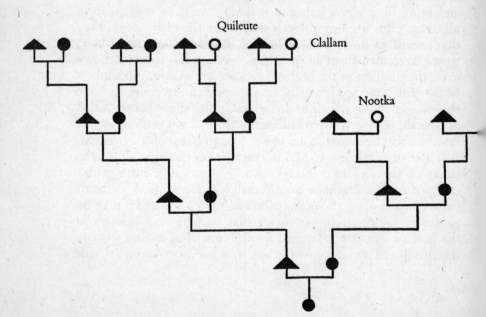

CHILD C

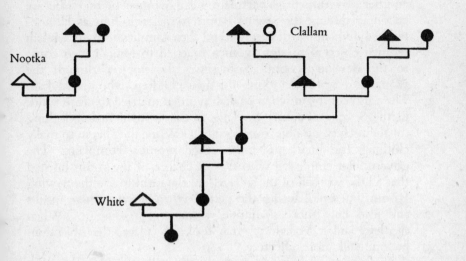

CHILD D

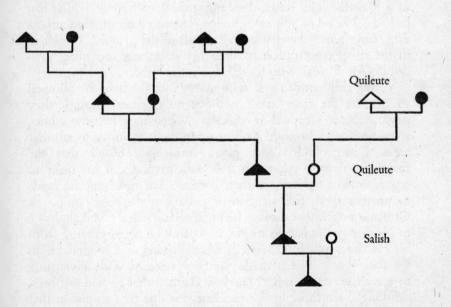

the Sewing Room established jointly by the Indian Service and another government department. All women of the tribe are encouraged to use the Sewing Room to make clothing and household equipment for themselves and their families. Many Makah women object if foreign women married to Makah men come to the Sewing Room. Sometimes they object though the women are sewing clothing for their children, who are Makah. They also complain when Makah women married to aliens work in the Sewing Room. So long as the women make clothing for themselves, no objection is raised. When they begin to make clothing for their husbands, other women complain. The government employee who was in charge of the room insisted that all the women of the village had the right to use the Sewing Room, but even during the period when she was there insults and jeers kept more than one woman from using it. When she left, and a Makah woman took her place, the objections became still more effective.

A woman who marries outside the tribe does not lose her membership in the tribe, even though she goes to live with her husband's people. At any time she has the right to return to the reservation and live there in full enjoyment of her position as a Makah. The status does not appear to be one which can be lost. I heard of nobody who has renounced his tribal membership, and no member has been cast out of the group. Nowhere in the tribal constitution is there any statement regarding procedure for formal withdrawal from the tribe.

Young children of those who marry into the tribe are allowed to live on the reservation without interference, though they never become accepted as Makah. When they become adults, some pressure is brought to bear upon them to move to another area. Older children are given immediate notice that the marriage of their parent to a Makah gives them no right to regard Makah territory as their home. Attempts may be made to prevent them following their parent to the reservation. A Quinault boy whose mother had married an elderly Makah drove to Neah Bay to visit his mother. Before he could emerge from his car, he was arrested for drunken driving and lodged in jail for the night. The next day he was released with a warning to leave the reservation. The boy claimed that he had not been drinking. He thought the incident was due to a suspicion that he might be planning to move to Neah Bay, and that the Makah were warning him off in advance. This interpretation was given force by a number of other incidents of similar nature which happened during the year and by statements from other alien Indians about the Makah attitude towards their presence in the area.

Summary

The case material quoted above makes it clear that the recognition of an individual as a Makah has nothing to do with the language that he speaks, the degree of Indian blood which he has, the customs which he practises. It is due purely to the recognition of descent from former members of the Indian communities about Cape Flattery, which is confirmed by registration as a Makah. A Makah may be seven-eighths white, speak only English, have been born away from the reservation and educated in the schools of the cities of the Sound area. Another person may have four Makah grandparents, speak only Makah, and have spent most of his life either at Neah Bay or at least on the reservation. He also is a Makah. The difference in the situations to which the two have been exposed demonstrates that the Makah themselves do not recognize a common culture as a necessary requirement for membership in the group.

In order to organize these heterogeneous individuals into a corporate group known as the Makah, however, we must include the factor of the existence of the reservation which is owned jointly by the group. The group is organized around the reservation in which all members have equal rights. The individual because of his property rights in the reservation thereby becomes a member of the social structure which has been created about it.[1] The territory of the reservation is regarded as their inheritance from lineal ancestors who fought for the land against invading tribes in the remote past and defended their possession of the land with their own blood. It is confirmed to them

---

[1] This is distinct from ownership of land on the reservation. A few aliens, of some degree of Makah blood, have inherited land on the reservation from Makah relatives. A portion of the reservation was allotted, and while the Trust Patent was never lifted so that it became possible for the owners to dispose of their allotments, the allotments could be inherited. But alien heirs own property rights in particular pieces of land, rather than in the reservation itself.

through treaties with the United States Government which recognized the Makah in their possession of the land around Cape Flattery. In the ideology of the group, it is their possession also as an inheritance from their more remote ancestors who were created upon the Cape. It is in their possession because their ancestors occupied the land since before the memory of man and because they themselves have spent their lives in the area. If the reservation should disappear, the group itself would probably disintegrate. This is recognized by the Makah themselves. One gave as their reason for combating the proposed sale of the reservation : ' The young people won't have any land if they sell now, and they will just wander around homeless with no more tribe. But if they force us to give up the land, we should just lease it for a few years. Then there will always be this place to come back to some day.'

MAKAH SOLIDARITY

The Makah do not form an isolated social unit, nor can it be assumed that a Makah associates primarily or even most frequently with other Makah. Individuals are in close contact with alien Indians and whites who have married into the tribe or who live near them in the village. With them some Makah spend more time and share more interests than they do with members of the tribe. A few make definite attempts to isolate themselves from the life led by most of the people of the village, including the majority of the Makah.

Isolation of a Portion of the Tribe

A few Makah belong to the Apostolic Church. They seek to isolate themselves from contact with all save those who belong to that sect. This draws them into close association with some whites and separates them from most Makah. In Neah Bay, the church is small. It has been able to attract only a small portion of the tribe, and has about twenty firm members, most of whom come from the same extended family group. A few are alien Indians of the Clallam tribe. They say that they are attempting to live only for God and that to do this they must reduce to a minimum contacts with those whose lives are not oriented towards this purpose, lest they be contaminated and drawn back to worldly things. While the isolation from the

' worldly ' people of Neah Bay is not complete, social contacts save with members of their own families and with other Apostolics have been largely disrupted. Members of the church avoid parties given by other people, especially those in which some attempt is made to include Indian games, stories, or songs. They do not go to dances, or to the cinema, or to any large gathering of people except in their own church. Rather than associate with other people at Neah Bay, they spend their time working towards the improvement of their church building or working on gifts for the Apostolic minister, a white man, who visits them from Port Angeles. These people are in closer contact with the Apostolic congregation of Port Angeles, composed of whites, than they are with most of the Makah at Neah Bay, and presumably feel a greater sense of community with them.

Another religious group has had something of the same effect. The Shakers [1] resemble the Apostolics in their attempt to isolate themselves from the life of the rest of the village, though they are less stringent in their prohibition of casual contacts. While they form a small cell in the community, the majority of them have more contact with Makah than they have with other people, including Shakers in other tribes. Moreover, many who were once strong Shakers and who still regard themselves as Shakers, although they rarely attend the church, are about the village at parties and mix indiscriminately with all Makah regardless of religious affiliation. There are thus social ties which connect the Shakers as a group with others in the tribe. This is not true of the Apostolics, who have formed their church at Neah Bay only recently and are still in the process of accumulating a circle of backsliders who serve as a medium of contact. The Presbyterians are much like the Shakers. A few attend only the meetings of the church, but most of them do not allow their religious ties to affect their social life.

Some individuals, independent of any religious feeling, form their contacts with whites at Neah Bay or outside the village and see little of their Makah neighbours. Emily Lester was one who did so. She said that she deliberately shunned her Makah compatriots with the exception of her immediate relatives because her neighbours hated her family and gossiped about it. Once

[1] This is an Indian Church founded in 1883 by an Indian living in the Sound area.

she said that any contact with people in Neah Bay could lead only to serious trouble. Her closest associations, besides those with her parents and her children, were with white friends of her alien husband.

But all the people whom I knew seemed to see a good deal of people who do not belong to the tribe. Despite this, the Makah do seem to feel that they constitute a body for more than political purposes, and that they have in common close ties that bring them together on a plane different from that on which they associate with others who do not have this background of shared interests.

Feeling of Group Unity

A feeling of unity is often expressed by older people, less often by younger members of the tribe. Older people seem to have a picture in which the society of the village represents every member of the tribe. Wedding parties are criticized if they take a form appealing only to younger people because ' they should be for everyone '. In such statements ' everyone ' means all Makah, though other alien Indians in the village who have lived there for a long time may also be included. An old woman once referred to the school teachers as ' the teachers of my children '. She explained that while she is childless, nevertheless she calls all the children in the tribe her children because they are all Makah. Even young people in their twenties and thirties like to talk of a time when everyone in the tribe came to the parties and spoke disapprovingly of the present when only a few appear.

Gradually, I realized that though at the moment some people take no part in the activities of the group, still they are parts of a small ingrown community, the members of which have lived together for so many years that they know each other intimately. Almost every Makah is related to every other Makah, though the kinship links may be distant. Most of them have lived most of their lives in close contact. The majority of them expect to continue to live together in the same village. They expect and hope that their children and grandchildren will do the same.

The actual solidarity and cohesion of the Makah is not reflected in the surface play of social interaction which is visible to the observer. It only becomes apparent when you understand that these people are relatives who have lived together, listened to the same legends, fought, and helped each other, intermarried, poisoned each other's relatives, and helped to lay out each other's dead. They are such a small group that every Makah who lives at Neah Bay knows every other Makah by sight, by name, by reputation, and by family history. They know their relative status within the group and what behaviour to expect from them. It is literally impossible for any Makah, save a small child, to meet a strange Makah. It is improbable that they meet individuals from any other group on so sure a foundation of knowledge of what can be expected. By comparison, even those whites whom they see daily in their village are strangers with an unknown background.

THE ORIGIN OF THE TRIBE

The feeling of group solidarity, as well as the political organization of the tribe, is of relatively recent origin. One or two old people have seen its whole development in the course of their lifetimes : the drawing together of members of several village communities to form one group which was given a foreign name and a superimposed political organization unlike anything known to the parent communities. About this group eventually developed a feeling of unity and of common interests, replacing the feeling of separateness which those who came from each original village held. Then the existence of economic and political privileges connected with status in the tribe gave rise to a new feeling of exclusiveness and a determination to define rigidly membership within the group and to keep the membership as restricted as possible.

The Old Villages

Most of the older members of the tribe were born not at Neah Bay, but at other villages which existed along the coast at the time the reservation was created. At one time there were five villages. bIída?, east of Neah Bay, was abandoned long before all save the very oldest were born. No one living today ever lived within it. dí.aˣ, wá?ač, c'úEs, and osé·IX̌ existed until a later date, and some of the people born within them are still alive.

Each village was an autonomous unit, and on occasion one warred with another. There was no tribal political structure of which the villages were segments. Each village had its own territory, and trespass by individuals from other Makah villages was resented quite as much as was trespass by members of alien villages. The common practice of village exogamy gave most individuals kin in all villages, but this did not create bonds which overrode the feeling of independence. They recognized, however, that the inhabitants of all villages shared similar customs and a common language, and that in this sense they were one. The whole group bore a name which designated them as a unit set off from people living in other villages in nearby regions. They were called qw'édiča?at^x, ' people living at the Cape '.

Development of the Tribe

In speaking of the former villages, informants say that they were all ' one tribe, because they all spoke the same language '. Nevertheless, the tribe as it exists today is regarded by them as a recent development resulting from the existence of the agency and the reservation.

They received the name Makah in 1855 when they made their treaty with the United States Government. The government interpreter was a Clallam, who gave the treaty makers the Clallam name for the Cape Flattery people. This has been the official name for them ever since. Today most people speak of themselves as ' Makah ', though some of the older people say that they dislike the name because it does not belong to them and they do not understand its meaning.

The treaty also began the development of forms of political organization leading to the coalescence of the villages into one body. Governor Stevens, who negotiated the treaty, appointed head chiefs over the entire group, with village chiefs under them. In the following years, their position was largely ignored, but a start had been made at the recognition of the Makah as belonging to one political unit. With the establishment of the agency, all the villages were placed under one jurisdiction. The old village and lineage claims to land were replaced by a common ownership of the reservation area. The people of blída? were moved into an area immediately adjacent to the houses of dí·a^x, without regard to the property rights of the dí·a^x people, when the agency officials decided to erect the agency buildings on their site.

For some time longer, however, the villages remained separate, and their inhabitants still retained their old village names. When older people who grew up in the other villages are asked what the Makah did when they were young, they usually counter that they do not know since in those days they rarely visited Neah Bay and therefore knew nothing of the doings of the Makah. Despite the formal recognition of the tribe by the United States, they still thought in terms of dí·aˣ, wá?ač', c'úEs, and osé·I✗'.

Neah Bay Emerges

With the development of Neah Bay from the Indian village of dí·aˣ, people from the other villages began to move to this centre. They were drawn by the advantages attaching to the site because of its possession of the best harbour along the coast. It was the place to which sealing vessels came to recruit hunters for the Alaska voyage, and men from other villages came there to find a ship for the long trip to the seal rookeries. While they were gone, their families lived with relatives at Neah Bay. Some built houses in the village in which they lived for part of the year, though they continued to spend the rest of their time at their homes in the old villages. When the agency established a school at Neah Bay and made schooling compulsory, there was a further incentive to settle permanently at Neah Bay. While the school was a boarding school, children were sent in from the other villages, and their parents remained at home. When the school was transformed into a day school, many families moved to Neah Bay to be near their children. Traders established stores in the village. It became a convenient place to dispose of fish, oil, or sealskins and to procure goods from the outside world. It was also more convenient than the Pacific Coast villages for those who wished to make the trip to the Sound area or to the city of Victoria, for trade or work ; for they avoided the trip around Cape Flattery or landward across the Cape. The children who grew up in Neah Bay while attending school began to settle there instead of returning to their own villages.

The Pacific villages were gradually abandoned. Finally only

a few old people were left at the village of osé·IX̱ʼ, which lay fifteen miles down the coast from the Cape and was the most distant of the Makah villages. It was beyond the boundaries of the reservation, but some preferred to stay there where, in 1882, a small reservation, a mile square, was created for them. But year by year, the elders left at osé·IX̱ʼ died, while those who lived at Neah Bay almost forgot about them. Finally only two old people were left. They joined their relatives at Neah Bay, and the oséX̱·Iʼ site was sold.

Today there are only Makah, though members of the tribe remember their divergent origins. The antagonisms which once existed between the villages have faded away and are no longer influential in affecting Makah behaviour. There is little indication of distinctions within the Makah group based on former village allegiance. They recognize that all have equal rights to the village of Neah Bay, to the reservation, and in the tribal organization. Even those descended from the people of dí·aˣ seem to make no claim to privileges on the ground that Neah Bay is within their former territory. There is little reason to quarrel since most people can claim descent from several villages. All four children whose genealogies are cited had ancestors in different villages. Child A had ancestors in dí·aˣ and osé·IX̱ʼ. Child B had great grandparents in osé·IX̱ʼ, wá?ač, c'úEs, dí·aˣ, and probably blída?. Child C is descended from inhabitants of osé·IX̱ʼ, wá?ač, and dí·aˣ. Child D had ancestors at osé·IX̱ʼ, c'úEs, dí·aˣ, and blída?.

Settlement within Neah Bay is somewhat affected by the original village affiliations. The lots and houses on the site of dí·aˣ at the west end of the present village are mostly owned by the descendants of these people. The blída? people settled to the east of them along the bay. When the wa?áč people began to move to Neah Bay, they were given unoccupied land at the back of the village away from the bay. The people of c'úEs and osé·IX̱ʼ settled either further east along the bay or at the back of the village where the land was drained and the swamp filled in to increase the area available for building. For some time there existed a division between the West End People and the East End People. The two groups competed against each other in games and dances, and each group had its own leader for these purposes. Today this distinction appears only in conversations, when older men and women tell of the parties given when they were young. In ordinary life, the distinction has vanished. Nothing that occurs today would lead one to suspect that it had ever existed. Even when the terms are used, it is apparent that the speakers are thinking of divisions within one village rather than of the diverse origins of the people in each section.

Today they are all people of Neah Bay, and the Neah Bays is a common synonym for Makah. The Makah themselves use it, and so do other Indian groups in Washington and on Vancouver Island. But in this usage the term Neah Bay includes only its Indian inhabitants. The whites who also dwell there, and do so in increasing numbers since the highway was built, are not regarded as Neah Bays. The term is not applied to them even in jest.

Factors creating Makah Exclusiveness

In eighty years, the entity of the Makah Tribe has been created from the descendants of the formerly independent villages about the Cape Flattery region. All members of the tribe associate on a common plane of political equality whatever their original village allegiance. But they maintain their identity as over and against all other people.

It was undoubtedly their common residence at Neah Bay and their status as Indians and wards of the government *vis-à-vis* the Indian agency which created the tribe from the former independent villages. But this alone was not enough ; for other people who lived among them—who were also Indians and under the jurisdiction of the Indian Service—were excluded from the group, and rejected by the Makah as their fellows. Thus many who have lived on the reservation for many years, who have shared in the life of the Makah and presumably are similar in culture with others of their generation, are not accepted as members of the tribe, though some of them have Makah ancestors. Whites are also rejected, and are not considered to be part of the Neah Bay community, though again some of them have spent their lives in close association with the Makah. However, their out-group status is not crucial, since they always had a particular relation to the Indian Service, and were never considered to be wards of the government despite their residence on a reservation. The real problem is why the Makah tribe should be created from inhabitants of the former villages, but should exclude alien Indians who are refused admittance into the tribe.

The answer probably lies in the rôle of the reservation. In the days before it existed, membership in the local group seems to have been based much more on residence than on descent. Those who came to live among the Makah seem to have been accepted as members of a village community. Slaves were certainly regarded as underprivileged citizens, and obtained their subsistence and their place in the community as chattels of the lineage groups which were reckoned as the property-holding groups. Each lineage had its rights to the resources of certain stretches of land, and protected these against outsiders, whether residents of the same village or trespassers from other villages. But the heads of the lineage invited aliens who were descendants of the lineage, whether through males or females, to visit and help exploit the fishing grounds and the other economic resources pertaining to the lineage. Thus a member of another community was privileged to exploit rights in the Flattery area. If he wished to do so, he might come to live with his relatives and seems to have been accepted without question as a member of the community, though his origin would be remembered. His descendants became merged with the community. Since the importance of the lineage in village life and in the intertribal exchanges depended to a large extent upon the number of members it could mobilize for defence or aggression, or to contribute property for distribution at potlatches and on other occasions, there were good reasons why the Makah at that period were not interested in defining citizenship qualifications too rigidly. Presumably it was only if an alien began to enhance his own status at the expense of the old members of the community, including the leaders of his lineage, that his presence in the area might be questioned and slurs cast on his right to speak as a member of the community.

After the creation of the reservation, and the changes brought about by the work of the Indian Service, the situation was altered. The rights in land which formerly vested in the lineages passed to the Makah tribe. Men who had welcomed the presence of alien relatives in the use of their own lineage resources, now found themselves having to share the resources of the tribe with those in whom they had no interest, while the presence of their own relatives would meet with equal objection from members of other lineages. As the old style lineage houses disappeared, and individual family units became the customary residential groups, the presence of aliens became more apparent ; for they lived as discrete groups and did not merge their identity with the old lineages on which they had a kinship claim. Moreover, the glory and advantage of the individual was no longer merged with that of the lineage. The presence of the agent, and other Indian Service officials, limited the occasions on which it was necessary for groups to muster large numbers of adherents. Warfare and intra-village battles were outmoded. Potlatches were forbidden. Moreover, in the last years of the potlatches changing economic conditions had made it possible for one man to accumulate a surplus of trade goods sufficient for distribution. The potlatch became more of an occasion for individual glory than for the stressing of the importance of the lineage. Then it disappeared altogether. There was no longer an incentive to press for the inclusion of aliens and to associate them fully with other members of the group.

On the other hand, there were new reasons for narrowing the group benefitting from the existence of the reservation. Under the early allotment acts it was envisaged that eventually all unallotted land on the reservation would be sold and the money divided amongst the members of the tribe. The amount each could receive was thus related to the total number who had a claim to receive a share. When the timber was sold, many of the Makah hoped that the money from the sale would be divided among members of the tribe. Again there was a strong motive to limit the number eligible to participate in the distribution. The incentive was the stronger since there was a new evaluation of wealth. Where formerly, the Makah reckoned their wealth in terms of the number of dependents they could hold and the number of people whom they could impress by distributions of property, they now reckoned it in terms of what they could obtain for themselves and in terms of an individual standard of living. The inclusion of aliens could thus be only a threat to the highest achievement in wealth, and was to be prevented wherever possible. This came out clearly

G

at the time of the sale of the tiny Ozette reservation. When the Indian Service prepared to distribute the proceeds to those who had a claim on the Ozette land, one of the two survivors successfully denied his paternity to prevent his reputed daughter and her children from participating in the distribution and thus secured himself a larger share.

Concern to differentiate Makah from non-Makah is thus a reflection of interest in property-rights. Makah do not object to the participation of aliens in the ordinary social life of the Neah Bay community. Aliens are free to participate along with the Makah, and no attention is there paid to their alien status. It is only when they seem to be encroaching upon the economic privileges of the Makah that their status is thrown in their teeth.

Since whites have no hope of incorporation within the tribe or of receiving Indian privileges because of their status as non-Indians, the battle against individual encroachment largely ignores their presence. It is against alien Indians that the Makah are most aggressive, and they protect themselves not only against those who are complete aliens but also against aliens who have Makah ancestors and who in former days would have been welcomed by their relatives into full participation in the life of the community. On the other hand, the Makah are realists. Since the treaty confirms the reservation to all Makah, who are defined as the residents of the Cape Flattery area, they accept without argument the participation, as Makah, of descendants of all five villages. They also accept into the tribe aliens who have a positive claim as descendants of former Makah inhabitants, but only if acceptable grounds for the exclusion of these people are lacking.

'ALIENS' IN THE MAKAH COMMUNITY

Aliens attached to Makah Households

There are aliens living at Neah Bay who are closely attached to Makah households. Some are men and women who live with their Makah consorts at Neah Bay. Others are the children of alien consorts, who live as members of the households of their step-parents. Finally, a few individuals of Makah ancestry live with Makah relatives, though they are not recognized as Makah.

In 1942, there were 97 Makah households with a total population of 410 people, of whom 56 or roughly 13·6 per cent were aliens. Those who are Indians probably have as diverse an origin as do the Makah themselves, since marriage beyond the borders of one's group is a common practice throughout the area from which they come. Most are drawn from groups in Washington or on Vancouver Island, though a few are from more distant areas.[1] They include people with the following ' tribal ' affiliations : Clallam, Quileute, Quinault, Clayoquet, Nitinat, Cowichan, Sook, Lummi, Shoshone, Siletz. There are also people from more remote tribes : one from the Colville Reservation in eastern Washington ; another from a California band ; several who have sufficient Dakota blood to be enrolled as Dakotas though they are largely of white ancestry and have spent most of their lives on the west coast. In addition, the aliens include eight whites, one Filipino, and one Mexican. All the whites are American citizens, though one has been naturalized. Their ancestors were English, Irish, French, German, and Scandinavian.

These people bring something of their own backgrounds into the households in which they live. Those who have children teach them something of the ways which they themselves learned as children in a different locality from bearers of a different culture ; 42 of the '97 Makah households are thus affected by the presence of aliens. The difference in cultural background is not the only effect of their presence. Though the aliens associate constantly with the Makah in their households and usually with other Makah, they remain aliens and never find unquestioned acceptance of their presence in the area. This in turn may have serious repercussions on the position of the household in the village and on its economic welfare, especially where the alien is the head of the household and the chief support of its members.

[1] In the coastal and Sound area of Washington the largest organized groups in pre-European times seem to have been the village communities. A number of villages might speak a common dialect but linguistic units did not mean political unity. In some areas, villages seem to have been fairly populous ; in others, they consisted of a single large extended family. Village exogamy was common, and intermarriage has given most individuals claims on a number of different communities to which they can trace ancestors. One person in his lifetime might change his village affiliation several times as he lived with one group of relatives after another.

The Makah are well aware of the heterogeneity in their midst. At times they seem to feel that Neah Bay has become a catch-all to which people from other tribes migrate. Some said, ' Everyone who has ever been here at Neah Bay gets to like it here and then they all want to move down.' Some expressed surprise that people of other tribes preferred to live at Neah Bay instead of on their own reservations, and at times they seemed to feel that unless some steps were taken to stop the influx that they would be inundated by aliens. I have heard them wonder : ' Whose reservation is this, anyway ? Makah or Dakota ! ' They feel apprehension despite the fact that few aliens settle permanently on the reservation unless they are related to Makah through either affinal or consanguineal ties.

Older Makah say that the infiltration is no new development. People from other areas, they say, have always been anxious to take over the Cape region. In the past there have been periods when the reservation has had an even greater diversity of population than at present. Women from Alaskan tribes have married Makah men and come to live at Neah Bay. Other Alaskan Indians have accompanied Makah children home from the Indian boarding schools, and then settled in the village for a period before returning to Alaska. During the days when the place was a rendezvous for the sealers and then for the early halibut fishers, many people came from Clayoquet, Clallam, and Quileute villages to live with Makah relatives for months and even years while the men were away with the sealers or fishermen. When Indians from Alaska and northern British Columbia first began to come south for hop picking in the Sound area, many of them made the journey along the Strait to stay with friends made when the Makah sealers were in Alaskan waters. Nevertheless, although many aliens have come and stayed a while, they have gone away again without attempting to incorporate themselves into the Makah group unless they have married a member of the tribe.

Unattached Aliens

The only alien Indians, unattached to Makah households, who are permanent residents of Neah Bay are the members of three family groups, a total of fifteen individuals. One family is headed by an alien who was brought up at Neah Bay as a member of a Makah household. His half-brother is a Makah, and his full-sister is married to a Makah. He thus has close ties with Neah Bay and its residents. The other two households belong to brothers. The two men were brought up on the reservation where their parents were employed by the Indian Service, although neither parent had any prior association with the area. Their parents were later transferred to another reservation, but the two men returned to Neah Bay to live, bringing with them wives of their own tribe.[1] They seem to regard Neah Bay as their permanent home, though they and their children continue to be regarded as aliens.

These families are in an anomalous position. Neither parents nor children have any right to the reservation nor can they acquire any rights no matter how long they stay. If they cause trouble, especially through violation of the laws banning the use of alcoholic liquor, the tribe has the right to order them to leave the area. But at the same time they regard themselves as Indians and are so accepted by the people of Neah Bay. Because of their Indian status they are also wards of the government and have such rights and privileges, as well as handicaps, as are inherent in that status. They thus stand half-way between the whites and the Makah. They associate more with Makah than they do with whites, but even the slow process of years of familiarity can bring them no closer to the Makah than they now stand.

Transient Aliens

A few other temporary residents of Neah Bay may be considered here because they rank as Indians. There were a number of them in 1942. They were drawn to Neah Bay by the opportunities to work on the construction projects in the Flattery area. These transients lived with Makah relatives or friends while they stayed in the village. Some rented rooms from relatives ; others stayed as guests. Most were men, but a few were accompanied by their families.

They were a heterogeneous shifting lot, and I was unable to discover much about their number or origin ; for hardly did I discover that they were living in the village than they were gone again. Among them were Quinaults, Quileutes, Lummi,

---

[1] Both women are more than half white.

Clallam, and a few Dakota. All had relatives or friends among the permanent inhabitants of the village, and many knew the area well from previous visits. There were also a few whites who were affinal relatives of the Makah.

A few were complete aliens in the sense that they had no kin or friends within the village when they arrived. Several claimed membership in some Alaskan tribe ; others were from eastern Washington or from Idaho.

These people were regarded as only temporary visitors. They were there only because for the time being good jobs were available. When they wearied of the work, they also wearied of the village and were gone. As they flowed in and out of the village, they were seen about the streets with Makah and other residents of the village. They borrowed money from Makah friends and lived in their houses. But they affected Neah Bay and the Makah but little.

Integration with the Makah

All of the permanent aliens are integrated in some fashion into the community of Neah Bay. Many of them have lived for years in the village and speak Makah as well as most of the members of the tribe. Recent comers to the village would have difficulty in disentangling them from members of the tribe. Certainly no whites, save perhaps the very oldest residents, and a few government officials, have ever gone to the trouble of distinguishing them.

Today the life of the Makah cannot be studied without attention to the presence of the aliens. Their presence is the principal reason, even more important than the present diversity among the Makah, for claiming that the term Makah today does not define a society or a community. The real community of Neah Bay includes the aliens. At the same time, however, the Makah reject the aliens and never forget their foreign origin ; for these people are not members of the Makah tribe and to the Makah themselves the tribe is a more important grouping than the village community.

SUMMARY

Today the name Makah refers to a group of people who are registered as members of the Makah tribe and thus hold property rights to the reservation owned by the Makah as a corporate body. They hold their membership in the tribe by virtue of descent from previous inhabitants of Makah villages. In a rigid sense, the term has no particular implications of cultural, linguistic, or physical similarity ; for those who bear the name show considerable diversity in all three.

Most Makah are today resident at Neah Bay, the only village upon their reservation. Although they are surrounded by whites and have intermarried extensively both with whites and alien Indians, those who live at Neah Bay are members of a small face-to-face community held together not only by membership in the same tribe but by close kinship ties and by a realization of their common historic background. Not all Makah today are members of this community ; for some live on other reservations and others have married into white communities elsewhere in Washington. A few of the members of the small community are not themselves Makah, but some have married into the tribe and others have spent long years closely associated with the Makah. They are generally regarded as members of the Neah Bay community, though they never become members of the tribe.

CHAPTER IV

THE MAKAH AND THE WHITES

IN this and the following chapter, I propose to examine the types of relationships which the Makah have with whites. This should provide some answer to the question of how far the Makah have adapted themselves to the customs of other Americans. If people are closely associated in their daily lives, they must have some understanding of each other's habits, customs, motivations, and symbols, and be prepared to show these some degree of respect. Where the association is close, the two may be said to share common definitions of the situations within which they meet and to exhibit similar habits of behaviour. To this extent, they then share a common culture.[1] Where contacts are reduced to only a few stereotyped relationships, such as the servant–master relationship, the common definitions need be very few. They may amount to no more than an understanding of the duties required and the wages and treatment to be given in return. As contacts include more and more of the total range of human relationships, the field of common definitions also widens. It thus becomes possible to use the intensity of social relationships between members of two groups as an index of acculturation, as well as of assimilation.

This chapter then will be devoted to a review of the types of relationships which the Makah have with whites. These will show the extent to which they now participate in the general American community. The eighty years which the Makah have spent as reservation people might have produced any one of a number of situations : (1) they might have been forced into a socially and economically depressed class having little contact with other Americans save in formal economic and administrative situations ; (2) they might have reacted to the pressure for conformity to the standards of the whites by withdrawing into a

[1] This seems to be the definition of culture followed by Redfield when he says, ' In so far as any defined human aggregate is characterized . . . by conventional understandings, it exhibits a culture . . . ' See Robert Redfield, *The Folk Culture of Yucatan*, p. 16. Chicago, University of Chicago Press, 1942.

world of their own from which retreat they repel all advances with a blank wall of indifference ; (3) they might have acquired a position and a comprehension of American customs which enables them to deal with whites on terms of easy familiarity.[1] Either of the two former possibilities would indicate that the Makah have not assimilated into American society but have received or created a special status from which they have little contact with the rest of the society. Even with these barriers against contact, it would be possible for them to acquire the customs of the whites, but the probability that they retained a culture peculiar to themselves or had developed peculiar customs in response to the situation would be enormous. In the third case, the channels of communication through which culture passes would be in full operation between the groups.

To assess the degree of interaction, it is necessary to look for diagnostic traits of social equality or social subordination. These are to be found in the particular types of social interrelationships to which individuals are admitted. Symbols of social equality are found in the sharing of a meal, the exchange of social calls, appearance together on different social occasions, membership in the same associations. They are displayed in the manner in which people greet each other. In the final analysis, intermarriage, when the children of the union receive a status not inferior to that of either parent, is the symbol of complete equality. Where this occurs, the two groups are rapidly amalgamating, and it is then probably inaccurate to speak in terms of two groups rather than of one.

THE WHITES OF NEAH BAY

A few years ago, it would have been difficult to learn how the Makah reacted to the presence of whites or the possibility of contact with them ; for within the boundaries of their own land they met few except officials of the Indian Service and these were hardly representative of white society. About 1930, there were approximately 15 permanent white residents in the village. By 1941, there were approximately 100 whites at Neah Bay, and many more at the lumber camp on the reservation. Then late in

---

[1] Two other possibilities, disappearance through extermination or through the absorption of individuals into the general population, have already been ruled out by the evidence that the Makah exist today as a group.

1941, the village began to be overrun by strangers who came to work on the defence projects already under construction on the reservation. The influx continued through 1942, with more and more whites appearing each month. Many were eventually housed in the temporary camp built some miles south of the village. Others settled in the village itself. With the declaration of war, soldiers were sent in to guard the coastline against possible invasion. Then naval craft with their crews were stationed at the Bay. The soldiers usually stayed in tent encampments some distance from the village ; the sailors were at the naval station about a mile from Neah Bay. But their wives and children came crowding into Neah Bay as the place nearest their men. Most of them stayed for a few weeks or months and then moved on as the detachments of troops were shifted about.

The transient whites were so numerous and they came and went so fast that it was difficult to make any estimate of the total number of whites in the village at any one time. My impression was that the size of the population doubled in about a year, and most of this increase must have been due to the presence of whites. This meant that during the time of my stay at Neah Bay the population was about equally divided between whites and Indians, with most of the Indians holding membership in the Makah tribe.

It is difficult to say whether these whites would be a reasonably representative sample of the American population or whether the Makah were being exposed to a small unrepresentative group. I should say, however, that they were reasonably typical. They fell into two groups, the transients and the smaller group of permanent residents.

The Transient Whites

The transients were the ones primarily responsible for the great increase in the Neah Bay population. They did not expect to fit into the village as permanent residents. They had no ties beyond that of their jobs which could hold them in the area. Most of them had never heard of Neah Bay until a few days or weeks before they arrived to find its hotel full, houses unavailable, and the housing facilities of the place taxed beyond capacity. Some of them came with trailer houses which they parked on some convenient vacant lot or in clearings close to the edge of the village. They were there only because of the jobs, or because their men were encamped nearby. Many of them found living conditions so unfavourable that they left abruptly without waiting until their jobs were finished. Those who left probably never expected to return to the Bay. Some of the men were planning to leave for Alaska and the building of the great highway. Others had heard of construction jobs in other parts of Washington or in more distant quarters.

Members of this group were held together only by common jobs and by the fact that for the moment they were encamped within the same locality. Their society was unorganized, save for the working life of the men, and the small family groups of couples with their children. In time, they might have shaken down into some semblance of community life, but time was too short. They came as strangers to each other. Once they left Neah Bay, it was improbable that most of them would meet again.

They were a heterogeneous lot. Most of the soldiers and sailors were young unattached males, completely cut off from their families for the moment, though a few were married men who had their wives with them. The construction group was composed of married men with their families, married men who had left their families in more settled areas, and single men. The number of women in the transient group was disproportionately small. I heard of no single women who came to the area alone, though some may have done so. The number of children also seemed to be small. There were no very old people. The transient group was thus unrepresentative both in age range and in sex ratio.

They came from all parts of the United States. The soldiers were in regiments drawn from New York, New Jersey, and Texas. Many of those from New York had never before been far from the city streets. The construction workers seemed largely drawn from northern states, and many of them had lived in Washington for some time. Ultimately many of them came from Minnesota, Wisconsin, Michigan, the Dakotas, Idaho, and Montana. But there were also some families from Arkansas and Oklahoma, who had drifted from one job to another until they found themselves in this far northwestern corner of the country. Among these were a few men who had some small fraction of Indian blood, though they were accepted as whites by their fellows. These were men with some claim to Cherokee descent, though they had either long since lost contact with any reservation or had never had any. In conversation they might mention their Cherokee blood, but it was as though a second generation American were to mention a German grandmother whom he had never seen.

During the summer when the fishing season was on and the bay became a haven for the small craft that fish the waters off the coast, the motley white population increased again and with a new element. Most of the fishermen lived on their boats rather than in the village, and they came ashore only to sell their fish, buy supplies at jetty or store, eat at the restaurants, or find a woman. Some of them were strangers ; others had returned to Neah Bay summer after summer for decades and knew most of the permanent inhabitants. Many of the fishermen were said to come from Southern Europe, but the few I met were of Scandinavian descent. In years past, some had brought their wives along and left them in rented cabins ashore while they spent their days fishing. In the summer of 1942, I heard of none who did so.

The economic and class status of the transients would be hard to define. Among the men working on the construction jobs were a few highly trained engineers. Among the military contingent were officers as well as enlisted men. Some of the fishermen were wealthy managers who owned their own boats, nets, and other fishing equipment. Others who appeared were rovers who came to the village with little more than their clothes. Some had wandered from job to job and from state to state. They had been miners, lumberjacks, carpenters, jackhammer men, bootleggers, and fishermen. Probably few of the transients had an education beyond the high school level. Many had not reached secondary school. It would probably be fair to say that the majority would be regarded as the rough element in a more settled community.

Many seemed to belong to a labouring class with a minimum of specialized skill. But at the moment, with high wages and good prices for fish, they certainly did not represent a depressed economic group. Even those working on unskilled jobs earned from eight to ten dollars a day, and received overtime pay for work on Sunday and at night. All the construction men belonged to labour unions since no one, except members of the Makah tribe, was hired unless he had a union card. Probably many of them were union members only by compulsion, and they had little interest in labour politics. A few, however, had been union men from a time when a union card might be a dangerous thing to display. Some of the older men had belonged to the Industrial Workers of the World in the days of its strength. Despite this, there seemed little consciousness of class status. The formal presentation of class systems worked out for some American communities seems inappropriate to these people. Most of them had never lived long enough in any one place to feel that a rigid social structure divided along class lines existed. Some may have thought in terms of capitalists and labourers, or of rich and poor, but the idea of social position interested them little if at all.[1]

Permanent White Residents

A small number of whites regard themselves as residents of Neah Bay, thus contrasting with the transients who only camped within the village. Most of them have either lived in the village for many years, or they hold jobs which are permanent positions in the economic, educational and religious organization of village life. Resident families include a total of 68 individuals.[2] A few have been at Neah Bay for more than twenty years.

The oldest resident is the trader, who came to the Bay as a boy of fourteen when his father bought the trading post. Now a man of sixty he lives in the village surrounded by his family, many of whom were born at Neah Bay. The trader's competitor is a newcomer by comparison, though he came to clerk in the trading post years before, and then established his own store. He and his family have lived at the Bay for the last fifteen years. A relative who runs the bakery has been there only

---

[1] The information on the transients was largely gathered during the time when I lived with a couple who belonged in this group. In their home I met a number of those engaged in the construction jobs. I also had casual contacts with a few other people in the same group, and learned something more about them from the Makah who knew different ones. It is possible that my information is not sufficient to justify even as much generalization as I have ventured to make.

[2] The figure is based on information obtained by questioning Makah and a few white inhabitants.

ten years, and his wife speaks of their being recent comers. Another long-time inhabitant is the manager of the fish jetty and power plant. He and the trader are considered to be the dominant figures in the economic life of the village and neither shows any sign of moving to another area. For them work a number of men. Those at the fish jetty are all old residents. At the trading store, several clerks have been there for many years; others come and go. In normal years perhaps the staff changes less frequently, but during this opening year of the war clerks came but to be drafted. A large oil company has a representative in the village, but the man in charge of the office is changed every few years, and does not develop intensive ties with Neah Bay and its people.

A number of people are employed by the government for work at Neah Bay. The doctor who does part-time work for the Indian Service is a recent incumbent of the position, but he has lived near the reservation for many years. A home economics teacher employed by the Indian Service was at Neah Bay for seven years before she was transferred early in 1942. The teachers at the consolidated school are mostly newcomers, though several have been at Neah Bay for three or four years. Married teachers have their families with them. The customs officer and his wife have been at Neah Bay for more than twenty years, and are active participants in its life.

One church, the Presbyterian, employs a white minister, who lives with his wife in the village. In the spring of 1942, after two years in the village, the incumbent was transferred, and another minister came to carry on the work.

Several other families are said to have lived in the village for a number of years. In 1942, the heads were all employed on construction jobs, and I failed to learn what originally brought and kept them in the village.

Although the village is upon a reservation, few white residents today derive their position from the existence of the reservation. This is a new state of affairs. Until the tribe was incorporated under the Indian Reorganization Act and the agency abolished, a number of whites lived on the reservation as employees of the agency. The agent himself did not live in the village, but a mile or so away near the present lumber camp. The forestry officer who guards the Makah timber interests and supervises the replanting of the area now occupies the former agent's house. In 1942, only the doctor and the home economics teacher remained in the village as Indian Service employees, aside from a few Makah who hold positions in the service. By the end of my stay, only one white resident was an Indian Service employee.

These people then make up the stable portion of the white population. Most of them have lived long enough in the village to know each other and the Indian inhabitants well, and they are known to the Makah. All of them are white Americans. Family names indicate English or Scandinavian origin. All of them come originally from the northern states, or from Washington itself. In social status and economic background, they show a fairly wide range. Two of the men are rumoured to be among the wealthiest on the Olympic Peninsula, and they have dominant positions in the economic life of the village. Others depend upon small business enterprises which are said to be tottering because of the inability of their owners to collect the backlog of bills resulting from the indiscriminate extension of credit. Most live on moderate, fixed salaries, and are probably less remuneratively paid than the majority of construction workers. Among them are university graduates, and people who have never completed secondary school.

Most residents live in family groups, but kinship ties rarely extended beyond the immediate family to bind two or more families into one related whole. The structural elements of their social organization seem only the immediate family, and each family is a little cell unattached to all others. They also share the factor of residence in a common locality. The men have brought their wives to live at Neah Bay. They have rented houses from the Makah under a lease system which allows them to retain possession for a number of years. Some of them have renewed the lease period after period, until they seem the real possessors of the site. Their children are being reared at Neah Bay, and many know no other home. Many have investments there. Most of them expect to continue to live in the village until some indefinite future when they will move to other parts of Washington to retire. One or two never expect to leave.

Summary

Today within the village, the Makah are in contact with an equal number of whites who represent a wide range of the present

American population. The whites include men, women, and children. Many are single, unattached males, but some men are the heads of families. All age ranges are represented save for the very old, the result probably of the recent move of most of the people into the area. The whites have a varied economic and social background. There are labourers, technicians, tradesmen, and a few professional people. Some are wealthy. Most live on the proceeds of their labour, but with the prevailing wages none can be regarded as poverty-stricken.

Most of them have come to the area because of work opportunities. Few are there because of any duties in connection with the Makahs, and only three or four have any power by virtue of their jobs to dictate to the Makah the terms on which they are to be accepted.

The Society of Neah Bay

Neah Bay today has a population drawn from five different categories of people : the Makah ; the Indian and white satellites of Makah households ; the transient Indians ; the transient whites ; and the permanent white residents. In so far as Neah Bay is a community or a society, it consists of all the people of the five categories who compose the local unit, and are in constant contact with each other.

Even those who attempt to isolate themselves from contact with other elements in the community are touched by their presence and forced to associate with them in the use of the common facilities of the village : the stores, the post office, the restaurants, the cinema, and the barber shop (the one new business opened during the year in response to the increase in population). All use the roads and the bus which connects Neah Bay with Port Angeles. Most buy vegetables and other goods from trucks which periodically visit the village. In the use of these facilities no pattern of segregation exists, and therefore there is no way of actually isolating oneself in Neah Bay any more than there is in any community where the conditions of life make it necessary to co-operate in the use of common facilities.

For their daily food, the people of the village, whether white or Indian, go to the stores, owned and operated by whites, where they are served by both Indians and whites. In the restaurants, both owned by Makah, they are waited upon one day by an Indian girl who has rarely been far from Neah Bay and the next by a white woman who has followed a soldier husband up from Texas. In their working life, the men are forced into constant association with men of all types, as they work on the same gangs at the construction projects or the lumber camp, and ride back and forth to work in the same trucks or sharing each other's cars. The children attend the same school and ride in the same school bus. Only the fishermen can be somewhat independent of the ties developed through this common life in a village community, and even they are wont to resort to the fish dock for their oil and gasolene and to the village stores for fresh supplies.

However, though people may buy at the same stores, or rub elbows upon the streets, and attend the same schools and churches, it is still possible for them to remain strangers to each other or to raise barriers against those whom they regard as inferiors or as aliens or as dangerous. The members of a small heterogeneous community may not be able to surround themselves with others of their own kind, but they are in a position to determine something of the types of contact which they will share with other inhabitants of the village. What type of contacts beyond the superficial ones do the people of Neah Bay share with each other ?

Economic Relationships

A few of the permanent white residents control the most important positions in the economic life of the village. They own the fish jetty and power plant, the hotel, the two stores, the bakery, and the oil business. Moreover, the lumber company and the construction companies which employed most of the Makah men in 1941–2 are owned and managed by whites, although the owners and top managers are not resident on the reservation.

A few Makah also own productive businesses patronized by most of the village. They own the two restaurants, the three tourist camps, and the filling station and garage. The latter, however, is leased to a white since the owner is old and ill. The Makah also own a fish house, for which they import an independent fish buyer who comes to the village during the summer months. This gives them greater independence in their fishing, and also forces the buyers at the fish jetty to pay higher prices

H

than if they had a monopoly in the village. Some white fishermen sell at the Makah fish house ; some Makah make a practice of selling their fish to the dock owned by the whites. The two businesses are competitive.[1]

Many Makah are independent fishermen for at least a part of the year. Fourteen men own fishing boats for which they recruit crews from among the Indians who have no boats of their own. In a few cases, white men join Indian boats on the same basis as the Indian crew, but the common practice is for Indians and whites to fish separately. The whites who live by fishing are transients who come to the Flattery area only for the fishing season. They compete with the Makah.

Since only Makah may own land, they are the landlords on the reservation. All who settle among them do so as tenants or lessees. Few whites bother to sign leases or make arrangements for long-term possession when they rent a house. Makah owners are thus able to evict undesirable tenants at a moment's notice, or they may use the threat of eviction to force tenants to pay a higher rent than that originally agreed upon. Against this the tenants have no redress. In normal times, their plight is probably not serious, but during times of expansion when the village is crowded, they have little chance to find another house at a moment's notice. On the other hand, they may decamp without paying their rent, and usually the Makah owners find it impossible to hold tenants responsible for damages.

Another monopoly held by the Makah is the production of firewood. Most people at Neah Bay heat their houses and cook their food with wood stoves. The whites cannot cut wood on the reservation to supply their needs. The Makah do not bother, but instead they search the Straits for driftwood which they saw and split for fuel. This has a ready market, and the few who work at woodcutting may pick their customers as they choose and sell at rates bringing them an income equal to what they could get if they worked for the construction companies.

Most people at Neah Bay, however, depend upon wages for the greater part of their income. The transients are usually entirely dependent upon the wages they earn as workers at the construction jobs or in the lumber camp. Most white residents

[1] In former years, Makah have also owned a number of stores and a hotel. At one time or another five stores in Neah Bay have been operated by Makah.

depend on wages for work in the permanent institutions of the village. Most Indians take jobs at the construction camps or in the lumber camp for at least the winter months when fishing is poor. The highest managerial and technical positions are held by whites ; the majority of whites and most of the Indians work at similar jobs. For similar work, they receive similar wages, and their working conditions are the same. However, the Makah have a technical advantage in applying for employment. When a company is granted a contract to carry out some enterprise upon the reservation, it must agree that Makah shall be given preference in getting jobs. In a boom period, the clause has little meaning, but if work slackens it means that Makah have a greater opportunity than whites to get jobs on the reservation.

Makah also take other jobs where they work for and with whites. During 1942, eight worked as clerks at the two stores, one became an apprentice to the white barber, several worked at the fish jetty, and one was hired as secretary by the oil company. Many of the women do some housework for the permanent white residents, coming in once or twice a week to help with the cleaning and the laundry. A few girls work as maids at the hotel. This is a traditional source of employment in the village, and most Makah women have worked at the hotel or as a household help for some white family in the village. Makah less commonly work for each other, though several are employed at the restaurants, and they occasionally do cleaning or laundry for wealthier Makah women. A number are employed by either Indian Service or the tribal council.

Whites are occasionally employed by Makah. The restaurant owners employ several white waitresses. A Makah who was building some cabins for rent employed a white assistant. In the past the Makah have employed whites on other occasions, but these are rare.

Economically, the Makah are in no inferior status to the generality of whites. They are in general the propertied class in the village. Most of the whites own nothing more than their clothes, perhaps a car, and a few items of household furniture and other equipment. If they have other possessions or rights in property, these are all beyond the area of the reservation. The Makah, on the other hand, have their possessions in the village where they live or close by. Most of them own their own homes, while many also own houses from which they derive rent. They own boats, canoes, and other productive tools. All of them either own allotments or assignments of land, or they are in a position to acquire the assignment of a certain number of acres for their own use. All of them have free access to any of the products of the unallotted portion of the reservation. Such access is either denied to whites or permitted only under licence. When they attempt to find work on the reservation, people from both groups are on much the same plane, save that the Makah have some slight advantage in competing for employment.

No sphere of the working world represented in the area is closed to the Makah because of their membership in the tribe, nor do they lack the skill and knowledge of work habits and situations which make it possible for them to compete with whites for employment. They can clearly be regarded as assimilated successfully into the economic organization of American society. There are complaints that Makah are less reliable than whites as employees, since they may absent themselves from work without notice and for slight cause. The opening of the fishing season is likely to cause a rapid loss of interest in other work, and the men quit their jobs without notice to cash in on the fish runs, despite the opposition of their wives who prefer the regular hours and wages of employment to the irregularity and gamble of fishing. Presumably, however, the same complaints would be made about the labour of the local population of any of the fishing communities along the coast where the men consider fishing their chief occupation and take other jobs only between seasons.

The gains which the Makah make from employment and from other activities are likely to be spent on direct consumers' goods, and to a minor degree upon the upkeep or increase in productive equipment, such as fishing equipment. Local whites complain that they make no attempt to save or to invest their surplus, and they are likely to attribute this to Indian improvidence, the persistence of potlatch values, and the Indian belief that government assistance will always be there if an emergency occurs and therefore saving is unnecessary. Probably the Makah spend a larger proportion of their incomes on hospitality than do many white groups, and they cheerfully admit that money burns holes in their pockets. But at the time that the local whites were complaining about the failure of the Makah to absorb American habits of thrift and investment, the newspapers were full of equally acrimonious accusations that throughout the nation defence workers were throwing their wages about in riotous or frivolous fashion. The proverbial saying, ' spending money like a drunken lumberjack ', might be applied to the Makah, but this certainly does not distinguish them from the greater number of Americans whom they have known.

Informal Social Contacts

In the stores and in the restaurants, whites and Indians are found talking together in mixed groups. Indians and whites exchange friendly greetings and raillery. Both men and women participate, and this is significant, for where a tendency for segregation exists it is usually shown most clearly by women. At Neah Bay it is possible for Indian and white women to associate freely and with every appearance of equality. Among people of older generations, cross-sex joking less commonly involves people from the different groups, but even here it occasionally appears.

When new families come to the village, they frequently form their first acquaintances with the Indians, and they take it for granted that these associations are natural developments. One Makah woman was on extremely friendly terms with two white families who rented cabins next door to her house. She saw more of them than she did of other Indian women. They visited back and forth with gifts of food and offers of assistance. When they entertained, they borrowed each other's chairs, dishes, and cutlery. With one woman she started a fish peddling business. They often ate together, and when their men were away at work they commonly lunched together rather than prepare separate meals. The white woman came to the house to use the Makah woman's sewing machine. They rode about the village together in the Makah woman's car, and drove to Port Angeles to shop together. The same white woman was on good terms with women in four other Makah families, and her husband joined with her in parties with Indian couples. They had few dealings with other whites, save for a few of the transients.

Another white woman who was only recently married came with her husband to Neah Bay when he got work there. They came to the village knowing nobody, and made their first contacts with Indian neighbours. Later they met whites and had some social life with other whites, but their closest associates continued to be a number of Makah of about their own age. For a while they kept open-house for the young people. A Makah boy brought his gramophone to the house, and they held dances in their tiny cabin for Makah youngsters, young construction workers, and soldiers and sailors. The woman and another white neighbour had a surprise birthday party for a Makah woman whom they knew, the party consisting of the three women and their husbands. The three couples were often together.

Another couple formed a close friendship with a young Makah woman, who often visited their house. They in turn were invited to her home, and then began to visit her relatives. Frequently they were to be seen together in the streets or riding about in the car belonging to the whites. Michael and Winona Clarke had intimate friends among several white couples. With one the friendship started when Michael brought home a white man with whom he was working on a construction job. The man later brought his wife to visit the Clarkes. The same man was also a visitor at other Indian homes. Another couple who visited the Clarkes had lived in the area for several years, and now had a small homestead close to the boundary of the reservation. Another transient knew many of the Indians. He worked with them on the job, drank with them away from the village, and visited them in their homes. On one occasion, he was invited to a large birthday party given for one of his fellow-workers and found himself the only white guest present.

In these instances, the association took place between Makah and recent comers among the whites. It is possible that a longer residence might develop in the transients a greater discrimination against social relations with Indians and that such incidents do not reflect the attitude of whites with regard to the acceptance they are willing to give the Makah in any more orderly and permanent life. Nevertheless, the very fact that it is possible for them to come into a strange place and live on terms of equality with the Indians indicates that the latter are enough assimilated to American standards not to arouse a feeling of estrangement in the newcomers. It also shows that at least some Makah are willing to accept association with whites, and that they are not attempting to barricade themselves off from contact with them.

Many of the permanent white residents have comparable relations with their Makah neighbours, indicating that the acceptance of the Indians is not entirely a feature of a fluid social system in which the transients find themselves. The home economics teacher kept her door unlocked day and night to encourage Makah women to come and visit her. This was done partly in line with her duties, since she was supposed to work with the Indian women as much as possible, but it was obvious that she was on intimate and friendly terms with many of the women. Once I found several Makah women having tea with her. She spoke of attending parties given by Makah and the big tribal Christmas party. Indian women liked to recall how she came to their houses and sat talking with them. This did not hinder her fitting into the white group at Neah Bay; for she seemed on good terms with the other whites. Another of the white women who has been in the village for many years is on equally intimate terms with the Indians though she has no duties or responsibilities in connection with them. She and her husband attend Makah parties, and ask Makah friends to dine with them and meet white friends. They gave a dinner party to introduce the Makah candidate for the school board to some of the newcomers among the whites. There are other men and women at Neah Bay who seem to mix freely with both Indians and whites. On the other hand, two or three white women considered to be the social leaders of the whites (if there are such at Neah Bay) do not invite Indians to their homes or exchange visits with them, though they sit talking with Indian women in the restaurants and chat with them in the streets.

Friendly relations begun while a white family stays at Neah Bay may be continued after they leave. Mathew and Rose Grove are friendly with a number of white families who have lived near them at one time or another. These people have now left Neah Bay, but they occasionally return to visit their friends. One family left their young daughter behind to spend a few days with the Grove children during a visit in 1942. When the Groves go to Port Angeles they visit their white friends.

With so much friendly interaction between adults of the two

groups, it can be expected that little discrimination will be shown among the children. This seems to be true. Most parents make little attempt to keep their children away from children of the other group, or to impress upon them that they are different. I heard of only one instance where white parents tried to prevent their children from associating with Indian children. Rose Grove complained of a white neighbour who lived near her for a number of years. The woman made a practice of calling to her children, ' Stop playing with those dirty little Indians ! ' Usually Mrs. Grove excused her on the grounds that she was too ignorant to know better. Other similar reports could all be traced to this one woman. I myself saw nothing of this type of behaviour. Occasional clashes occur between children. I once heard Brenda Sterne, six years old and in her first year at school, quarrelling with her brother. She shouted, ' You're a dirty Indian. Louis is an Indian.' When I asked her where she heard these things, she said, ' Everyone says that.' On another occasion I saw a group of boys of about ten years of age. The group included one white boy. A Makah child had him tightly by the front of his sweater while he shouted at him. But within a minute or two, the whole group went off together amicably enough.

Children's play groups are formed by neighbourhoods rather than by ' race '. The Porter children, who are half-breeds, play with both Indian and white children. The play group in another area includes both white and Indian children. At the back of the village still another group includes small tots and grade school-children of both groups. In all play groups, however, Indian children predominate. This is due to their numerical pre-ponderance in the village rather than to any attempt to segregate the white children.

Schoolchildren, including those in the secondary school, con-tinue to associate together both in and out of school. For a while the teen-age group had a craze for horseback riding, and one little group of riders was composed of two white girls and two Indian girls. Another white child spent most of her time with an Indian girl of her own age. The Makah child's father owned a small open truck, which was usually filled with the two girls and with other Makah children. In this case, however, some of the whites criticized the girl's guardians for allowing her to spend so much time with the Makah, but the guardians continued to permit it.

Occasionally Indian boys were seen with white girls, or white boys with Indian girls. One couple, the boy an Indian, attended school events together frequently, though the parents of the girl finally objected and sent her away to a girls' school to end the affair. At high school dances, Indians and whites dance together, though here there is less mixing between the groups.

Formal Social Contacts

In two of the churches in the village, whites and Indians are in close contact. The Presbyterian church had a Makah minister and white missionaries for many years. About 1938 the Makah minister resigned because of ill health. The mission was then changed into a regular church congregation with a white minister sent in from outside. The elders of the church are drawn from both groups represented in the congregation. When the minister is absent, the old Makah minister or one of the elders takes the service. Makah as well as whites teach in the Sunday school, in which Indians and whites sit in the same classes. At the Christmas programme, children of both groups perform in the Christmas play.

The congregation of the Apostolic church is entirely Indian, though not exclusively Makah. The church, however, is closely associated with the Apostolic church in Port Angeles whose minister, a white man, comes each month to the village to hold services. Members of the Port Angeles congregation usually accompany him and join the Neah Bay people in the service. Afterwards, Makah members serve dinner to the visitors in the house of one of the members. They in turn visit Apostolic people in Port Angeles, where they say they are always made welcome. The Shaker church is again composed exclusively of Indians, but during 1941–2, it was beginning to co-operate with the Pentecostal church which had members among the white transients in the village. Weekly prayer meetings in the tourist cabin rented by a white couple drew both whites and Indians. At joint services in the Shaker church, both Indian and white leaders took charge, and the congregation was drawn from both groups.

The consolidated public school located in the village draws

children from the village, the lumber camp, the construction camp, and from the cabins beyond the eastern border of the reservation. Whites and Indians are taught the same subjects, in the same classrooms, by the same teachers. However, all the teachers are whites who come from outside the village. Only two Indians have any connection with the school in an official capacity. These are one of the three members of the school board and the truant officer. All white children and all Indian children are at some time in the school. In 1942, only one white child was sent away to a school in another locality. Makah children may be sent off to an Indian boarding school when they are ready for the secondary school. More drop out of school entirely once they are past the legal school-leaving age. A few finish secondary school in the village. The class that graduated in 1942 was composed of three Indians and two whites. All schoolchildren are allowed and encouraged to come to school affairs, which include athletic events, plays, dances, and picnics. Teachers are quick to oppose any discrimination on the grounds of 'race'.

Cases that come to their attention are immediately dealt with. Lincoln Grove started to school in the fall of 1942 for the first time shortly after his sixth birthday. On the second day he returned in tears because some white children had called him 'cute little Indian boy'. He maintained that he was 'an all American boy' and refused to return to school. His mother reported the matter to his teacher, who called the children in and told them not to call each other names and to remember that each one was as good as the next. That afternoon Lincoln came home beaming with the announcement that he was now friends with the white children whom he had promised to 'slug' if they called him Indian again.

The school teachers said that white and Indian children come from a sufficiently similar background so that teaching them in the same classes gives rise to no particular teaching problems. A white member of the school board said that scholastically Indian children are on about the same level with the white children. She felt that there is still sufficient difference in the background of the two to make this an impressive achievement for the Indians. The school teachers said that within the Indian group were both some of the best and some of the worst students.

On the whole, however, they thought they could see a greater difference between children of different families than they could between children of different groups.

This comprises all the formally organized social life within which members of the two groups participate. Since the political organization of the village is that of the tribe, the whites are excluded from the political structure of the local unit. They have no voice in the election of the tribal council, nor may they hold office on the reservation. All Makah who are over twenty-one may attend tribal meetings, vote for officials, and stand for the tribal council. Both groups, however, are to some extent under the jurisdiction of the tribal authorities. The Makah are expected to accept the decisions of their council and to respect the legal authorities of the tribe. The whites are required to pay a fee to the tribe if they conduct any business enterprise on the reservation. If they break the peace, they may be arrested by the local Makah policeman who is appointed by the Indian Service, and they may be tried before the judges appointed by the council. The whites are thus to some extent subjects of a local authority in which they have no voice. The fact that both are citizens of the state and of the nation does little to associate them in any political body.

There are no fraternal organizations in the village. The few whites who belong to these organizations go to Port Angeles or to Forks, a small town some forty miles away, to attend meetings. The only regularly organized clubs that exist, save for the church groups, are composed exclusively of Indians, or include only whites married to Makah. These clubs are the Progressives, the Wranglers, the Sharp Shooters, and the Makah Day Association. All have been in existence for some years, but were largely inactive in 1942. The Makah Day Association held a number of meetings and succeeded in organizing entertainments for Makah Day; one of the other clubs organized the tribal Christmas party. Two of the others did not even meet.

Occasionally public dances are held, usually at the school, and these are attended by members of both groups. Indians and whites may dance together and stand talking together during intermission, but most people stick to others of their own group.

The Appearance of Segregation

So far I have stressed the occasions on which whites and Indians join together in friendly fashion. Not all whites at Neah Bay are pleased that friendly relations go as far as they do. Some indication of this has already appeared. Their fellow-whites notice this and are affected by it. One of the transient white women who had many friendly contacts with the Indians told me that it was the first place she had ever been where people looked at you askance if you were seen with an Indian woman. She accused most of the whites of being ' standoffish ' and ' unfriendly ', and in this she referred to the permanent residents rather than the transients.

Today there are a number of occasions on which segregation occurs. Those who have lived long in the village regard them. as recent developments due to the increased white population.

When the women of the Presbyterian church planned a dinner for soldiers stationed nearby, Makah members of the congregation complained bitterly because they were not asked to help and the committees were composed entirely of white women. On a number of occasions I saw cars parked in front of a house occupied by a white family. When I asked what was going on, I was told that it was a meeting of ' the four hundred of Neah Bay ', who met weekly for bridge, and that they never invited Indians.

In the summer of 1942, when Red Cross work was organized at Neah Bay, the white women who took the lead in planning the work arranged to have two groups, one for Indian women and one for whites. The white women organized and met regularly. The Indian women remained completely inactive as soon as they heard the plan for separate groups. The whites said they could not understand the lack of interest. One who mentioned this to an Indian friend was promptly told that none of the Indian women liked the idea of having two groups instead of one. The same Indian woman later told me that the Makah women wondered where the whites thought they were living : ' If they lived someplace else, they could run their clubs the way they like. So long as they're on a reservation, well we don't think they have any right to keep us out of any club.'

Another Red Cross activity was a sewing group which met in

the building erected by the Indian Service as a centre for Indian women. It has now been turned over to the tribe, which pays a Makah woman to keep it open two days a week. The white women arranged to use the building one day a week, but only two Indian women attended their sewing meetings. One was the woman in charge of the building. The other was Maude Allan, an alien Indian brought up away from any reservation and now married to a Makah in government employment. She said she found the white women pleasant to work with and that she was surprised that more Indian women did not come. When I asked other Indian women about the sewing group, they said that they were too busy to spend the afternoon, or that the white women would make them feel out of place if they went. On the days when the Indian women were in the building, no white women appeared, nor would they have been welcomed if they had come.

The Ladies' Aid Society formed by the wife of the new Presbyterian minister soon after her arrival consisted of herself and a number of Indian women, though by that time the congregation was half white. None of the white women of the village ever attended. Two white women from the neighbouring lumber camp came to one meeting and despite their promise to come again never returned.

In affairs organized by the Makah, there is also some exclusion of whites. At wedding parties given by Makah, to which all members of the tribe and members of their households are invited, whites rarely appear. On two occasions in 1942, one of the spouses was white. All the guests were Indians or white members of their households. On one occasion, the wedding party was given by a staunch Presbyterian, who invited the minister and his wife, and they came to the party. That was the only time when a white received a formal invitation.[1] Occasionally some white might come in to see what was going on after the dinner was over and the dancing or games had begun. Several times soldiers, on hearing the sound of drums and singing, appeared near the door of the hall in which large parties are held and stood there watching. Once when guests were playing a

---

[1] Anthropologists do not count. When I lived with an Indian family, the family invitation was widened to include me. When I went to live with a white family, I usually received a special invitation.

game which requires shooting with bow and arrow at a target, soldiers were invited to come in and try their luck.

Whites are thus not rigidly excluded from these parties. Rather the Makah make no effort to include them or to urge them to come. This may be due to a feeling that whites would not be interested, or that they might object to eating food cooked by Indians. But since many have white guests at their houses and a number of whites show an interest in Indian games and dances, this explanation does not seem the true one. Probably the explanation lies in a feeling that these parties are something for the tribe as such and therefore whites do not belong among the guests unless they are attached to Makah households. The parties are demanded by the Makah through small informally organized groups. These chivaree newly married people and demand a dinner and a party. Only Indians, and frequently only Makah, form the parties that hold the chivaree.[1]

Whites at Neah Bay also chivaree people, but apparently only members of their own group, and in these chivarees only whites participate. A white girl who had grown up at Neah Bay married a construction worker during the year. Although she was well known to most of the young Indians with whom she had gone to school and with whom she had been on close terms, the party which chivareed her was said to be composed exclusively of whites, most of them men who worked in the same crew with the young husband.

Weddings are not public affairs at Neah Bay. Either the couple go quietly to Port Angeles to be married there, or they are married in the village with only a few people present. They are not occasions for exhibiting tribal solidarity. But the funeral of a Makah is an occasion when all Makah are expected to appear. The church is always crowded, but the only whites who are likely to appear are one or two of the old permanent residents. In 1942, the only funeral attended by any number of

---

[1] The custom of the chivaree has been borrowed from the Americans, amongst whom it was once a fairly common practice. Shortly after a wedding, a group of friends of bride and groom gather outside the house where they are staying and proceed to make a racket with any available implements —banging on wash tubs, tins, etc. They continue the uproar until the couple appear at the door and then offer to leave them in peace in return for a consideration.

whites was held in the Apostolic church, and the whites were
members of the Port Angeles congregation who had come to
help in the service rather than people from Neah Bay. Again
there is no formal bar against the attendance of whites, and I
think the families of the dead would be pleased if white friends
came. However, the funerals like the wedding parties have
about them the air of a tribal occasion which is not for outsiders
unless they are closely affiliated with the main participants in
the event.

The only general tribal occasion to which whites come in any
numbers is the Makah Day celebration, and in this they are both
spectators and performers ; for they are permitted to compete
in the athletic contests that take place in the afternoon. Older
Makah, however, complain that Makah Day has lost its meaning
under the influence of younger members of the tribe who are
trying to turn it into a tourist attraction. At the Christmas party
for the tribe, which is organized and run entirely by Makah, a few
white guests are usually invited. In 1942, several whites appeared
on the programme. This meets with less resistance from the
older Makah, who consider the Christmas party a village affair
rather than a tribal occasion.

On all other occasions, only a few whites ever appear, and these
have usually received invitations. Small private parties are more
likely to be shared with whites.

Intermarriages

The surest indication of social segregation is the absence of
intermarriage, which prevents the appearance of members of
different groups in the same familial structures.

Social discrimination at Neah Bay has not introduced any
signs of a caste relationship. Intermarriage is not only theoretically possible, but it actually occurs and fairly frequently. Both
white men and white women marry Makah and live with their
spouses in the village.

In 1942, two white women married Makah men, though one
soon deserted her husband. Another white woman has been
married to a Makah for some years. All three women lived
for a few months at Neah Bay before they married, and met their
husbands on the reservation. In one case, the woman met with
considerable opposition from the people with whom she was

staying, though her parents cheerfully accepted her choice of husband. In another, the relatives of the husband objected strongly to the marriage, but eventually accepted the situation and treated the wife kindly. One of the women complained that after her marriage the other whites ostracized her, and that they looked down upon the Indians and discriminated against them socially at all times.

These were not the first white women to marry into the tribe. Perhaps ten years earlier, a Makah boy married a white girl he had met in southern Washington, but according to his relatives he eventually returned her to her parents because he found her too expensive to keep. From all accounts she fitted into the village life with little difficulty, and spent much time with the old people learning Makah songs and stories. Two or three other Makah men have been engaged to white women, but have not married them.

Marriages between white men and Makah women are common occurrences. They have more support for Makah from tradition than the previous type, for such unions have taken place since the early days of contact between Makah and whites. Not all have been legal marriages recognized by whites, but many white men have contracted unions with Makah women which have been recognized by the tribe as legal and which legitimated their children. Others, especially in the last thirty or forty years, have gone through legal marriage ceremonies. In 1942, five white men were living on the reservation with Makah wives, and one man whose wife had died lived there with their son. No particular stigma attaches to either spouse, though the men are regarded by other whites in the village with some disapproval. Their wives so long as they remain in the village are still considered by both whites and Indians to belong to the Indian group. Whites living elsewhere or on first coming to the village are likely to disregard the village attitude and accept the women as though they were white women. The marriages certainly do not outcaste the men from their own families. Their families may visit them at Neah Bay, cheerfully accept introductions to their Indian affines, and urge the couple to visit them in return. They may leave other sons or daughters behind to stay for a few months in the village with their brother and his wife. They welcome their grandchildren with warm affection. Some of the men who marry Makah wives take them away to live in other parts of the country.

Intermarriages between Makah and whites consist of only a small proportion of the total alliances contracted by Makah. Neither group considers them to be ideal. The whites are likely to consider that the white partner has lost in prestige and the Indian partner has gained none, but the white person is not outcaste nor is he or she condemned by all members of his group. The whites at Neah Bay say that the unions are bad because of the difference in cultural background between Indians and whites, or because they think that the attitude of other whites may make the position of the couple difficult. They speak vaguely of the difficulties of adjustment for two people who come from such different backgrounds, but they do not condemn the alliances as unnatural or as evil because of a difference in physical type, or as wrong in themselves. This may be their real feeling, but verbally they are culturalists.

Among the Makah, as among the whites, there is a divergence of opinion about the desirability of these unions. Most of those with whom I talked do not condemn intermarriage as such, although a few condemn them in general terms. Jim Frost told me once, ' Whites and Indians married together don't seem to work out.' The general Makah objection seemed based on the effect of intermixture in the offspring, and more importantly on a dislike for intermarriage with people whose social status they do not know. In conversations, they never referred to differences in background, nor to the effect on the social status of the children *vis-à-vis* the whites. They are interested in status only within their own group in this respect and are anxious to keep their descent lines pure of ' common blood '. The possibility that intermarriage as such may affect the social status of the couple or of their children in an injurious manner does not seem to enter into their thinking. Probably this is due to the fact that in a mixed marriage, the Makah spouse retains his or her position, and it is the white partner who has his or her status changed most drastically in relations with his or her own group.

Nevertheless, Makah express some objection to intermarriages either with whites or with those with some white blood. Winona Clarke once said that she was the one blot on her family line and that her grandparents had never forgiven her mother

I

for marrying a half-breed. 'Grandma and grandpa think Mamma should have married the man they picked out for her instead of my Dad. Then the whole family would be pure blood. I don't see that it makes so much difference to them actually, but they don't like the idea of their family mixing up with white blood.' Another half-breed said that he had a miserable childhood because the other people in the village always held it against him that he was not a full Indian. His only close friend was another half-breed boy who like himself was under partial ostracism. The other children would refuse to play with them, and if they attempted to join in the games, their white blood was cast at them. He may have been exaggerating his sufferings, since the boys he mentioned as most vocal among his persecutors are themselves known to be half-breeds. However, Joan Hewitt who is considered to be a pure-blood said that when she was a child, her father and stepmother used to call her from the beach where she was playing with a little half-breed girl, using voices loud enough for the whole village to hear, 'Come away from that little white girl. She'll harm you.' They seem to have raised no objections to her associating with other half-breed children, and it is likely that they were using this reproach only because of their feud with the child's relatives.

Whites seem to regard all living in Indian households who have any Indian blood whatsoever as Indians. The Makah distinguish half-breeds from those regarded as full-bloods. A white says, 'That Indian'. A Makah referring to the same person will usually say, ' that half-breed ', unless the speaker himself has some known white blood or unless the person is present. The term frequently has no particular emotional tone of contempt, dislike, or favour. Sally Grove, one of the older Makah who is also regarded as a full-blood, once formulated for me the feeling the Makah have for such people. She was speculating about the heredity of one of her small relatives and wondering what kind of a man his great-grandfather was. She said he was a white man, and this led to a discussion of the status of mixed bloods. She felt that Makah accept mixed-bloods as they do pure-bloods so long as the white men who beget them are living with the mothers in some form of recognized union. But if a Makah woman conceives a child in adultery, or if an unmarried girl conceives a child by a white man in too casual a manner, the child will have little status and his white ancestry will always be a delicate matter to broach in his presence. For that reason the white ancestry of her small relative was nothing of which the family was proud.

The position of the half-breed for the Makah is therefore not due solely to the fact of racial intermixture. It is complicated by the factor of legitimacy. For some their white blood can only be a disgrace in the eyes of the rest of the community. In such cases, it is never mentioned by themselves or their close relatives.

A few Makah are said to favour intermarriage with whites rather than marriage with other Indians. One woman married three daughters to white men. Another woman who is not married is said to have refused to take an Indian and been unsuccessful in trying to attract white men. A woman whose daughter left two children, one by a white man and the other by an Indian, chose to bring up the child of the white man. Others in the village said that the other child was ' too Indian ' for her, but it is equally likely that she felt she could rear only one child and that she should take the one which had no paternal relatives to look after it.

Liaisons between Makah and Whites

Men of neither group are prevented from casual sexual adventures with women of the other group. This seems to rouse little more scandal than if they confined themselves to their own group.

I heard a white woman, talking of a Makah boy, laugh as she said, ' I saw a sailor's wife going into the woods with young Bill Elliot. That boy certainly must have something, but I don't know what.' Those who overheard her, both whites and Indians, laughed without any particular outrage. The speaker herself appreciated the gossip value of the incident, but her voice betrayed no other emotion. The Makah themselves do not think it particularly dangerous for a man of their group to approach a white woman of doubtful reputation. For a while a woman with peroxided hair was about the reservation. One night a Makah woman came in laughing. She had been with a Makah couple who saw their son obviously trying to pick the woman up. She said, ' Sam swore and then he laughed, but I don't think Sylvia liked it much.'

Only once has an affair given rise to a serious incident, and that case is still much discussed by the Makah and remembered by the old white residents. A few years earlier, a Makah man was accused of raping a white woman then living in the village. After two or three trials where the jury could not agree,[1] he was finally sentenced to hang. On appeal, he was declared innocent. The case split the village at the time it occurred, but the split was not along racial lines. Some Makah believed him innocent ; others said he was guilty and refused to testify in his behalf, a stand that still rankles with the man's close relatives. A distant relative said that Makah who knew the man to be innocent, and could prove it, refused to come forward in his defence. He was finally acquitted on the evidence of a white woman. After his release he returned to Neah Bay, where the whites treated him as before.

The significant thing is that so little ' racial ' feeling was aroused. In this, as in affairs which receive no publicity, both groups seem to feel that these are private matters affecting the individual rather than attacks upon the standing of the whole group.

The same attitude is shown towards affairs between white men and Makah women, though these are much more common. During 1942, many young girls and a few married women were seen with white soldiers and sailors. The situation created considerable scandal among both whites and Indians, especially since girls in their early teens were involved. The parents and relatives of the girls blamed the women themselves rather than the men. They were able to do very little to curb the women though they beat them and sometimes had them jailed. This was not, however, a situation completely foreign to them. Before soldiers were stationed in the area, Makah women were sought by men from the lumber camp or by fishermen, and before that by sealers and other whites who visited the reservation. The Makah have never evolved a method of dealing with the situation. A few women are known as prostitutes who quite openly ply their trade.[2] Other women accept only such

---

[1] The case was tried in the federal courts, as rape is one of the ten crimes for which Indian tribal courts do not have jurisdiction.

[2] Three girls, all in their late teens, were known to the fishermen by their prices rather than their names. They were ' Two Bits ', ' Half a Buck ', and ' Six Bits '.

men as they like, and although they expect gifts, they do not regard themselves as prostitutes.

As far as I could judge from talking with older members of the community and from conversations with young women about their own affairs and those of their age mates the white men are not using a superior position to coerce the women. The Makah are not in a position where they are unable to protect their women against the advances of white men. They are in a position where they cannot control their own women. Most of them admit this. At one time, the tribal council did arrange to have the soldiers stationed in the village moved to a camp some miles away and to have the village placed out-of-bounds. The only result was that the girls developed a passion for walks in the country or for horseback riding.

The few white girls in the village were said to be as soldier-wild as the Indian girls, but white parents usually retained better control over their daughters. This was not because they were in a better position to protect them, but because they were less strict. Many Indian parents refuse to admit that friendships may exist between men and women. They assume that if their daughters are seen with men that it is only for one purpose. They therefore beat their daughters for any casual encounter with men, and the girls' reputations suffer equally whether they walk down the street with a man and sit with him in a restaurant, or whether they sneak into the woods with him. The few Indian parents who allow their daughters to bring men to their homes or to be seen with them only in the restaurants or on the front streets of the village seem to have little more difficulty with their children than do the whites.

DEFERENCE PATTERNS

There is no systematic subordination of one group by the other in the life of the village, despite the existence of some discrimination. The lack of subordination is also shown by the absence of observable patterns of deference exacted by one group from the other. Makah and whites address each other and refer to each other in the same terms. Friends or acquaintances use each other's personal names or nicknames. Even the trader is addressed familiarly by the Makah, though they consider him the most important white in the village. Those who do not know each other well give each other the titles of 'Mr.', 'Mrs.', and 'Miss'. They shake hands and greet each other familiarly on the streets.

In the stores, it is usually first come, first served, without members of either group being given preferential treatment.

The whites are not in a position where they can discharge their aggressive feelings directly against the Indians. The only cases of physical violence involving people of the two groups occurred when the Indian policeman arrested various whites for drunkenness and took them to the jail. The whites may choose to accept the decision of the tribal court, or they may ask to have the case transferred to the county courts. In 1942, all chose to have their cases tried by Indian judges and accepted their fines without further objections. They said they got fair treatment from the judges. The Makah, therefore, are not using their political superiority on the reservation as an aggressive weapon against the whites.

Verbal quarrels between Makah and whites are more common. In these Makah are in a position to give as well as take. One of the more outspoken of the tribe quarrelled with her next-door neighbour over their boundary mark. She felt that she came off winner in the encounter, and had a lovely time retailing all the things she had said to the white woman. Another woman went to whites who were renting a house from her husband and ordered them out at a moment's notice. She raved and stormed at them and accused them of running a bawdy house in a voice that could be heard throughout the block. The whites moved out without taking any action against her, although some of the Makah said they would have sued her in court for slander. I heard other Makah engaged in arguments with whites, and in no case did they show themselves intimidated by the thought that they were combating someone of an alien group who might be able to enforce his views. Instead, many of them said that if the whites did not like what they did on their own reservation, then the whites could move off, and that it might be a good idea, because they had no right to be there in any case. When the Presbyterian minister's wife reprimanded a Makah Sunday school teacher for not attending the service one Sunday, the woman promptly intimated that she had no desire to teach a class and would like to be released from the duty. Later she told me :

'This woman tries to tell me what I should do and what I shouldn't do. I'm not used to doing what other people tell me to do. I'm used to thinking for myself.' To a large extent that sums up the attitude of the Makah in their contacts with the whites. They are prepared to think for themselves, and if the whites object they can be reminded that they are aliens upon the reservation.

The only whites who could completely ignore the threat of eviction were the soldiers stationed in the area. They may have shown some arrogance in their dealings with the Makah, but it would be hard to prove this since if they roughed up an Indian found wandering along the coast they excused themselves by saying they thought they were dealing with a Japanese invader. However, on one occasion they found the Indian policeman attempting to enter the barracks. They immediately threw him out with speed and vehemence, to the great rejoicing of most if not all the Makah.

Most whites are careful even in their verbal utterances not to offend the Indians. Occasionally I heard a white say, 'those dumb Indians', but never when any Makah were present. The super-intendent of the school was accused by the Makah of having said they were irrresponsible and shiftless because they spent money on cars rather than on improving their housing conditions. Some of the whites made accusations of filth and disease against all Indians, as a blanket and sweeping indictment rather than applying it to specific cases. But such statements were rare. I heard few myself, and what is more, even those Indians who complained loudest about the attitude of the whites could give me almost no instances of this 'name-calling'. Most of the whites in the village tend to deal with Indians as individuals, rather than in terms of a general stereotype. There is a general lack of derogatory terms applied to Indians. Elsewhere in the state, people speak of the 'Siwash', a general derogatory term applying to Indians in the western portion of the state. I never heard this term used by any white resident in the village, although in Port Angeles it was common enough.

The Makah, however, have their own term for whites which from their point of view is derogatory, although few whites who heard it probably realize its significance. This is bábáX̣ld, which means 'those who live on the water'. The Makah explain that the name was given to the whites in the early days because no one knew where they came from and they seemed to have no homes but their ships. From this it is an easy transition to the thought that the whites were originally landless and have obtained places to live only through pitiless robbery of the original owners of the country. Most Makah whom I knew well presented this picture at some time or other during the year. But in their ordinary contacts with whites, the unfavourable implications of the word do not intrude, and it certainly arouses no emotional response in the whites who hear it.

CHAPTER V

MAKAH VERSUS WHITES

THE Makah are in close and extensive contact with a population of whites within their own village which seems fairly representative of the white population in nearby areas. In their associations, there is little appearance of segregation, though discrimination does occur. Their relationships are not governed by a system which subordinates the members of one group to those of the other directly, although the Makah have certain political and economic advantages over the other inhabitants of the village.

The two groups share a sufficiently large body of definitions and assumptions for their members to meet on common ground in most of the activities open to the inhabitants of the village. They are able to use the same schools and enter into the same church congregations. They enter into economic relationships and compete for the same jobs. They may belong to the same cliques and form close friendships. They may exist in the same familial structures and in the same households. It is therefore probably valid to assume that they share a large body of common culture. To this extent at least the Makah are assimilated into the world of the whites.

Since most of the whites with whom they associate have come to the village only recently, and few had any previous association with any Indian group, it must be assumed that this assimilation is due to the taking on of American patterns of behaviour by the Makah rather than to the creation of a hybrid culture in which whites have accommodated themselves to Makah behaviour.

Yet despite the similarity of behaviour, the apparent friendliness between many individuals of the two groups, and their co-operation in different spheres, there is good evidence that the Makah still regard themselves as a people apart, distinct from other Americans.

ANTAGONISM TO THE WHITES

Through much of the thinking of the Makah there runs a current of antagonism against the whites which seems irrational to the observer watching the present adjustment of life at Neah Bay. In many respects, they react in a manner typical of a people suffering from repression and discrimination, even where nothing in the situation justifies this reaction.

It is difficult to document the existence of the antagonism, since it is rarely expressed verbally. Yet the antagonism seems widespread. It is phrased by the Makah not in terms of specific white men and women, but as a general antagonism to the whole white group and to individuals because they are members of this group.

The Spoilers

The commonest accusation against the whites is that they are intent on robbing the Makah of all their possessions. Grace Sterne, in scolding her married daughter for friendliness with whites, told her that she should never trust any white because while they might seem to like you they were only after something. She ended : ' They took all our lands. They are trying to take our place. The white people are all like that.' Howard Sterne grew furious when a dealer tried to sell him a car on the instalment plan. He said : ' All white men are bad to Indians. If I owe just five dollars on this car, you'll send the sheriff after me. You just want to take what us Indians have.' Lydia Morris, the veteran of a marriage with a white man and of many years' residence in Seattle and other white communities, said that when she and Sheila Day were complaining about the recent influx of whites they were told by a woman who came from a California tribe : ' That's nothing to what they did to my people. They took all our land and left us nothing. That's what you can expect from the whites.' Mrs. Morris and Mrs. Day agreed heartily with this dictum.

Many times during the year I heard Makah make this same general indictment of the whites, that they were greedy monsters ready to take the land, against whom constant vigilance was necessary. Older people would suddenly interrupt a story or ethnographic detail during formal interview periods in order to relate some act of aggression by the whites. They would say that at the time of the treaty they asked for a large reservation, and the whites made it small. They would refer to an attempt by whites to settle on the reservation in the 1870's, and maintain vehemently that it was only the action of Makah leaders who appealed directly to Washington over the head of their agent which finally forced the men from the reservation. They said that early agents had tried to inveigle them into signing away their control of the reservation. They asked advice about how they should proceed to recover damages from the government for their summer houses on Tatoosh Island which they said had been burned by the lighthouse keeper early in this century—the island by then having been taken by the government, although the Makah still made annual visits there. They brought up the shutting down of the sealing industry by the government at the end of the nineteenth century when sealing schooners owned by Makah were seized for poaching. Nor in their indictment of the whites did they forget that it was the entrance of the whites as fishermen upon the halibut banks and the waters of the Strait that led to the decrease of the ocean fish.[1] Old men contrast the time when they were boys, when a man could return within a few hours with a canoe load of fish. Now with better equipment and with boats that enable them to cover a greater area, they may fish for hours or even for days and return with nothing or with only a paltry load insufficient to pay for the petrol used in getting to the fishing banks and back. The disappearance of the whales which were hunted by the great men of the tribe is also laid at the door of the whites, who are said to have swept the whale from the seas.

Most of these incidents took place in the distant past, many before the majority of the Makah were born. Some took place before their parents were born. But nearer events also make them wary of the whites, and these are represented as additions to the long chain of encroachments upon the possessions of the tribe. Suspicion against the Indian Service and its officials is rife. Although accounts are subject to Federal Government audit, officials are accused of conspiring with the local whites to dispose of the reservation timber at much less than its value and then to embezzle a portion of the funds that were realized. People frequently threaten to hire lawyers to investigate their claims and to force the Indian Service to give them their due. They complain that neighbouring tribes whose members received allotments on the Quinault Reservation have received much

---

[1] The white fishermen seem to have begun serious fishing of the Flattery area in 1891.

larger sums for the timber on their allotments than they themselves have.   Some would agree that the timber stands on the
two reservations are of not the same value.   Others see only that
they have received less than their neighbours, and cite it as
evidence of their helplessness before the tactics of the whites,
who in this, as in all else, find a way to cheat them of their inheritance.   The attempt of the Indian Service to prevent them from
dissipating funds paid by outsiders for the use of particular
allotments by doling the money out in small sums for living
expenses, or for some definite purchase of capital equipment or
improvement in living conditions, infuriates them.   They argue
that they have as much right to control their funds as any white
man, and either deny or shrug aside the evidence of extravagance
which officials can produce from recent history, where people
have obtained control of considerable funds which were used in
a revival of potlatch parties or somehow disappeared without
trace.   Their acquaintance with white loggers, sailors, fishermen, construction workers, bootleggers, smugglers, and various
others, suggests to them that they are not unique in spending
their money for the maximum immediate enjoyment, and they
see no reason why they alone should be penalized for doing so.
They feel that the Indian officials in pursuing this policy must
have some ulterior motive, and that it is a further instance of
the general oppression of the Makah by the whites.

· During 1942, there were constant rumours that the government intended to take over Neah Bay and to evict all civilians
for at least the duration of the war.   One week, the rumour
would be that plans had been drawn up for turning the area on
which Neah Bay is built into an airport, and that houses were
to be either burned or moved elsewhere if their condition made it
worth while.   The next week, someone would appear with the
story that everyone was to be moved to Puget Sound, and that
temporary quarters for their reception had already been built.
With the turmoil and uneasiness on the coast at the time, these
rumours were easily accepted as true, no matter how many times
they were proved groundless.   But a good deal of the acceptance
seems due to the Makah premise that nothing the Indian possesses
is safe so long as the white man wants it.

The tradition is also upheld by the battle to preserve the tribal
right to fish without restriction at Hoko River.   Although the

mouth of the river is not on the reservation, it lies within their former territory, and by their treaty they are confirmed in their right to fish at their accustomed fishing sites throughout the area ceded to the government. Now the State of Washington, urged on by sport and commercial fishermen, was attempting to assert its right to prevent the Makah from fishing on the river except under the restrictions applying to whites and Indians of other tribes. The Hoko fishing is an important source of income for every Makah family containing fishermen, and this means nearly every family in the tribe. Some men made four to five hundred dollars from the Hoko catch, and the loss of fishing privileges in the river worried them considerably. The case was being tried in the courts in late 1941 and early 1942, and finally the decision was given against the Makah, to their considerable dismay. The reasoning of the state that unrestricted fishing by Makah is as disastrous to the conservation of the fish resources of the area as is that by whites interested them little. Their picture is that again they are being despoiled by whites and that nothing they can do will prevent it.[1]

These are very real grievances which involve the whole tribe. But almost every individual has some private complaint against the untrustworthy white man out to rob the unsuspecting Indian. Sally Grove enlarged in great detail upon the whites who leased a schooner belonging to a Makah, and sent it out upon the Straits with an insured cargo with instructions to the captain to sink it so they could recover the insurance money.[2] Grace Sterne was bitter against a white man whom she claimed had ruined their business. He had lived with them for a period and worked in their store, and had extended so much credit and given away so much that the Sternes were unable to meet their bills. Mrs. Sharpe claimed that an early trader appeared upon the death of her husband to collect on large bills which they had already paid. Another woman declared that a white friend borrowed a negative from her and with the print won a prize in a photography contest which she kept herself along with the honour. Everyone has grievances against white traders and others who have operated business enterprises in the village. From these grievances they

[1] The Tribal Council was considering having their lawyers launch another appeal.
[2] This occurred in 1893, but the Makah have not forgotten it.

proceed to generalize about the ethics of the white rather than the ethics of the business man.

The frequency with which such incidents appeared in conversation seems indicative of a general deep-seated distrust of the white. The distrust, I believe, is at least partially based on other causes than the economic deprivation which they cite, much of which took place many years ago.[1] In actual fact, they have suffered less than most Indian tribes. Their reservation has been secure for generations ; they have continued to exploit their resources without great hindrance. The presence of the whites has enlarged their markets and given them new opportunities. Even today they can still earn an adequate living by fishing.

But as the reservation symbolizes and ensures the existence of the tribe, so Makah feelings of insecurity before the whites are symbolized by the picture of the aggressor whites with designs upon the actual area and resources of their reservation. For while the whites have left them in possession of the reservation, they have deprived them of a way of life which the Makah regard as their own.

Cultural Losses

Though most Makah never knew this way of life before it fell before the attacks of the whites, they feel deprived of something vital which properly belongs to them. Those who lived through the agency period said : ' We never thought the whites would ever be interested in anything we had, so we tried to forget about it and learn the ways of the white man. Now

[1] It is possible that the frequent references to double-dealing by whites is indicative not so much of anti-white feelings as it is of a typical Makah reaction to other people. The great mass of anecdotes in my field notes which deal with other members of the tribe usually picture them in an unfavourable light. Makah freely accuse each other of lying, thieving, and even murder. Probably much of this unfavourable material can be explained by the fact that I was someone outside the group to whom they could speak with less likelihood of reverberations and therefore they unburdened themselves of thoughts which they would not reveal so freely to other people. But allowing for this element in the situation, the Makah do not take an optimistic view of human nature, whether it be Indian or white. The significant thing about the references to whites is the tendency to generalize from them to blanket condemnation of the whites.

that we have forgotten and live the way the whites do, people start to come around and ask us about what we had.' Others said : ' If I had ever thought that the whites would be interested in our doings, I would have listened to what the old people said. But we thought it was all gone and there was no use trying to learn the old ways any more.' Even those most assimilated to American standards may suddenly show this feeling of loss. Announcements of new discoveries in medicine lead to statements that the Makah formerly used something similar which early doctors only laughed at. ' And now look, after all these years they find it really is good.'

One of the young men who had completed a term or two at the University of Washington, and who had lived much in Seattle, interrupted an interview with his grandmother to say : ' You're here too late. The old people who really remember things are gone. When I was a boy there were still a lot of old people around and when they had parties, they would sit around and sing songs and tell stories about the old life. But the agents stopped them from doing that. They called our ways heathen without knowing that the Indian ways were good too. You had to respect these people here. They went out in little canoes, just about the size you see on the beach, clear out in the ocean hunting whales. I've been out myself in those canoes, and I don't see how they were able to stand it. They stayed out for days at a time too. They had to know what they were doing. And they had to remember all the places along the shore and the fishing grounds and how to locate them. I remember going out in a canoe with Jack and he gave the names for all the points along the coast. But I never learned them or remembered any of them.' [1]

There is a reverse side to this picture. Makah contrast themselves with Indians from Canada whom they say are less civilized because their government never tried to educate them whereas the Makah were ' civilized early '. They are equally proud of being more ' civilized ' than the Quileutes and attribute this to their greater opportunities for education and for contact with whites. There is also an open rejection of the old customs. June Grove, about eleven, listening to her father tell stories of

---

[1] The man is probably only about a quarter Indian, as his father was a white man and his mother was not a pure-blood Indian.

the old days, broke in to say : ' I'm glad I'm not a dumb old Indian. I'm glad we know things now.' Her ambitions were to learn to speak French and to play the piano rather than to learn anything about Makah culture. Her brother, about twenty-four, refused to listen to his mother's accounts of the old life, with the statement : ' Oh, Mom, why bother us about those old stories. We're civilized now. Who wants to hear about those things ? ' Judith North, the daughter of a man who considers himself a leading exponent of Makah custom and who takes an almost professional interest in incorporating ethnographic information from other tribes into his account of Makah life, told me once that she thought everything her father recounted was stupid : ' I've heard it all so often, I never want to hear it again. I don't see what you want to listen to that stuff for.'

Most young people, indeed, are rebellious at any attempt to force them to accept the old standards of life. Joan Hewitt once snapped out : ' My father still wants to boss me. That's because he always listened to what his father said even when he was old. But they've got to get used to us modern young people. Times have changed.' I heard the same warning note from other young people. On the other hand, I knew only one young woman ever to make any statement that she intended to guide her life by any of the old standards. This was Louise Armstrong, not a Makah according to members of the tribe, who often said that she wanted to take the best of the Indian customs and the best of the white and combine them in bringing up her children. The appreciation the others show is either in an unconscious acceptance of Makah standards or in an admiration for customs which are safely ensconced in tradition beyond hope or fear of being practised again.

Even among the older people there is no complete respect for the old customs. Arnold Black, who is past seventy, refused to act as an informant and said that everything worth knowing was in the Bible. This was not an easy way of dodging my request for information, since he said the same thing to other Makah. Sally Grove told me :

'I don't think Arnold knows very much anyway though he is older than I am so he must know something. But he thinks it's smart to say that the old Indian ways are "just ignorance". He always goes around saying that about everything : stories, games, dances, and everything. He said that if we know about those things it is just going back to the days before we learned better things from the whites. He just believes in Christianity and white ways. One time everybody went down to Sail River to have a big party there with gambling games and Indian doings. There was still an agent here then so we went down there so he wouldn't find out about the party and stop it. Arnold Black went along and went from one bunch to another telling them it was just " ignorance " and that we shouldn't be doing this. I said if he felt that way he shouldn't come and try to spoil everyone else's good time. He could have stayed home. But that's the way Arnold always is. He just wanted to show off to the others. Finally he came to the group Warren was in. Warren decided he wasn't going to hear any more, so he said, " Well Arnold when your boy was in trouble, all the tribe helped you then. We weren't too ignorant for that ! " '

Most older people are more ambivalent. They want to be regarded as equal to the whites in ' civilization ', and they speak with apparent disgust about different customs—which they remember having seen or having heard about—and say that they are glad that such things are gone. But at the same time most of those who are beyond their thirties have within them a feeling of loss, and for this at least they directly blame the whites. ' We were kept from learning what the old people knew.' ' We were told that there was no use learning any more Indian things.' ' We were told that the old ways were superstitious and wrong and only the white man's way should be followed.' ' We were young and foolish and believed what the whites told us about forgetting the old things. Now that we could have our old ways again, those who knew about them are all dead and there's no way to learn.'

In almost every interview old Howard Sterne showed this feeling of belonging to a group which is gradually losing its identity before the onslaught of American culture. ' Every year it gets less and less. These young people don't seem to care or want to carry on the old ways. I try to talk to them, but they don't want to listen. When I die, and Peter Fisher and Jeffry and Virgil, I guess there'll be no more Makah Indians. Then we'll be just like the whites. But I think maybe the old ways were better. Of course, I came too late to see most of the old things. The whites had already changed most things then.'

Part of this nostalgia may be attributed to the general

K

phenomena of old age which leave the old certain that times have changed for the worst. But it is strong in the Makah who feel themselves less powerful and capable than their ancestors. Sterne told me :

' I was talking with Nick Mead yesterday, and I was talking about this selling livers for nine or ten hundred dollars in a few days. I said, " Bet you ten dollars, Nick, if the old fellows were around here yet, bet you they'd make lots of money." You know the old fellows used to fish for dogfish every day, year round, saving two or three livers every trip they went out. And they made something like a hundred fifty or two hundred gallon of oil. And he said, " Howard, I think you're right. Today we can't do it now." I said, " I bet the old people would be rich today." And he said, " Well, Howard, it's going fast. It's just like if it's going fast, fast every year. We don't know what we doing now today because we can't fish. I'm too lazy to fish, and you're too lazy to fish." I said, " Nick, I'm not too lazy to fish. I'm a sick man. If I was well, I'd try to fish for liver." " Well, that's me. That's my brothers. They know the price of liver today, but they don't try to do it." And I said, " It's that way now, Nick. Everything is fading away all the time. We ain't travelling like the old people used to do. Even the old people—old man with a cane used to go walking, walking along slow. But we ain't doing that now." So everything is changing today.'

The young who have never had personal contact with the old Makah life have less of this feeling of personal loss. But even from them come resentful statements about what the whites have done in outlawing or ridiculing the old life.

The Whites as Snobs

Along with the picture of whites as despoilers, the Makah also hold the view that the whites are snobs who look down upon Indians and discriminate against them. The more outspoken Makah declare that whites are all snobs who think they are better than other people. As a result of this premise, the Makah are quick to see snubs and signs of discrimination even where the whites have no intention of being offensive, and they magnify the incidents that do occur.

They complain that at one of the stores they receive bad service and that the store tries to unload upon them spoiled goods which cannot be sold to whites. They say that the baker sells them only old bread and reserves fresh supplies for the whites. A white woman who peddled fish with an Indian woman was accused of selling fish only to whites as though Indian money was not good enough for her. The Presbyterian minister is accused of spending most of his time with whites when he should be working with the Indians. The school superintendent and teachers are said to cater for the white children and to look down upon the Indian. When I asked Sally Grove if I might bring a school teacher to see her, she replied that it was all right if the teacher was not ' stuck up '. She explained this by saying, ' Some of them don't want to come into an Indian house.' The Indian woman employed by the oil company was said to have difficulty in dealing with a white employee under her direction because ' he doesn't like to take orders from an Indian. Quite a number of the whites are like that '.

Some feel that whites avoid physical contact with them. Emily Lester who has lived much in Seattle, said that she dreams a good deal and that it is always the same dream : ' I am with a large crowd of people, and they're always white people. They won't have anything to do with me. They all try to get as far away from me as possible, and won't speak to me or touch me. They say I smell bad. In my dream I think that can't be so because I bathe often to take all the body smell away, but those people won't have anything to do with me. It makes me feel terrible. Even when I wake up, I still feel unhappy about it. I always wonder why I have that dream. It's been a long time now since I had it. I'm always careful about myself and bathe often—more often, I think, than lots of white people do—and I change all my clothes. But still in my dream they won't have anything to do with me.' Joan Hewitt in reporting the opening of the new barber shop commented : ' He even cuts Indian hair.' Asked why this should be odd, she said that in many places the hairdressers do not like to have Indian customers, and that when she went to a shop in Seattle, the operator gave her a bad permanent wave ' because they don't like to have Indian women come in '. Sally Grove also thought that whites avoided Indian contacts and when she was ill and in hospital in a nearby town, she carefully thanked her nurses ' for being so good to me when I'm Indian '.

The Makah feel that most whites in their behaviour towards Indians follow stereotypes which have been worked out for all Indian groups and that they do not treat them as individuals. The Makah woman with whom I lived sometimes neglected her housework for several days and sat around the house in an old bathrobe. Then she would suddenly remark, ' I'm just like an Indian squaw who never gets a thing done and just lives in dirt.' She would follow this with the comment that whites think all Indian women are like this. I have heard her laughing with a friend about their being ' just squaws ' who let their houses go all day and then rush home to pick up the place a little while they get dinner for their husbands. Ruby Hare, who shows little trace of her Indian blood, was laughing once about sitting in a bar in Clallam Bay. She said : ' It's part of the fun I guess sitting there expecting him to say any minute, " Get out of here, you fat Indian squaw ! " I'd die if he ever did.' [1]

Some of the Makah asked me if I were not afraid to live among Indians. They would then explain that most whites seemed to be afraid of them and that the whites still regard them as ' wild Indians '. Louise Armstrong once grumbled about a landlady she had in Seattle who called the police when a group of Indian young people spent the evening singing Indian songs and telling stories. ' I suppose when she heard us singing, she thought we were planning to go on the warpath next. I guess she was afraid of Indians,' was Louise's final comment on the incident.

The stereotype which they think the whites hold of Indians may be summed up as : ' Indians are dirty, immoral, and stupid. They are dangerous and all of them love liquor. They can't be trusted with property or to do a job properly or to judge the amount that they can drink.' In all the indications that cropped up in their conversations and actions of the picture they had formed of this stereotype, I never found the Makah attributing to it any of the good qualities which they feel are theirs. To them, it appears as though the whites think of Indians only in condemnatory terms, and in this thinking all Indians are placed in the same category. Those who are most explicit about this complain that Indians realize that there is a difference among whites but that whites never realize that Indians are individuals and differ among themselves, that some of them fit the white

[1] It is a federal offence to sell liquor to Indians, either on or off a reservation.

stereotype, and that others are as ' civilized ' and responsible as
the whites themselves. In their complaint, of course, they are
blind to the existence of their own stereotype of the whites.

THE FAILURE TO IDENTIFY WITH THE WHITES

The Makah show also their failure to identify themselves with
the rest of America. Though all are citizens of the United States,
they reserve the right, at least subconsciously, to dissociate themselves from the fate of other citizens. Soon after the Japanese
attack on Pearl Harbour, the dreams told me made frequent
allusions to this feeling that they as Makah belong in a distinct
category from other Americans. In one dream, Mrs. Sharpe,
regarded by other Makah as strongly identified with the whites,
saw Japanese come to the beach at Neah Bay and start to divide
the people of the village into two groups. All Indians were
placed in one group which was to be set free ; all whites were in
the other. She gathered her children and grandchildren about
her and told them to stay close to her so that there would be no
possibility of their being placed in the white group despite their
European features. One child who speaks little Makah was told
to keep quiet, and the others were ordered to speak Makah to
prove they were Indians. Although Mrs. Sharpe did not make
any interpretation of her dream, the dream seems based upon
the belief that whites and Makah deserve different fates, and that
the Makah cannot be regarded as responsible for what the whites
have done.

Another indication of their feeling of belonging to a distinct
group is the common usage of the term ' white '. The Makah
say ' that white man ', ' that white woman ', ' the whites ', when
there is no apparent necessity to point out the distinction. In
contradistinction, they identify themselves as Indians and tend
to identify themselves with other Indian groups. In speaking of
themselves, they are apt to refer to themselves as ' Indians ' as
well as ' Makah '. I observed too that when I accompanied
them on trips away from the reservation, that the whites they
saw roused little comment. The sight of anyone who might be
Indian brought an immediate quickening of interest, and the
murmur would go through the group, ' There are some Indians
over there.' When I went to Seattle, they questioned me on
my return as to whether I had seen any Indians about Pioneer

Square, the congregating point for people of many tribes. The same thing happened when I went to Victoria—then they were curious to know if I had been able to visit any of the Indian villages near the city, and not at all interested in any other places.

They mention other tribes frequently, and measure themselves by whether they have retained more or less of their own culture than other peoples known to them. When they talk of the fame of their families and of their own names, it is always in terms of the number of Indian groups which know their names and family histories. At times in these conversations, I was left with the feeling that they see only the network of relationships between Indian tribes throughout the extent of their world, and that the whites are unregarded objects which the Indian social life surrounds but yet ignores.

There is some feeling that their natural friends and allies are other Indians rather than whites. Old Louis Keller complained that his daughter who is married to a white man has no right now to live on the reservation : ' He's a white man, and she ought to live with his people.' His granddaughter asked him if he meant that she too should leave since her husband is an outsider. Keller replied, ' You're married to an Indian. That's all right.' Actually the two men have about an equal amount of Indian blood, very little in either case, but the husband of the granddaughter is registered as an Indian while the other man is not. Winona Clarke, who is one-quarter white and who has lived much away from the reservation, complained that her cousin turned sulky when they joined forces with some Indians in Seattle rather than with the whites they expected to meet. The Indians were from another tribe, and neither was known to the two women. Winona later said : ' I don't see this having nothing to do with our own people. We're Indians too and we ought to stick together.' Her cousin, who is regarded as a full-blood, repudiates this attitude. She frequently said that she married a man of another race because she thought he would take her away where she would never have to live with Makah again.

Another indication of this identification with a wider group than the Makah Tribe which is in opposition to the white group is the pride that members of the tribe take in the Cushman Hospital and the Indian boarding schools. They refer to these as

' our Indian hospital' and ' our Indian schools'. These institutions belong to them as members of the Indian group and create ties which bind them to other tribes no matter how distant. Older people also at times refer to the accomplishments of a member of another tribe with the phrase ' one of our Indian boys' or ' one of our Indian girls'. They speak of enjoying themselves with ' our Indian dances', or ' our Indian songs and games'. Those who read *Indians at Work* cite Hopi or Navaho accomplishments as examples of what Indians, and therefore they themselves, can do.

Following this identification, they have taken over certain practices which they regard as Indian and which are generally regarded as Indian by the whites. They recognize that the making of small wooden totem poles, which they carve badly and paint with atrocious combinations of colour, is a recently acquired practice borrowed from other tribes. Though they may sneer at it as something they do only for tourists, it has an interest for them that the arts of the whites do not have, because they feel that it is Indian. They know that the woven baskets which the women make are not of the old Makah type. They borrowed the type from other tribes because of its appeal to tourists. The designs with which the baskets are decorated are used because tourists regard them as ' Indian' designs. Nevertheless, they feel that this work belongs to them because it is ' Indian'. Several men have visited the Ethnological Museum at Victoria to copy designs of northern Indians for use on their own dancing outfits. Many of them wear Navaho jewellery, though this may not be because it is Indian.

On the day when the Makah give a series of dances supposed to represent their own heritage, many today use costumes in which the Plains Indian warbonnet is an important and highly visible part. Others have adopted moccasins for the occasion. Even young people deny that these are Makah styles, but the costumes are prized by their owners and countenanced by others because they represent something Indian. In their dances and in their parties they unhesitatingly use dances or songs borrowed from other tribes. Some I observed were said to originate in Alaska, others in northern British Columbia. Some came from Yakima, others from Oregon, and a few were said to have been brought back from California. The use of an American song in such a setting would be regarded as inappropriate, although on other occasions American songs are sung.[1]

To some extent, then, the Makah have accepted an identification with a general 'Indian' group. Nevertheless, the old feelings of enmity have not entirely vanished. When they talk of other tribes, Makah like to speak as though their own superiority was generally acknowledged. They look down upon all groups on the Olympic Peninsula, and probably on all south of the Strait. They do not claim that the Nootka people of Vancouver Island are their inferiors, but they do say that all tribes have always looked up to the Makah and that it is a thing of pride to be a Makah or of Makah blood. It is still possible for older people to say that the Clallams hate the Makah because of the old warfare between them, and that the Quileutes are wild quarrelsome people inferior to the Makah but still to be dreaded. But when they think of the whites, they tend to ignore the barriers between themselves and other groups, and to represent themselves as a common class in opposition to the whites.[2]

The Makah show little tendency to identify themselves with other minority groups. They dodge the problem by identifying the whites as aggressors, who oppress both the Indians and other minority groups. They express little sympathy for other minorities, but blame the whites for the treatment these mete out. They comment that the whites ought not to treat other peoples the way they do, that the whites always think what they do is right and what other people do is wrong, that the whites think themselves superior to everyone else. This is a stereotype, therefore, of the whites as aggressors and offenders against all non-white groups. For this they condemn the whites, though they themselves express great antipathy for any group of people of darker skin than themselves. Their references to negroes, Mexicans, and orientals are anything but complimentary, and any attempt to class them together with these people or to indicate that they have anything in common would bring a violent answer. They object to the theory that the American Indians

[1] A few dances borrowed from the whites in the days when they were just another group to the Makah are treated as though they were borrowed from another tribe.

[2] As we have seen in Chapter III, identification with other Indians disappears completely in relation to rights to the Makah reservation.

come from Asia originally and argue that they had a common origin with the Europeans.

The Makah then tend to think of themselves in relation to the whites in terms of two categories of experience. They think of their own contacts with the whites in their village, and they also think of themselves as members of the Indian group which has been systematically despoiled and repressed by members of the white group who regard the Indians as their inferiors and fair prey. The whites are also regarded as actively aggressive against other peoples, and while the Makah resent this aggression because it reminds them of the white treatment of the Indians, they grant the premises of inferiority upon which the expression of that aggression is based. But for themselves, they deny the inferiority of the Indian, and are quick to resent any expression of prejudice.

Thus despite some fusion of race and a considerable degree of social equality and social intercourse between all elements in the Neah Bay community, the lack of economic discrimination, and the failure of segregation to appear in spatial distribution, there are two opposing groups in the village. Their relationship to each other is conditioned by a recognition of differences in race and in cultural background. It is also affected by the emotional response of the Makah to the knowledge that whites in their contacts with Indians have deprived them of property and a way of life. It is moreover affected by the existence of the reservation, which proves a powerful factor in preventing the complete coalescence of the two groups.

The Reservation as a Focus for Segregation

Two aspects of the present-day Makah social system distinguish them from the whites. Most whites live in discrete family groups which have no connection with the kinship relationships of the Makah. Makah are bound together by a network of kinship relationship which ultimately make all Makah kin to each other if the descent lines are followed far enough and thoroughly enough. This at least the elders in the village are prepared to do, and the younger people are aware of a vague feeling of kinship, though they are prepared to ignore specific relationships with distant kin. The other factor is the existence of the reservation which makes the Makah into wards of the government and also unites them in a political body which expresses itself in the form of a general tribal meeting each year and in a tribal council which is the governing local body. This is elected from Makah by Makah. The whites are excluded from participation in the group created by the reservation.

Political and Economic Implications of the Reservation

The organized political structure of the tribe is similar to that of American political organization generally in that it is composed of regularly elected officials chosen by secret ballot in conformity with a written charter and constitution. The elected officials bear the same titles and perform much the same functions as they do in white communities. Nevertheless, the actual body politic which supports this structure is based on a theory of blood descent which has little to do with the American theory of residence as the factor entitling members of a community to partake in the life of the community. Therefore the tribal structure separates the Neah Bay community into two groups which may loosely be regarded as whites and Makahs though there are a number of individuals of Indian blood who are also excluded from the Makah category. The tribe, moreover, is an organization directly under the control of the United States Indian Service, whereas no white political community is. This political structure therefore differentiates the Makah from the whites. Though the structure itself has been developed under the tutelage of the Indian Service, the theory underlying the structure is alien to the political organizations in which other Americans live.

The existence of the reservation also makes it possible for the Makah to form a corporation which holds property. The tribe receives funds from the sale of the reservation timber and for the use of reservation resources. It has the right to collect fees from non-members of the group who are settled on the reservation for business purposes. There is a Tribal Trust Fund held in trust for the Makah by the Indian Service. Members of the tribe complain bitterly that they cannot obtain control of the fund or even learn how much it contains, but nevertheless its existence is of great moment in binding individuals to the tribe. Its existence also conditions the attitude of Makah on the subject of tribal membership. They resent attempts by outsiders to add themselves to the tribal membership because that would mean that they and their descendants would be claimants to the Trust Fund if this is ever divided among members of the tribe. Indeed, wherever the existence of the tribe and reservation may benefit individuals, the Makah show themselves jealous of their rights and eager to defend themselves against encroachment. Special privileges for fishing at sites beyond the reservation are defended against whites, members of other tribes, and any residents of Neah Bay who do not belong to the tribe.

The Whites resent the Reservation

To those whites and alien Indians who live as members of Makah households, some of the advantages derived from the existence of the reservation accrue, and they can regard these advantages as the legal prerogative of their Makah children.[1]

To the rest of the whites, the existence of the reservation is a stumbling-block rather than an advantage. They share in none of the direct benefits of the tribal organization, and Makah property rights prevent them from acquiring permanent holdings on the Cape. Even those who are born on the reservation and spend their lives within it can acquire no permanent right to live there. The Makah firmly believe that old residents among the whites are plotting to have the reservation abolished so that they can acquire land holdings in the area, since if the land were allotted to individuals who were permitted to sell their individual holdings they would have a greater chance to buy up the land they desire. One of the older white residents probably represented the attitude of the other whites during his conversations with me. He clearly resented the existence of the reservation and hoped that it would eventually be done away with. He said it was a barrier in the way of further ' civilization ' of the Makah. He disliked the fact that he could never own his own home in the village and the fact that when he retired he would have to move further up the Strait to acquire land upon

---

[1] The Indian Service tries to prevent white men from registering their children as Indians in order to secure them the benefits of Indian status, but it is not always successful in its efforts. The Indian Service defines an Indian as ' any person of Indian blood, regardless of degree, who through wardship, treaty or inheritance has acquired certain rights '.—*Report of the Commissioner of Indian Affairs*, 1937, p. 249.

which to build. His investments in improvements on the house he occupies at Neah Bay were a loss to him because he can neither acquire the house nor can he recover the money he has spent upon them.

Differential Treatment of the Two Groups on the Reservation

As individuals, the Makah and other Indians have all the privileges given to whites as citizens of the state and the nation, with the exception that they are not allowed to buy liquor. They may vote in state and federal elections. The State of Washington pays old age pensions and pensions to the blind and disabled. Old people are provided with free spectacles and false teeth. The Makah are as eligible as any other citizens of the state to receive these benefits, and many of the old people are recipients of state pensions.

In addition to the ordinary privileges of citizens, the Makah have special privileges as members of the tribe.

Though they are citizens of the state and benefit from this status, they are not subject to its laws.

From the earliest years of the Republic, the Indian tribes have been recognized as distinct and separate political communities, qualified to exercise powers of self-government, not by virtue of any delegation of powers from the Federal Government but rather by reason of their original tribal sovereignty. The public usually thinks of Indians as wards of the Federal Government, which exercises over them individually the kind of power and protection usually exercised by a guardian over a minor. Many people, otherwise familiar with Indian affairs, do not realize that Indian tribes are legal entities, subject to Federal law to the exclusion of State law, and entitled to exercise their inherent rights of self-government so far as is consistent with Federal law. An Indian tribe possesses all powers of a sovereign State except those which have been specifically taken away from it either by treaty or by act of Congress. Tribes are subject to the legislative authority of the United States, that is to Congress. They are not subject to State laws except where Congressional action has so decreed.

While the Congress and administrative officials have in numerous instances frustrated the exercise of tribal powers, the courts have repeatedly upheld them. And while these powers have been restricted somewhat by treaties and acts of Congress there still remains to the Indian tribes a large area in which the inherent powers of self-government may function. A tribe may determine its own membership, regulate domestic relations, control the distribution of the property of its members in the absence of contrary legislation, administer justice in connection with every offense not specifically made a Federal offense, and exercise many other rights and powers.[1]

Whites and Makah have thus a different legal status. In many small ways, the difference in status is emphasized, and this adds to the irritation of the whites. Indians on the reservation do not pay the state sales tax ; whites do. Indians on the reservation do not need fishing licences ; whites do. Indians on the reservation can hunt when and how they please, in season and out ; whites are not supposed to hunt or fish. Indians do not pay the entertainment tax on tickets for the cinema ; whites do. Makah who drive cars only on the reservation need no state car or drivers' licences ; whites must have licences. In the schools, while it is emphasized that Indian and white children are equals and are to receive equal treatment, Indian children receive a hot lunch, prepared by a cook hired by the school, without charge to them. Their lunches are paid for by the government. White children either carry their lunches or pay from family funds for what they receive at the school. Indian schoolchildren have their teeth cared for by a visiting government dentist without charge. White schoolchildren must go to the towns

---

[1] *Report of the Commissioner for Indian Affairs*, 1942, p. 245. The denial of state jurisdiction is also due to ' the concept of Federal guardianship over Indians which exempts Indians living within reservations from most of the laws and law-enforcement machinery of the States and localities in which they live, and which creates confusion with regard to the jurisdiction of the several courts ' (1939, p. 56). At the present time, ' The United States courts have jurisdiction only with respect to 10 major crimes which have been specifically designated by Congress. The State courts have jurisdiction only with respect to crimes committed off reservations. All other crimes and misdemeanours, if punishable at all, are under the jurisdiction of special courts of Indian offenses which have been established in a large number of reservations. They follow either the code promulgated by the Secretary of the Interior or ones which have been devised by their own tribal councils acting under the authority of their own constitutions adopted under provisions of the Indian Reorganization Act of 1934 ' (1939, p. 46).

The Makah judges told me that the tribe has a written code, but as they have never been able to understand it since the lawyers put it into proper legal language, they dispense judgment according to their own sense of what is fitting.

for dental care, and this is paid for by their parents. Indians receive free medical care from the doctor attached to the reservation, and they have access to other government doctors who either make periodic visits to the village or who can be consulted at the Cushman Hospital in Tacoma. Whites must pay for medical attention.

The whites of the village who refuse to pay their bills may find that a garnishee has been placed on their pay cheques, or they are subject to some other action taken to recover the money from their property. The Makah are protected against this. Many families have bills at the stores of two and three hundred dollars which have been on the books for years.[1] There is no way for the store owner to recover this money unless he can hire some member of the family as a clerk and deduct from the monthly salary a portion to be set against the bill. Many Makah owe large bills for electricity at the power plant. In some cases, the manager of the plant retaliated by cutting off electricity to their houses. Frequently he did nothing ; for some Makah threatened to persuade the tribe to instal its own power plant if they were not given free electricity. One who did this never again received a monthly statement, but his house remained attached to the power lines.

One story told about the reservation shows the attitude that many Makah take in these matters, although I was never able to discover whether the incident actually happened or whether it is only folklore. It was said that, a few years before, a sewing-machine salesman came to the village and sold a number of machines on the instalment plan to members of the tribe. He was proud of his record, until none of the succeeding instalments were paid. When he attempted to follow the usual procedure and recover the machines, he found that he was forbidden to remove them from the reservation. Makah who told the story regarded it as highly entertaining. When I was there, the white husband of a Makah woman had a garnishee placed on his pay cheque because he refused to pay the instalments on a car he had purchased in Port Angeles and also refused to return the car to the dealer's yard, although he was willing to have the dealer come and collect it. When the notice of the garnishee arrived, his wife was furious both with the bill collector and with her

---

[1] This I was told by the Makah who owed the bills.

husband, and wanted to know why the car had not been put in her name so that they would be safe from reprisals.

When this attitude is shown, the Makah justify it on the grounds that whites always attempt to cheat Indians and that they have taken everything from the Indians. Therefore the Indians are only getting something of their own back. Everyone I spoke with cursed one of the storekeepers who, it was maintained, was continually cheating them. They use this as a justification for their failure to pay the bills they owe at the store. Actually, their failure to pay their bills seems in large part due to the acute realization that they have a preferred status which enables them to do these things with an impunity which is not accorded to whites, since all stores ever operated by Makah at Neah Bay have failed, and it is commonly said that this is because people refused to pay their bills. They demanded unlimited credit, and then ignored hints that the accounts be settled. At the present time one of the restaurants owned and operated by a Makah is said to be in a bad financial condition because the proprietor cannot refuse people credit, and they will not pay their bills. I never heard any suggestion that the proprietor was not dealing fairly with the people, and he was liked by other Makah and by the whites. There are people who do pay their bills and who are still able to buy on credit at the stores in Neah Bay. Others pay cash for everything by choice. But many families have exhausted their credit throughout the town, and there is much joking among them about how they have to go to Clallam Bay to cash pay cheques, because if they cashed them any place in Neah Bay they would be forced to use part of the cheque to settle a bill.

The whites with whom I talked also realize that there is a difference in status which puts them at a disadvantage, and they sneer at the Makah for being dishonest in taking advantage of the situation. Many of them, however, take advantage of their own greater mobility to disappear suddenly from the village before news of their intention to depart has circulated and thus escape with their pay cheques and without paying their bills. They leave the business people and their Makah landlords with unpaid bills on their hands.[1]

[1] The high prices in the village stores, and they are higher than in nearby towns, are at least partially explained by the increased cost of transport to this outpost and the precarious matter of credit.

The differences in sentiments and attitudes which differentiate the two groups, and the feeling of Makah solidarity and alienation from the whites, are bolstered and perhaps partially created by this difference in status. The differential treatment accorded to the Makah because of their status is a constant reminder that they come from a background different from that of other Americans. In the nature of the case, it is an ascribed rather than an achieved status. The holders of the status realize thoroughly the advantages that they gain from it and would fight any attempt to alter it to their disadvantage although they may be loud in their demands for equality with other Americans and sneer bitterly at any imputation that they are less capable or less ' civilized ' than the whites.

Summary

For the last three chapters, we have been considering how far the Makah still represent a distinct group, and what the bases for their separation from the general American population are. Attention has been centred upon the situations in which the people of Neah Bay interact with each other and upon their attitudes towards each other.

The examination of the data seems to show that the existence of the Makah as a distinct group today is a phenomenon due not so much to the survival of a set of customs obviously differentiating them from the whites and the creation of a class or caste system on the basis of these differences as it is to the creation of a separate status for the Makah by the reservation system. The result is not strictly comparable to conditions found in most heterogeneous societies ; for in Neah Bay the lines of division are not bolstered by an economic structure favouring members of one group at the expense of the other. It is not a simple case of superordination-subordination, with the members of one group owing deference to the members of the other. The situation is more complex than this.

The programme of the Indian Service in the period prior to the Indian Reorganization Act seems to have been successful in so far as it has abolished the Makah group as a culturally distinct body with an integrated system of customs and practices preventing its holders from entering into the body of American citizens. But in pursuit of its goal, it established barriers in the form of the reservation and ' Indian status ' which set the Makah apart as a people in a separate legal and social status. These prevent the further assimilation of the Makah into the general, American population. The status is now self-perpetuating because with it are privileges which are regarded as vested interests by those occupying the status.

Racial, linguistic, and most cultural differences may vanish, but so long as there continues to be a Makah Indian Reservation and a policy of special legal and economic benefits for those who are Indians, the Makah will continue to regard themselves as a group with a peculiar position in American society. This feeling is also bolstered by the ideology that they and other Indians are a class despoiled of their possessions in lands and culture by an aggressor white group, and that any benefits derived from their peculiar status are but partial repayment on the debt which whites as a group owe to the Indians. The debt itself can never be satisfied. Any attempt to readjust the situation so that the status differences between Makah and whites are lessened or increased will be complicated by these developments. At the same time the difference in treatment makes it impossible for Makah and whites to meet on the same footing. The difference in status will undoubtedly result, as it already has, in differences in culture ; for culture is responsive to the situations in which people find themselves.

The early Indian Service policies which were framed as a means for promoting the rapid assimilation of the Indian into American life have thus been instrumental in transforming a difference in status due to a difference in cultural background into a structural difference within the American social system. This may not be true of certain large Indian tribes where cultural differences are still striking and far-reaching ; but the Makah are now for all obvious purposes a part of American society. They still have customs and practices alien to those of whites with whom they associate, but these have less effect upon their relationship with whites than does the development of the Indian status and the ideology of a despoiled people.

CHAPTER VI

THE MAKAH AND THE OUTER WORLD

BEYOND the borders of the reservation lies another world. Today the Makah are in close touch with this outside world, despite the tradition of isolation which still prevails in the village. They seek it often, and it in turn impinges upon them in their village through many channels.

INFLUENCES ENTERING NEAH BAY

Tradition of Isolation

Once this was not true to any extent, and Neah Bay was a world apart. Sally Grove who is over sixty often said that they were accustomed to call their village ' the lost land ', because it was so far from everywhere that they knew nothing of what was happening in the outside world nor did those who lived there know what went on within the reservation. In the village, life went on within a closed circle with only the people of the agency, the missionaries, and the owners of the trading store to remind them that there was a world beyond their immediate horizons.

Old residents among the whites speak mournfully of the days before the early 'thirties when the road was built along the northern edge of the Olympic Peninsula to connect Neah Bay with the rest of the United States. They say that in those days the village was a tightly knit community. Its people were dependent upon their own resources for their social life and for the goods used in their daily lives. Social life was much more homogeneous and the few whites participated more fully in the life of the Indian inhabitants.

Makah, especially those over thirty, also speak of this time, and wonder what has occurred to destroy the old community feeling, which has weakened the bonds not only between whites and Indians but also those existing between the Makah themselves. Formerly the majority of the tribe gathered for social affairs ; now only a few appear at parties. They attribute the change to many factors : the increased white population in the village ; the increased Americanization of the young people ; the development of religious groups which refuse to countenance social life with any save their own people.   Most of them maintain that the change is due directly to the building of the road which allows people to visit at will over the surrounding territory. Before the road was built, few whites came among them save the fishermen who appeared during the summer.   The Makah themselves stayed more at home.   When they did leave the reservation, it was for long trips of weeks' duration.   There was no constant travelling back and forth between the reservation and the outside.   During the bad weather of the winter they might never leave the village except for short journeys along the shores of the reservation, and even the mailboat might not be able to approach the dock to land its cargo of letters and newspapers.   In those days, the big event of each day was the coming of the mail, brought by boat from Clallam Bay where the highway ended twenty miles east of Neah Bay.   Three times a week, a steamer made the trip from Seattle and back carrying freight and passengers.   Some travelled out by steamer ; others went by canoe or by the gasolene-propelled fishing boats owned by Makah men.   But by water it took almost a day to reach any more settled spot than their own village, and when the weather was bad it was better to stay at home.   Thus isolated, they built up their own life within the village with little dependence upon the inhabitants of the rest of the world.

As the people talk about the former isolation, there is a nostalgic feeling for a lost simplicity and quiet.   One woman pointed up the contrast between the present Neah Bay and that of ten years and more ago by describing the impact of the first world war upon its people.   The earlier war meant little to the people tucked off at the end of the Strait.   The papers came in three times a week, but no one paid much attention to the news which concerned them little if at all.   Only one man from the village was taken for military service.[1]   He went overseas with the troops, but this aroused little interest in the war.   Weeks passed without the inhabitants of the village being pressed into awareness of what

[1] Indians were not drafted for the first war.   They were given American Citizenship in 1924, by an Act of Congress.   This made them liable to draft on the same basis as other Americans.

was happening half a world away. Food did not worry them since they subsisted chiefly upon fish caught within their own waters and depended little on what was bought in the stores. But now, they, like the rest of the country, were in the thick of world events. Their radios announced the latest news reports. The daily papers glared with headlines. Past their harbour limped ships torpedoed by enemy submarines. Their shores were guarded by men in uniform who warned them off from some of the beaches. Their boys were drafted into the army and navy, and scattered in training camps or embarkation points. The village was under blackout regulations similar to those affecting the rest of the coast. Their food was rationed, and, now largely dependent upon the food bought at stores, they felt the effect not only of rationing but also of high prices.

The Neah Bay people can no longer regard themselves as isolated and far outside the currents that affect other Americans. Instead they have been invaded and surrounded by the outer world which has become a part of their daily lives. This they recognize. They reiterate again and again that while once they were independent and able to live by their own efforts they have now learned to use the things of the white man and cannot live without them.

Channels of Communication

Daily the mail is brought from Port Angeles, bringing letters, the daily newspapers, and magazines. Every Makah on the reservation over school age is literate with the exception of six old people. They are not only able to read ; most of them do so to some extent. Many families subscribe to Seattle or county newspapers or buy them locally. Those who do not take a paper still glance through copies lying on the counter at one of the stores or on the tables in the women's Sewing Room. They also buy magazines. Even the few old people who cannot read like to study the pages of *Life* and other pictorial magazines and thus learn something of what is happening beyond their immediate ken.

The men, even if they are not interested in general news, buy papers to learn the market prices of fish or to read the weather reports. Women buy fashion magazines. They also buy the usual run of women's magazines from which they cull patterns and recipes as well as ideas on the life of other women.[1] A larger number obtain the *True Story* magazine and other ' confessional ' periodicals each month. From these the young girls obtain something of their philosophy of life. When they describe their own experiences or those of their friends they tend to fall into the phrases and emphases familiar to them from this type of reading. Other popular reading material are the detective magazines, which are read by both men and women. They have some impact on Makah thinking. Dave Grove, about twenty-five, told me that when he fought with his wife he shoved a pile of detective magazines at her with instructions to read them and see what happened to jealous women because if she would study them she would be saved a good deal of trouble.

Even more popular are the books of comics filled with fearsome adventures of supermen and master criminals and weird animals. These are bought whenever a new issue appears in the stores. People of both sexes and all ages look through them and are conversant with the characters, who have passed into the folklore of the village. The tribal policeman was dubbed ' Hawkshaw ' after a comic strip detective, and beyond his hearing his own name is rarely used. The whites borrowed the name, and probably recent comers have never learned what the man's real surname is. Another Makah who performs Indian dances for different white gatherings and who boasts that he is a descendant of chiefs with a rank above most of the other dwellers in the village was nicknamed ' Chief Wahoo ' after a comic strip Indian. Since everyone understands the references, these terms are as effective a means of ridicule as can be found.

Other periodicals though less popular still have some circulation among the Makah. Members of the different churches receive denominational publications. Children are given Sunday school lesson sheets. A few people subscribe to *Indians at Work*, a publication of the Indian Service. This is the only publication entering the village specifically aimed at an Indian audience, but it seems of limited appeal. The Christians read their Bibles, but other books have little sale among them. However, one of the stores began to carry paper-bound reprints of popular books, and some Makah occasionally buy these.

[1] I have seen *Good Housekeeping, The Woman's Home Journal, The American*, and other similar magazines on the tables in different Makah homes.

Finally there are the catalogues of the mail order houses : Montgomery Ward, Sears & Roebuck, and the Chicago Mail Order House. These are guarded treasures in most houses, and a catalogue is popularly known as 'the Bible'. People spend hours poring over them and talking of what they will send for when the next pay cheque comes.

Literacy alone has opened much of the world to the Makah. If much that they read does not present them with a realistic picture of the life lived elsewhere, at least it makes them conversant with symbols current among other Americans, and with the common folklore that is circulated by the printing press throughout the nation.

Another medium through which information and entertainment comes flooding into the village is the radio. Every house I entered with only one or two exceptions had a radio. Some are powerful sets for long-range reception. Most of them are in constant use. Only the few old people who understand little English seem unable to endure the constant flow from one programme to another ; the rest are immune to the sound and are within earshot of a radio most of their indoor moments. From their radios, they learn of current happenings. Ordinarily they may not be interested in news broadcasts, but in 1942 they kept their sets tuned for the latest bulletins. They also hear the latest popular music, radio plays, and all the other features available to the rest of the nation. These are now a part of the life of the village. Many of the women listen to the serial plays and will give long descriptions of the plots if offered any encouragement. The children listen to dance orchestras and to the children's programmes. Some of them send in messages to be broadcast on request programmes over local Washington stations. Those having birthdays are not unlikely to hear selections dedicated to them by their relatives. The stations to which they listen most frequently are those in Seattle and Vancouver, but these are connected with the broadcasting networks which cover the continent, so much of what they hear is of nation-wide distribution.

The Makah are also being educated in the customs of the world outside and learn much of its external features through the films brought to the village each week. The first films to be shown there commercially began in the 'twenties, and since then they have always had cinema showings. The man who now runs the business comes each week from a small town thirty to forty miles away and pays the tribe a fee for a permit to show the films. The inhabitants of the village have no control over the selection of what they are to see and they are given the regular films released throughout the country. Most films are shown a few months after they are first released. When I asked people for their preferences, they usually said they liked best films about the South Sea islands and musicals. The building, however, is crowded no matter what is shown. A few old people who understand little English or who are deaf or blind do not attend the weekly showings ; strict church members who regard films as sinful are also conspicuously absent. Almost everyone else goes to the cinema often. Most go every week if they are in the village and have the money.[1] The next day small children playing in the street try to enact some of the episodes of the picture.

The pathway of the Strait and ocean still lies open to connect the village with the outer world, and through it some fragments of the world come to Neah Bay. But this old highway is now of little importance. It is used chiefly by the oil tankers and the fishing boats, and the most important means for the movement of goods and people in and out of the reservation is the road. In the years immediately preceding the war, it brought in tourists in large numbers. The road is also the highway along which most of the supplies of food and other goods used in the village are brought. Supplies for the stores are brought in by big freight trucks which comes lumbering into Neah Bay. Other trucks make weekly visits to sell produce from house to house, competing with the regular stores for the trade of the villagers. These bring fresh meat, vegetables, fruit, and coal. Occasionally someone from the eastern end of the Strait appears with a load of clams or crabs for sale. In the spring, Quinault Indians bring smelts caught in the river on their reservation to sell from house to house.

[1] Some Makah seem to think it behoves them to attend every film if they are in the village. When the cinema manager decided to have showings twice a week, a number were furious and wanted the tribe to ban the project because they said they had the money to go only once a week and now they would have to find the funds to go a second time.

Other mediums of communication are of less importance though perhaps they emphasize even more thoroughly how closely the dwellers on the Strait are now linked to the inhabitants in other areas. There are telephones, which though few in number emphasize that the Neah Bay people are no longer protected from interference by their distance from other centres. In 1942, three Makah households had telephones, but the majority of the population resort to the stores to make their calls. Those stranded miles from home can phone their relatives for money. Those worried about some absent members of the family can check upon their well-being by telephone without the need of making a trip to see how they are. There is also a small airfield at the Coast Guard Station where an aeroplane is kept ready for emergencies. When someone is seriously injured, a doctor can be summoned from Port Angeles to arrive in a few minutes by air ; or a patient can be flown off to a hospital. While it is little used, the people of the village know that the plane is available and it narrows the distance between them and the outside.

Material Contributions from the Outer World

Most of the items used in the daily life of the village are derived from some contact with the outer world. When I attempted to inventory the goods used by the Makah and the items found in their homes, it soon became obvious that they are dependent for their existence upon the channels of communication. Despite the persistence of a tradition of self-sufficiency in all essentials little is produced on the reservation either by whites or by Indians for direct consumption. The few things which they do produce are sent into the outside market to be sold for a money return rather than used in the direct satisfaction of their own needs.

The people of Neah Bay are primarily dependent upon the world beyond the reservation for their raw materials ; for in an emergency and sometimes from choice the Indians, at least, are capable of manufacturing many articles they need. Men still build their own houses, but they import the materials used in the construction. Lumber and shingles are purchased from lumber mills or lumber yards. Other items come from hardware stores and junk yards. When hard pressed by the shortage of materials, they can turn to improvised materials, but this is done with grumbling and a feeling that they are subject to real inconvenience. In 1942, one man who could not get metal pipes used wooden drainpipes of his own construction in a house he was building. He also used shingles split by hand from a piece of well-seasoned cedar that had drifted ashore nearby. But as he sat working on his shingles, he explained to the onlookers that this was the way they used to make houses when he was a boy before they had access to other materials. In normal times, no one would make his own shingles, or cut his own planks.

Some of the boats owned by Makah are built by men who live in the village, and frequently by the owner himself. During 1942, one man went to a quiet place beyond the village and made for himself a dugout canoe. Few today make dugouts. Instead they buy milled planks from the lumber dealers further up the Strait, and build dories or small fishing boats. Fishing boats are always built of imported planks, and the fittings are also imported. So is the paint used for preserving the wood, and the engines which run the boats. These come either from boat fitters or they are old car engines from the junk yards of the Sound area. The fuel used to run them comes from outside.

All the tools used for building boats and houses come from outside. So do the axes, saws, and power-driven saws with which most of the firewood burned in the village is cut. The rest of the firewood is imported from dealers off the reservation, as are the stoves in which the fuel is burned. Some families now own oil burners, and then both stoves and fuel are imported.[1]

Almost all fishing equipment used by the men in their work is purchased : lines, nets, hooks, and lures. A few halibut hooks are made at home by fishermen in the traditional shape of the aboriginal wooden ones, but these are now cast from copper which is bought in the form of bars or thick wire. Other lures and hooks are altered by the fishermen. Some of them paint their metal lures with bright fingernail polish. None are fashioned from materials obtained in the area.

---

[1] In 1942, it was cheaper to run an oil stove than to have a wood range. Peter Morris had converted his oil-burning range into a wood range, and then decided that he would have to reconvert it back to oil because the price of firewood was above that of oil and the firewood was almost unobtainable. This was because all the men were busy and cut little wood for their own use. The population had increased, and more people demanded wood. The few men making a business of providing wood could not supply all the customers.

Household furniture, including sewing machines, washing machines, radios, and gramophones, is almost entirely imported, although a few families have home-made benches or stools. Bedding, dishes, cutlery, cooking pots, and pans are all purchased, and so are the soaps and cleaning fluids used in keeping the dwellings clean. In most houses there are a few small wooden totem poles, and these are carved in the village, but the paints used to decorate them are purchased from outside. Most houses are also equipped with a few baskets, usually of a twined work. These again are usually home products, but the raffia with which they are woven is bought from commercial firms in Seattle, and so are the dyes used for colouring the strands. Much of the cedar bark used in the framework of the baskets is also purchased, but from Indians on Vancouver Island rather than from commercial firms in the city. The only local materials used in the baskets are a white seaweed and a small quantity of cedar bark.

Clothing is purchased from outside, though many women buy materials and make the clothing worn by their families. Shoes invariably come from outside, and some women manage to acquire twelve or more pairs a year. Jewellery almost invariably comes from outside, though a few women have small copper pins in the form of a halibut hook which have been fashioned for them by a fisherman relative. Most of the women buy cosmetics, though a few use an elk tallow, obtained either locally or from other Indians, for a face cream.

Most of the food is imported. I would estimate that roughly 80 per cent of the food used by the Makah is shipped in from outside. The amount purchased varies greatly from family to family. Some families are still largely dependent upon a fish and potatoes diet, and rely on the stores and vegetable trucks only for supplementary foods. Others serve fish but rarely, and then it is likely to be extracted from a tin rather than from the waters of the Strait. This was especially true in 1942 when men were employed on jobs, and most people bought meat since there was no fish to be had.[1] Some, however, had dried or canned large

---

[1] It was one of the peculiarities of Neah Bay life that it was practically impossible to buy fish even when the fishermen were successful and arriving with large catches. They sold their catches to the fish houses, and neither place had a retail licence and therefore could not sell to people in the

quantities of halibut and salmon the previous summer, and could draw on these supplies. In 1942, a few families raised some vegetables in small gardens, but I found only seven gardens at a time when there were 97 Makah households in the village. In previous years, gardens were more common. From the gardens, a few families obtain supplies of potatoes, and also carrots, beans, and cabbages. Six families own stock, which they either sell to a cattle buyer or butcher themselves. One family keeps pigs which they butcher for pork. But the meat produced in the village usually supplies only the families of the owners and their immediate relatives, and is insufficient for their needs. Several families have milch cows, and one man sells milk but is able to supply only a small number of people. Ten families own small flocks of chickens which keep them supplied with eggs. One woman sells her surplus either to the stores or to her neighbours. Most people have to rely on tinned milk and imported eggs. In the summer, women gather sprouts and berries which vary the diet, and some preserve berries for the winter. But today the common method of preserving berries calls for sugar, which is imported.

These are the only local sources of food available with the exception of shellfish which are collected in small quantities when the tide is right. Few women are able to produce a meal without a trip to the store for needed supplies. This means that ultimately most of their food comes from sources beyond the reservation. It is imported by the stores, the produce trucks, or by individuals who shop in the towns and hamlets close enough to the reservation to permit of frequent shopping trips. Many Makah say they find it cheaper to do their shopping some miles away or even to go to Port Angeles than to buy at the stores in the village despite the state sales tax which they must pay once they are off the reservation and the added expense of gasolene and oil. Many of them also wear their tyres thin journeying to nearby towns for supplies of liquor as this cannot be obtained at Neah Bay.

In return for these goods, those who live in the village have only the fish which they catch, their timber, their baskets, and

village. The fish were shipped to the Puget Sound markets for distribution there. Those who had no fishermen in their families had to waylay a fisherman before he sold his catch to obtain a fish.

their own services to offer. Most of these therefore go to obtain a money return which can then be used in obtaining the other possessions which the people desire. But the return on what they have to contribute is governed by conditions in the world outside rather than by their own needs. The price of fish is determined by conditions of a world of which Neah Bay is only a small part. The larger portion of fish caught by Makah fishermen is sold to the fish houses in the village which base their prices on those quoted at the Seattle markets unless the fishermen are unwary enough to accept lower prices. Only a very small portion of the catch is consumed by the village population. All the timber cut upon the reservation is sold on the outside market. Men carve small totem poles and toy canoes which they sell to the stores or to chance comers. Women produce baskets, which also compete on an outside market. Most of them sell directly to the trading store at Neah Bay which then either sells to tourists visiting the village or ship to outside dealers. Others supply outside dealers direct. A few baskets are sold directly to customers who ask a basketmaker to supply a particular basket, but this accounts for only a minute portion of the number sold.[1] The labour for which they are paid is one in which the price is set by the conditions of labour and the legal provisions of labour legislation. The Makah are thus bound both as consumers and producers to a world in which Neah Bay is not an important factor, nor are the conditions of production and consumption altered for its peculiar conditions.

Summary

Neah Bay is thus no isolated community. Most of the currents which affect Makah life are formed outside the village and then sweep in upon the backwater which is Neah Bay, changing and overflowing the currents which are peculiar to the place. The economic world in which the people of the Bay live is determined by the economic conditions of the world outside : the demand and price for fish and the demand for lumber are immediately translated into terms impinging upon the world of the Makah. They are also affected by the prices and supply of the goods

---

[1] At the trading store, they receive a standard price based on size. Little attention is paid to quality. As a result few women attempt to produce fine work.

they purchase. The materials which they use to build their houses, and the goods with which they furnish these come from outside. Most of the food they eat, and often the recipes by which it is prepared, come from outside. The clothes they wear come from outside.

The music which they hear, the dance steps which the young people learn, the entertainment which offers itself in the form of the films, radio programmes, recordings, come from outside. So does all that they read : the comic books, the *True Story* magazines, the newspapers, and the women's magazines, and all the rest.

These items are all manufactured for mass consumption. Almost nothing, or perhaps nothing, that the Makah receive from beyond their own boundaries is fashioned with any thought to their tastes or desires. It is rather directed at the great mass of American people. From the range of items offered to them, the Makah may select, but they are not numerically important enough for their desires to affect the nature of the product. Theoretically nothing now forces the Makah to accept these objects instead of depending upon their own resources. The fact that they are dependent upon alien manufactures indicates the large degree of assimilation of American standards and tastes.

It is also apparent that since they are dependent upon the outside world for so much of their material goods they have had to adjust themselves to the economic life beyond their borders. The economic relationships within a small closed community might be readjusted to their particular needs or desires, but in those in which they are enmeshed, they are dealing with people who know nothing of the Makah save as consumers and small producers.

The people of Neah Bay recognize this dependence upon the outside world, and regret it. As they present it, they feel that almost everything they do is a product of the world beyond their borders which has replaced the things which their ancestors knew and practised. They claim that even the religious faiths they hold come from the outside : the Presbyterians, Shakers, Apostolics, and Pentecostals regard their religions as importations, and know the dates when these were introduced into Neah Bay to replace the religion of their ancestors. The education their children receive is determined by the decision of people living away from the Bay, and in accordance with the State standards for public schools. The instructors to whom the children are entrusted for their education are all derived from outside rather than recruited from within the Neah Bay population.

With the outside world pressing upon them from all sides, even within their village, it becomes impossible for the Makah to have sufficient isolation to allow them to develop a new culture of their own in adjustment to the changed conditions in which they live. Instead, their adjustments must be made to the continuous invasion of new ideas and new objects, all of which are tailored to fit general American tastes and ideas, and none to fit the Makah so long as they remain unassimilated.

They seek New Experiences

The Makah are not content to stay at home and wait for these new ideas to come crashing in upon them. Instead they seek the world outside. But when they go, they go as individuals or in small family groups, out beyond the influence and moral support of the tribe. They leave behind the firm anchorage of the reservation with its privileges which cushions their position.

Background of Emigration

Movement from the reservation has a considerable backing by the weight of tradition. Though Neah Bay is the centre to which they return from far-reaching expeditions and is the centre of their group life, and though the Makah usually represent themselves as a stable group bound to the reservation, they have always been travellers with an urge to seek distant areas.

Their parents, grandparents, and great-grandparents made trading trips as far as the Columbia River to the south, eastward to Puget Sound, and northward to Nootka Sound before the whites ever penetrated the region. When ships first appeared on their coast, Makah men signed on for trips of varying duration. Some were carried off for long voyages. In the village today, when the old people gather in their parties and tell their stories of the distant past, they fall to arguing about which countries their ancestors reached on these voyages. Some, they think, were taken south to California to serve as seal hunters ; others reached the Hawaiian Islands. Others were taken to China and

Japan, or so their descendants like to think. Makah men were also carried northward on vessels going to trade for furs with the northern tribes. Later in the great days of the sealing industry they set out in large numbers for the Bering Sea. At first they went as crews or hunters attached to schooners owned by whites. Later, Makah men bought schooners and hiring whites as navigators set out for themselves to participate in the profits of the trade.[1] Both men and women made the long voyage which lasted for months, and in Alaskan waters they mingled with other sealers and with the natives of the coast. In 1942, five old men and one old woman were left from those who took part in these expeditions.

Inland they ranged to the settlements of the Sound and to Victoria, the Hudson Bay Trading Post on Vancouver Island. There they traded their seal furs, their whale oil, and fish for the goods of the white man. When the sealing industry was forbidden by international treaties in 1894, the eastward migrations became still more important, for they were now dependent upon a money economy and there was little as yet upon their reservation which would enable them to obtain money or goods for trade although they began to ship fish to the Sound in large quantities first in 1891. Whole families now moved off up the Strait to be gone for months and even years. Some went to work in the salmon canneries early established near the city of Vancouver. Others went to eastern Washington to work in the hop fields. Others settled in Seattle, or went to work in the lumber camps which were calling for workers. During the summer months, Neah Bay was almost deserted. Many families did not return even when the winter months came.

Young women who were graduates of the Indian boarding school at Neah Bay took jobs as houseworkers in Port Angeles, Port Townsend, and Seattle. Youngsters went off to Indian boarding schools in Washington and Oregon. There was a general scattering of the tribe throughout all parts of the state. Some went even further afield. In the early 1920's, two men with their wives were sent to Idaho for training in a Presbyterian mission school which prepared Indians to return to their own tribes as ministers and missionaries. One man went to the Indian

[1] The first schooner bought by a Makah was purchased in 1885. The man made such a large profit, that in the next year he bought a larger boat.

college at Carlisle in Pennsylvania and later with his wife, also a Makah, worked for many years as an Indian Service employee in schools on reservations in Arizona and New Mexico. One man went to France in the 1914–18 war as a member of the American expeditionary force. A youngster in his late teens found himself in a reform school in Nevada.

The Makah as individuals have had considerable contact therefore with the outside world and have found it possible to adjust in situations where they are not protected by their reservation.

Geographical Mobility

Almost every Makah I met sooner or later mentioned having lived for a while in some other locality. Their conversations were studded with phrases such as ' This happened when we were picking hops at Yakima one year ' ; or ' When Jack Gray and his mother and brother were working in the cannery over at Vancouver—we usually went too, but we didn't go that year ' ; or ' I heard this story from my cousin one time when we were waiting for the tide to go out. That was when we were digging clams over on the canal. Most people used to go over there every year when it was so hard to make a living down here.'

I did not realize the importance of the question at the time, and therefore did not make systematic inquiries about whether or not people had lived and worked away from the reservation for extended periods of time. However, when I went through my notes afterwards, I was able to get some indication of the extent of the movement : at least 56 of the 104 men and 53 of the 99 women over the age of twenty-five have lived away from the reservation. This includes people who lived in other areas while attending boarding schools, while in hospital for long periods, while working, and while living with relatives. Some of them went as children ; others as adults. Some made repeated sojourns away form the reservation ; a few had gone away but once or twice. They amount to 53 per cent of the total population over twenty-five resident at Neah Bay in 1942. These figures minimize the mobility of the population, since undoubtedly others have lived away from Neah Bay although I did not happen to hear about it.

I was also able to find in my field notes some information on the actual mobility of the population in 1942 : 30 men and 40 women over the age of twenty-five left the reservation for a period of more than several weeks either because of a job in another area or because they went on a long extended visit. This involves a much larger number of the total population, since in many cases the whole family moved. Thus when one man took a job in the shipyards in a city on the Sound, he took his wife and two young daughters with him. Another who found a job as second mate on a ship whose home port was Seattle took his wife and three babies to Seattle. In other instances, part of the family went, while other members stayed at Neah Bay. Women and children from eight families went to the berry fields near Seattle, leaving their men behind.

Almost everyone made trips of short duration which took them some distance from the reservation. They would be away only a day or two at a time, but over a year this amounted to a considerable period spent away from Neah Bay. One family was probably either of average mobility or perhaps slightly more mobile than the majority. They owned an old car in which they went to Clallam Bay and other neighbouring towns once or twice a week. They made several trips to the headquarters of the Indian Service in southern Washington, which is about 150 miles from the reservation. Five or six times during the year they went to the Quileute Reservation thirty or forty miles by road from Neah Bay. About twice a month they went to Port Angeles. One member of the family visited the Sound area five times, to be gone from several days to a week, and then complained that she never had an opportunity to travel the way her neighbours did. Others in the village made trips of a similar nature, and some departed for more distant places. A number visited Vancouver Island. A few went to Portland, or to Bellingham, or to Yakima. A few disappeared and returned to say they had been to California. Some of the trips were made by bus or by boat ; short trips were usually made by car. There were forty cars owned by Makah households, or about one car to every two and a half households. Not all were in running order at the same time, but whenever they were serviceable they were in constant use.

It is almost impossible to find anyone who knows only Neah Bay or the immediately surrounding country, but the majority of Makah have never been beyond the State of Washington and the southern coast of Vancouver Island which lies only a few miles across the Strait from their own village.   At least this was true until the beginning of 1942, when there was a further scattering out of the younger men and older boys, as the Makah were either drafted or enlisted.   Some went to camps in the southwest or far east.   Some received their training in the middle west.   Most were moved from one camp to another so that they saw a good deal of the United States.   Probably most of them eventually went overseas.

Even the children have seen something of other parts of the state, although a few have never been far from Neah Bay. Lincoln and Corkie Grove, six and eight, told me they were once as far as Forks, about forty miles away, and that they have been promised a trip to Port Angeles some day.   Their ten-year-old sister, however, has been taken by their parents in migrations about western Washington and lived for a time in Seattle and Port Angeles.   Her small brothers are probably exceptions among their age mates.   I found no others with as limited an experience.   Brenda Sterne, at six, has visited Tacoma and Seattle a number of times, has lived near Seattle with a relative for some months, has gone hop-picking with her mother to Yakima in eastern Washington, and has been in a hospital in Tacoma on three occasions.   Sonny Clarke, at seven, has lived for some months in Port Angeles with his parents and other relatives and once spent a year with a relative in Seattle.   Some of the older children are probably as much at home in cities on the Sound as they are at Neah Bay.

Older people wander afield frequently.   One woman left her children with a relative and went to Seattle for a month, where she stayed with her cousin and another Makah girl who were working in the city.   She found a job in Seattle, and then returned to Neah Bay to arrange for the care of her children so she could go back to the city.   In the intervals when she lived at Neah Bay, she was always venturing off to Port Angeles or to other towns on the Peninsula.   Emily Lester and her husband were even more mobile.   They frequently vanished on drinking bouts that took them from the village.   Early in the summer they decided to move to Port Angeles where the husband found work.   In the fall, they returned to Neah Bay, and then began to lay plans to move to Seattle for the winter. The Clarkes wearied of Neah Bay in the summer and moved to Port Angeles, leasing their house in the village until the end of the year. After a month and a half in Port Angeles, they moved back to Neah Bay. Mrs. Clarke, however, continued to visit Port Angeles at least once a week, and was trying to persuade her husband to take a trip to California. Peter and Lydia Morris visited Vancouver Island for several weeks, then went to Seattle for a week, then spent some days on the Quinault reservation, and then when a relative joined the navy and was posted to Seattle used to visit him there every week or so.

Even those who consider themselves the old people of Neah Bay are eager to travel and have no hesitation about setting out alone. The oldest person in the tribe considered going off to Yakima for hop-picking accompanied only by his elderly wife. Another man who is well past sixty caught the bus one day and went down to California to visit a grandniece who had followed her soldier husband to his camp. Another old couple who say they are past seventy went off to Victoria and Seattle. Mrs. Sharpe who is over eighty was always eagerly planning trips which her feebleness usually prevented her from taking, but she did succeed in visiting Victoria.

Permanent Emigration

With all this mobility of the population, it is surprising that Neah Bay has a Makah population. But Neah Bay is the lodestone which draws them back from trips however distant or however far. Only a few Makah who have been raised in the village seem to have left it for good. These are people who have either married into other tribes or women who have married white men. I could discover no trace of any couples which have left Neah Bay permanently where both spouses were Makah. Some of those who left during 1942 may be gone for good, but the odds are very much against their departure being anything but temporary.

Several factors seem at work to draw them back. For one thing, it is easier to make a living at Neah Bay, and should an individual have no money there are always relatives at Neah Bay to fall back upon. When Louise Armstrong planned to move to Seattle, old Warren Grove told her that since she had to pay no rent at Neah Bay and could get what she wanted to eat without paying much, it was ' silly ' to go to Seattle. Her cousin told her much the same thing, and added that he would ' rather be poor in Neah Bay than Seattle because here I'm always sure of eating. Even if I have no money, the people here will feed me.' The thought of these supporting relatives is a powerful one. Emily Lester once shook her head over a Makah woman who was living at the Quileute Reservation and said, ' I wonder how she can stand living down there where she has no relatives ! '

At the same time there is a pull in the opposite direction ; for many young people are restless and claim that if they have a chance they will leave Neah Bay for ever. Three young women talking one night about a woman who had left her husband and then returned to him, agreed, ' If we ever had a chance to get away from Neah Bay, catch us coming back here ! Don't see why Marie ever came back.' Others felt the same way. One recent graduate of the Indian boarding school at Chemawa, took a job at Seattle and came to Neah Bay for only short visits. Her mother said that the girl ' has been away to school so much, at Chemawa ever since she was twelve, she feels strange down here. She can't make friends. She says the other girls just stand off and look at her, and they say she feels stuck up. So she says she doesn't like to stay down here where everybody just looks at her. She never was one to make friends down here.'

One might assume that other young people who have been away at Indian boarding schools might feel the same way, but they have all returned and settled in the village with the exception of a few girls who have married outside the tribe.

Nevertheless, approximately 42 per cent of the Makah households contain individuals who have a close Makah relative living in some other locality. By close relative here I mean, a brother, sister, father, mother, son, or daughter. If grandchildren, nephews, nieces, aunts, uncles, etc., are included, then there is probably not a household which does not have such a link to the outside world. With them they keep in touch by letter and visits.

How they fit into the World Outside

When the Makah leave their reservation, they go as individuals ; and in the outer world they must establish themselves as individuals. They do this with some measure of success, though their position in the larger society which they enter is ill-defined. They are neither rigidly excluded nor completely accepted. Since there is no well-defined pattern to govern their relations with those they meet, individuals must find their place by a process of trial and error. The majority of them become a part of the labouring class, both in the types of jobs they find and in their living conditions and associations. A few, but only a few, are able to secure a more assured position.

Types of Jobs Available

The majority of men and women who leave the reservation go as unskilled workers. They lack technical or professional training which would fit them for better jobs. Three men have attended universities, but only one completed his course ; three women have had a business or nurse's training. One of the men with University training worked for some years as a teacher in the Indian Service. One of the women with a business training worked for a period as a typist for the Indian Service ; another works as a trained nurse in a city on the Sound. These are the only Makah who have ever held ' white-collar ' jobs. The rest lack the training to compete with whites for employment in these fields.

Instead they drift into unskilled jobs. They easily find work as seasonal labourers in the hop fields, berry fields, and on the potato farms. This work, however, lasts for only the period of the summer and fall, and then they must either find fresh employment or return to Neah Bay. None of them have become professional migratory workers following the crops throughout the length of the Pacific Coast. Instead, they may move from berry fields to hop fields and then to the potato farms, but this is the limit of their wanderings. This leaves them dependent upon some other means of obtaining a supplementary income. But in the field work, they compete on equal terms with other labourers. A few Makah women act as labour contractors for the owners of the big farms, and arrange to obtain additional workers from their own people to help with the crops. Others go as ordinary labourers. While they work, they camp in the fields besides Indians from other tribes (many of whom come from British Columbia), orientals, and white migratory workers. At the berry fields, they are usually employed by Japanese who own most of the berry fields in the Sound area, and are supervised by either Japanese or Filipino foremen. On the hop and potato farms, they usually work for white owners.[1]

The wages they receive vary from year to year according to the supply of labour available. The Makah themselves, however, seem to regard the money they earn as of secondary importance. The trip to the berry fields and the excitement of mingling with other people attract them whether they are in need of money or not. Some claim they go not because they expect to make any money picking berries or hops, but because they usually reap a good return from the gambling games that go on about the camps in the evening. Within a few months, they tire of the work and then even the added attractions provided by their employers, such as trips to weekly films or visits to some neighbouring fair, will no longer keep them on the job. They either move to some other area, or are off to the cities for a few days or weeks to spend what they have earned, or they return home.

Whole families may co-operate in the work of picking : men, women, and children working side by side. Some children earn enough for their school clothes. During 1942, however, none of the Makah adult men went to the fields to work, since they were engrossed in fishing or in construction jobs on the reservation. Ordinarily they also go, perhaps as much to keep a vigilant eye on their wives as for any other purpose ; for the berry fields are notable places for acquiring a new marital partner or merely for casual liaisons.

In ordinary years there is scant possibility of finding better or more permanent jobs, unless the men go into the lumber camps. Usually they prefer to work at the lumber camp on the reservation rather than investigate other camps in Washington. Still at least 27 adult men in the present population have supported themselves, and perhaps a family, away from Neah Bay by a job other than seasonal farm work. Several men have worked on coastal steamers. Others have worked in lumber camps, or as night watchmen in the cities. Several have worked as labourers on construction projects or found work in

[1] With the evacuation of all Japanese from the West Coast in 1942, the farms were in the hands of Filipinos or whites.

shipbuilding yards. Several have held jobs as forest rangers. In 1942, with the big demand for defence workers, finding a job was comparatively easy. Ten men and boys took jobs in aeroplane factories, shipyards, or machine shops.

Ordinarily few openings exist for women other than those in the fields. The greatest opportunities for them lie as house-workers. Fifteen or more women have taken such jobs, though I was told that most Makah girls do not work out and do not know how to do so. A few have held other jobs. One was asked to act as housekeeper at a Port Angeles hotel, but gave it up after a day or two. Another was first cook and then matron at an Indian boarding school in Tacoma. In 1942, one woman found work in a Seattle bakery ; and three girls took jobs in defence factories, but this was regarded as a new departure for Makah women. A middle-aged woman said that she once supported herself in Seattle by the sale of baskets. A few women have earned their living as prostitutes. Only two have ever held a skilled job.[1]

It is clear that most Makah, as far as jobs and economic status are concerned, are kept in the lower stratum of society, and form their contacts with other members of this class. A few individuals have been able to escape from it because they earned enough through fishing or other enterprises at Neah Bay during summer months so that when they went to Seattle it was simply to spend the winter and not to work. One family at one period customarily wintered in Seattle to be near a married daughter, and so that younger members of the family might have the advantages of Seattle schools. But this is a thing of the past ; and all those who go to Seattle now go either to work or to live on the bounty of relatives or the government.

Living Quarters

In neither their jobs nor their living quarters are they segregated from whites who are on the same economic level. In the fields, migratory white workers share the same camps and the same living conditions as the Indians. They work side by side. In the cities, most Makah frequent cheap lodgings, which are also patronized by whites. During 1942, three Makah girls roomed

[1] Cf. above, p. 165.

together in Seattle, but usually those who go live scattered about the city, and the only concentration of Makah is the immediate family group. In Seattle, at least, there is no section of the city given over to Indians, though most of them usually visit Pioneer Square at some time during their stay to see what other Indians are around, and many of them congregate around the First Avenue district along the waterfront.

Those who make short trips to the cities stay in hotels patronized by whites, though the hotels most generally frequented would be regarded as third or fourth rate. One hotel popular with the Makah is over a noisy dance hall where incoming sailors gather. One of the hotel chambermaids swore that she would not stay in the place overnight, that it was bad enough to have to work there during the day. However, both white men and white women stay in the hotel which was once one of the good hotels in the city. Others from Neah Bay patronize hotels in quieter locations, which are said to have better reputations.

Social Life

No restrictions discriminate against Indians as such in their relations with whites outside of Neah Bay. The two peoples trade at the same stores, though Makah make most of their purchases at inexpensive department stores or second-hand stores. A few, however, patronize the more expensive department stores in Seattle, or are careful to say that they do. They go to the same theatres and to the same restaurants as whites, and at the latter they appear to be served without question.[1]

If they are church members, they go to the same churches as the whites. Their children attend Sunday schools and youth conferences with other young people. The Apostolics are welcomed eagerly at any Apostolic church, and a number of them go to the annual summer conferences held in Portland to which Apostolics from all over the country come.

Those who live in a locality for any length of time seem to make friends with their white neighbours. Women told me of

[1] The only actual segregation of which I heard took place in Canada. Some of the Makah said that when they were on Vancouver Island they were told to sit in certain portions of the theatres which were allotted to Indians, and that they were not expected to enter most of the restaurants.

how they visited their neighbours, and exchange advice on housework, family matters, and business ventures. When they return to Neah Bay, they correspond with these friends, who sometimes come to visit them at the Bay. When they go back to the cities on short visits, they may stay with white friends, and usually call on them. The Makah are thus able to adjust themselves to social relations with whites away from their reservation, in situations where they are known as individuals and not as landlords or holders of political power.

How the Whites regard Them

Many whites whom they meet thus obviously accept them on equal terms. Nevertheless, there seems to be a greater tendency for whites away from the reservation to regard the Makah in an unfavourable light. Away from the reservation are people who may call them ' Siwash ' or refer to the women as ' squaws '. The whites I met in Port Angeles made slighting comments on Indians and said they were stupid, dirty, and uncivilized. I heard women in Port Angeles championing separate schools for Indian children so that their own children would not run the risk of contamination from the ' diseases ' which Indians have. But in such face-to-face contacts as I saw between Indians and whites, no unpleasant incidents occurred. I heard of a few cases of pointed discrimination from Makah and whites, but when I accompanied Makah in restaurants, hotels, and stores, I saw no apparent discrimination.[1]

Whites show a slight tendency to regard Indians as a picturesque element in the population fit to provide entertainment on a pioneer occasion, but this only touches a few members of the Makah population. One man is frequently asked to dance before different organizations ; several have been invited to Seattle to dance for some big men's clubs ; a number have taken part in frontier parades in Tacoma. The Makah for some years have had a booth at the county fair in which they display the few treasures of Indian handiwork which they still preserve and their own basket work. This was arranged by an employee of the Indian Service who hoped that the exhibit would give the Indians

[1] My European features would not act as a protection here, since many Indians in Washington have such features.

a greater prestige in the eyes of the white communities near the reservation. Several women have been invited to Seattle to teach basketry in the Y.W.C.A. there. One of them also goes to an Indian boarding school to demonstrate basketry. She refers to this work as her ‘ charity work ’.

Most whites away from Neah Bay, however, are completely ignorant of the Makah as a people. Even the Port Angeles people who live in the same county with them know little or nothing about the Makah as such. They do not distinguish between the different Indian tribes found in the area nor do they regard them as an artistic element in the community. Instead, *Indian* to them means ‘ those people on the Plains who are a much higher type of person than our local Siwash. They’re supposed to be the lowest form of humanity.’ The majority of whites seem never to have met an Indian except casually on a street or in a business dealing across the counter of a store. When they do meet an Indian, they tend to deal with him in terms of a general stereotype rather than as an individual.

Summary

It is not their ‘ Makahness ’ which keeps the Makah from being more successful in making an assured position for themselves in the outside world. They are perfectly capable of adjusting themselves to the demands made upon them to conform to the behaviour of the various people that they meet, and they success-fully deal with whites in many types of relationship. They fail to raise themselves into a secure position, because they lack the skills that would enable them to find better jobs, and because with the reservation and its ties they tend to look upon their jobs as purely temporary and make no effort to associate themselves with some enterprise and gradually work themselves up into more skilled posts.

They are also hindered in forming close contacts with many whites because of the prejudice of the latter, which is based on the stereotypes about Indians and their behaviour and capabilities. These are held whatever the actual behaviour of the Makah, and therefore are immune against evidence of individual abilities. Where whites are willing to accept Makah on their own level, the two meet as equals and friends with common interests and a common sphere of understanding.

In Makah dealings with whites beyond the reservation, therefore, it is white prejudice and their own lack of technical skills rather than any survival of Makah custom which prevent full assimilation and the chance to participate in every aspect of American life.

CHAPTER VII

THE MAKAH AND THEIR TRADITIONS

INTRODUCTION

IN relationships between Makah and whites there is little to distinguish the behaviour of the Makah from that of other Americans. Their adjustments to whites are in terms of mechanisms available to them in the white culture or in terms of mechanisms fostered by the reservation system. To understand these adjustments, it is unnecessary to know much about the Makah as the possessors of a traditional way of life different from that known to the whites. Much the same thing is true of the adjustments which the Makah have made to the economic system in which they find themselves.

If we try to understand the social relationships which exist between Makah and the interests which mark them as a group, this is no longer true ; for in the interaction of Makah with Makah there are usually a large number of meaningful associations not shared with whites. Most of these are regarded by the Makah as their direct legacy from ancestors who have succeeded in passing on to them something of their own tradition. This may be referred to as the *Traditional Culture* of the Makah, or as the *Tradition* ; for to the Makah there is still a distinction between the things which they do in conformity with white standards and those which they feel to be a following of the ' old ways '.

It is possible to treat the traditional culture under two categories. One may be termed ' latent culture '.[1] It is rarely expressed otherwise than verbally in the forms of reminiscences about the past, though a few treasured heirlooms also represent the tradition. No attempt is made to carry the knowledge of the ' latent culture ' into actual practice. It is not applied in everyday life as a mechanism of adjustment to those environmental and social problems that must be met today. At the same time, interest

---

[1] Linton speaks of culture elements becoming a latent part of cultural equipment. See Linton, 1940, p. 480.

in it is strong among the older people who in their youth participated in much that is now only tradition. It is strong even in
those of middle age who came in time to see a few of the old
customs carried out and who lived as children and young adults
in close association with those who were firmly anchored in the
traditional life. Among the younger people, it begins to fade
away.

The other category of the Tradition is the ' manifest traditional
culture ', which is still expressed in the life of the people—
verbally and by other means—and which affects their adjustments
to each other and to other aspects of their present way of life.
It consists of the things they do which they regard as ' Makah '
customs.

The Makah differ from the whites with whom they associate
both in ' latent ' and ' manifest ' traditions. The whites are
immersed in the present and little inclined to show an interest
in the customs of their own parents and grandparents. Moreover, since they are recent invaders of the area who came as
individuals or in small family groups in recent years, they have
no traditions of a group past which includes the particular people
with whom they associate at present. In this sense they have no
common history. The Makah do. Analogies though dangerous
are useful, and the Makah may be compared to the members of
an old tradition-conscious New England village little affected by
emigration or immigration until recently. The whites are comparable to a population of workers invading the village, who have
been drawn from a wide area and are unconscious both of the
traditions of the village and lacking in any unifying traditions of
their own. The older Makah, like the elders in most long-lived
communities with relatively stable populations, tend to talk in
generations—a practice that keeps before them their common
past. As they speak of people whom they remember or of
whom they heard their parents speak, they are led to recall
changes in customs and to re-emphasize the differences and
similarities between the present and the past. At the same time,
the young people who came too late to take part in the activities
described, who never knew the individuals whose names are
mentioned, acquire some knowledge of what their ancestors were
like and of the life they had.

Though much that is described has ceased to be a standard

urged upon those now growing up, though much has vanished completely from everything save ' stories ', the tradition still assures the Makah that another way of life than that which they follow at present may exist and has. They are aware of alternative modes of behaviour and belief from those current today, though the knowledge of and respect for the alternatives vary from one individual to the next.

The whites, with few exceptions, know little or nothing of the tradition that forms a background against which the present life of the Makah is enacted. It does not enter into their relations with each other, nor is their behaviour towards the Makah affected by it.

THE LATENT CULTURE

Participant Knowledge

Among the Makah there exists a body of traditional knowledge held by people who lived at a time when many of the customs were still current. Certain skills now long since passed into disuse for all practical purposes were acquired by older men and women when they were children and youths. They no longer practise these skills or carry out the activities learned, which still form part of their culture in the sense that they at least think of themselves as capable of carrying out the customs, and they are still interested in talking about them and in describing them to all who will listen.

The Makah can be divided into four categories as far as participant knowledge of the tradition is concerned : There are a few old people who as adults made and handled the artifacts used, who practised the skills, who took their places in different social situations, who played the traditional games and helped to organize them, who had experiences in the traditional manner with the supernatural. There are other individuals who as youths stood by and watched and perhaps were called to help in some small capacity. Others looked on at a distance as small children before they were aware of the implications of what they were seeing. Finally there are those who were born after all save verbal tradition was gone and who have only a hearsay knowledge of the different customs. There is a sliding scale for this gradation, however, and those who came too late to see some aspects of the old culture were as adults full participants in other aspects.

For example, the very oldest people can describe the building of the old ' smokehouses ' as it was done when they helped in the construction.   Those in their sixties and early seventies lived in the old-style houses as children until they went to the boarding school, but they returned home to live in ' modern ' houses. They can describe the appearance of the houses and the arrangements of people and furnishings, but they rarely mention any details regarding methods used in the construction of the buildings.   Others in their fifties never lived in the old houses, though they visited older relatives who still inhabited the few remaining structures.   Those under fifty have only a hearsay knowledge of the old smokehouses, the methods of construction, the arrangement of the interiors, and the manner of life led within them. But from the oldest in this group down through the age grades there is no rapid diminution of knowledge.   I obtained almost as complete a description of a smokehouse from Joan Hewitt, aged twenty-four, as I did from Mrs. Denison, who is fifty-five and who saw the last smokehouses.   The gap is much greater between the descriptions of those who built smokehouses and lived in them as adults and those of people who only saw the buildings as children than it is between the descriptions of the latter and those who came a generation or so after the structures were completely demolished.

A similar gradation in knowledge occurs in relation to subsistence techniques.   Two men remain who served as harpooners in the whaling expeditions and were thus known as ' whalers '.[1] They went through the ritual search for power and were taught the requisite prayers and techniques by older relatives.   In their homes, they preserve floats and harpoons which were part of the whaling equipment they used as young men before the disappearance of the whale led to the abandonment of the activity. There are also two women who were married to ' whalers ' at the time when the men were still hunting whale, and who therefore had to observe certain rituals and taboos to ensure the success and safety of their husbands.   A few men who accompanied whaling expeditions in some capacity other than that of harpooner can also tell of their experiences in the pursuit of the

[1] One died in the middle of 1942.

great mammals. They too know something of the whaling songs and the whaling techniques and rituals, from participation in the activity. Those close to fifty have mingled with the crowds around the carcasses of whales drawn up on the beach after the hunt and have listened to the accounts of older relatives who took part in the hunt. Those born since 1910 have never seen any part of the whaling complex except for some of the costumes and songs displayed on Makah Day and the few whaling implements left in the village after collectors swept away much of the old paraphernalia in the early years of the twentieth century. It was then that the Makah saw their old life vanishing and turned towards the white man's life under the pressure of edicts from their agents and the necessity of discovering new ways of making a living after the ban on fur sealing and the disappearance of the whale. Most of the younger people have never tasted whale meat, once an important item in Makah diet, or have eaten it only when members of the tribe have been able to purchase meat from whales which have drifted ashore on the Pacific Coast. Nevertheless, even children in their teens and some much younger know that the Makah were great whaling men, that whale meat was an important food, and that whalers prepared for the hunt by seeking a guardian spirit through an ordeal of fasting, bathing in hidden spots, and roaming through the woods sleepless for many days and nights. At the same time, there is no pretence that the skills involved in whaling have been communicated to the younger people. The old people claim that most of the complex is now forgotten save for the few men who actually took part in the expeditions.

The Makah are still fishermen, as their ancestors were before them, but many of the skills known to the latter have fallen into disuse. Older men claim that they have much of the technical knowledge but that with modern boats, compasses, and fishing equipment they have no use for it any more. This is especially true of the old weather knowledge and the landmarks for the fishing banks which the older men can describe but which the younger men have never bothered to learn. Sterne said that in the old times old men and women were invited by the family of a growing boy to eat with them and afterwards the old people lectured the boy on the family history and the different kinds of knowledge he would need to know.

' So, this man, when his boy is growing up, he's always wishing to have an old man to have supper with his boy. It's just like if they made a law for the Indians. They tell everything. Even tell them the fishing grounds. Now today, I always kind of laugh at the boys. I always have a bunch of boys along. They don't even know the landmarks because the old men are gone to tell them. Each place all along the fishing bank is named, and they all go by landmarks. But these young fellows here, they don't know that. That was what the old fellows were for, to tell everything about how this boy was going to go about when he's growing up to be a man. And they know the weather too. They listen to the sound on the beach early in the morning. But today, some of these boys, they don't believe that. It's very few of us know. Two years ago, we didn't believe it. Warren's father told me that when you going out fishing, before you pass that point, there will be little breeze running out. Then you turn back no matter if it's fine day. So one morning I was going out. It was blowing hard in that little bay, and no wind the other side. So I told the boys, " Going to be south wind today." " No ! No ! Going to be fine day ! " So we went out. Soon as we got out, we could see the cloud coming from the south, and we run into big southeast storm coming home. And Bob Mead came to me when we got home. " Howard, how did you know that ? " I said, " Old Man Grove told me that if you run into little breeze at that point, turn back. Stay home." So the old timers used to study all these things because they used to go out in the ocean with pole and paddle. No propeller. Why we don't much care, we got propeller on the boat.'

Sterne learned his knowledge of the weather and the landmarks in the days before they had boats with engines. Mead who is a few years younger stayed longer in school and then worked away from the reservation and never absorbed the old skills. The young men have no incentive to learn. They listen to weather reports on the wireless rather than the sound of the waves on the beach to learn what weather they are likely to encounter. But they know that their ancestors possessed knowledge that enabled them to foretell the weather and to guide themselves to the fishing banks and back, and that they had small sheds upon the beach where the old men sat to watch the weather. Of specific details which would enable them to do the same, they are ignorant. In this respect, again, those born long after the particular skills were outmoded seem to have

N

nearly as much information about them as do those who came but a few years later or who were young children at the time.

The women also have their traditional knowledge of subsistence techniques. A few old women can remember gathering and preparing different plants for food. Younger women remember details learned from older relatives who were still using the plants, but never bothered to make any use of them themselves. Still younger women know only that their mothers and grandmothers knew a large number of plants for which they know not even the names. Older women learned how to cut fish for drying and helped to dry them in the sun on the roofs of the old smokehouses. Those of middle years know the technique of cutting fish, but they learned to dry fish in special smokehouses built for this purpose behind the ordinary dwelling-houses. Young women in their twenties and thirties have seen fish prepared for drying and smoking, and have eaten the dried product, but many have never learned the skills involved and have learned methods of canning instead. Ross North complained of his daughters : 'My wife does all the fish drying. The girls won't even try. They think they don't need to work, that their parents will live forever. When my wife and I are gone, the kids will learn.' The older women learned to cook using wooden boxes and stone boiling technique, or earth ovens, or roasting on coals. Younger women know that such methods were used, but most of them have never seen the processes actually carried out. None of them have used these cooking methods. Instead they have learned to cook on stoves with metal and enamel pots and pans.

A similar gradation of knowledge occurs with regard to the ceremonial life, particularly the old ceremonial societies. A few of the very old adults have sponsored *kloqwali* parties for the tribe, though they feel that the *kloqwali* ceremonies in which they participated were very different from what their grandparents described as the proper style. All Makah over fifty were initiated into the *kloqwali* society as small children. Those under fifty have seen nothing of the ceremonies except for the few dances and songs used on Makah Day. These, however, are but a small part of the entertainment offered at a regular *kloqwali*, and nothing of the organization of the society is represented in the Makah Day celebrations. I once talked with Mrs. McBride, a woman in her late forties, and asked if she had come in time to see *kloqwali*. She replied :

' It wasn't real *kloqwali* when I was young. They were just showing the children how it used to be, but it wasn't the real thing. They just showed lots of dances and songs. But my grandmother used to tell me how it was when she was young, and I used to be glad it wasn't like that any more. Now we're civilized and don't have those old savage ways. They were real savages, seems like, long ago. They used to cut themselves. . . . When I was a girl, they weren't having the cutting any more. The white people wouldn't let them, but I remember one time—it must have been when I was about eight because I was real small yet—somebody at Ozette had a *kloqwali*. He was going to show us the real old way, and two old women were willing to be cut. They were real brave. After the *kloqwali*, they started cutting themselves with knives. My grandmother said it didn't really hurt, but I didn't like to see it done. I don't think I could bear to be cut like that. I think it was the last time it was done.'

Yet *kloqwali* is still a familiar word in Makah life. It occurs often when the older people are talking together. Songs still used are described as ' *kloqwali songs* ' ; dances which are occasionally presented are referred to as ' *kloqwali dances*'. Even young people know that formerly a society existed whose performances only the initiated could watch, and that most people were initiated as children through being taken away by ' wolves ' and then recovered by the society. At the same time, people of younger generations have little interest in such matters, and older people who remember participating in the activities of the society feel that most of the *kloqwali* has vanished completely even from the memories of those who were once initiated. Sterne told me that several years before Peter Fisher, a man close to seventy, gave a party in which he tried to revive the songs and dances associated with *kloqwali*, and that at that time old Louis Keller said the old *kloqwali* had many more. Now no one is able to recall them. As for the actual organization, no trace of that is left so far as the Makah can see.

The two other ceremonial societies regarded as old Makah organizations are even less important in the present life of the tribe. A number of old people can remember being initiated into the *c'áyIkˣ*. Others can remember having seen something of its ceremonies from a safe distance and can describe costumes and motions used by members. Younger people have heard tales of the curing performed by the society and have seen the costumes displayed on Makah Day. The *dóƛub* society is now represented by only one man, who is the only living person in the tribe who was initiated into the society. Younger people, however, can remember seeing members of the society perform their dances during the *kloqwali* season, and they have heard tales of its ritual and origin. Children have heard the name of the society and know that it once existed. On the whole, however, much less is known about *c̓ạyɪk^x* and *dóƛub* than about *kloqwali*.

The tradition is not completely uniform in appraising the old ceremonial organizations. Members of Shaker families have been taught that the societies were concerned with the worship of ' devils ' and ' evil spirits ', and that their parents and grand-parents, as recently converted Shakers, helped to put an end to the societies. In other families, the older members never became convinced by the Shakers' arguments, nor by those of the Presbyterian missionaries, and they have taught the young that the societies were good things for the Makah.

War customs are almost completely within the realm of ' story ', though all are aware that the Makah used to be great warriors who raided up and down the Strait and northward along the west coast of Vancouver Island, and in return were prepared to repel attacks by other tribes. Old Louis Keller told me that the last man who knew about war customs through actual participation in war raids died without passing on his knowledge : ' He knew times had changed, so he never cared to talk to the boys about it, and now nobody knows.' The oldest person in the tribe, in his eighties, can only remember that as a tiny boy too small to realize what had happened he saw heads lying on the beach near the village : ' I saw those heads and wondered where the rest of the man was. I thought the bodies were buried in the sand.' Others were told as children what they should do if enemies attacked the village, and the boys were sent out to practise throwing rocks and using the bow and arrows so they might hope to repel attacks. But as tribal warfare faded into the past before the presence of American troops, these warnings were no longer uttered. Now all that survives of the war patterns is crystallized in the tales of past wars, in the pride that is taken in the martial record of their ancestors, and in the few war clubs that exist as heirlooms and not as necessary weapons. And it is only fair to say that some of the latter have been picked up in recent years from the sites of old villages, and have not been handed down from father to son. The pride in their martial ancestors has not led them to emulate their behaviour. Only one Makah fought in the first world war. Before war was declared in December 1941, the only Makah in the army had been drafted under selective service. In the first few months of the war, there were no enlistments. Later men and boys began to enlist, but this was said to be so that they could join the coast guard or the navy and thus avoid being drafted into the army. Though many were in the army by the end of 1942, the tribe gave them no public recognition.

Channels through which the Tradition is Transmitted

The latent culture, since it is expressed only verbally, is dependent upon verbal communication for its perpetuation. The closely knit village community favours its perpetuation. In the parties, on the streets of the village, and during informal visits, the older people are brought together and their conversations frequently turn to the past. The young people, and especially the children, who live in the same household are thus given an opportunity to learn not only what their own elders remember but also what is stored in the memories of the other old people in the village. Some of the older people take their responsibility as custodians of the traditional knowledge very seriously and rarely let slip an opportunity to lecture the younger people so that they may learn what the Makah once did. Others feel estranged from the young people growing up and make no effort to talk even with young relatives who live in the same house with them. The second oldest person in the tribe, well over eighty, was of this persuasion. She thought that all the customs would vanish with the death of her few contemporaries and that there was no reason to tell the younger people anything. On the whole, however, there is a lively interest in the tradition and much discussion.

The tradition is transmitted also through the folk tales which still have widespread currency among all ages, save perhaps the young adults who show little interest in these things. But they heard the tales a few years before when they were children and are familiar enough with the tales though they now neither bother to listen nor relate them. Through the tales, much of the tradition is outlined for each oncoming generation, since they include descriptions of artifacts, techniques of getting a living, games, prestige systems, and behavioural standards which are represented as characteristic of the customs of Makah ancestors. For though most of the popular folk tales are set in a time before the Makah and other Indians were created, the incidents of the tales are placed firmly against a background which the old people say is similar to that which they first knew or which their parents told them existed before they were born.[1]

The background is no longer visible to give point to the incidents, and therefore as the stories are told, the teller stops to explain the different objects and practices which belong to this vanished background. The storytellers describe the houses in which the characters lived, the food they ate, the canoes in which they rode, the tools and weapons which they used, as these items are introduced, with the evident feeling that unless these forms which are no longer to be seen can be explained, the tales themselves lose their meaning. Perhaps the explanations were partly due to the fact that many people who told me stories were older members of the tribe who habitually think in Makah. In translating their thoughts into English, an explanation is easier than finding the exact English word to fit the subject. But the tales are commonly told to children today in English, and the same explanations are necessary for them as for the outsider ; for the Makah children have no more opportunity than the latter to see the objects and customs which give the tales their contexts.

For example, when Dave Boone was relating a tale, he said :

' You see he started for this place. And he had on the wolf skin he used to wear when he was mad because he thought the wolf

---

[1] The tales, however, are not sacrosanct, and there is no feeling that they must be repeated exactly without additions or changes. Occasionally a storyteller puts in an obvious anachronism to the appreciative delight of his listeners. Grove, for instance, said, ' Then Kwáïti grabbed his gun.' His wife snickered, ' Gun ! Listen to that guy ! ' Sterne in describing Kwáïti's race before the wolves in which he created the different rivers and mountains, added, ' Then he got clear to Florida and kept right on running all around the world till he got back here.' His family laughed heartily.

was a fierce animal. That's the reason he had the skin to wear.
And his arrows were in a bag, a cedar bag. And he had a bag of
oil. He poured the oil into those wooden bowls they used to have
that they made themselves out of alder trees. After he put the oil
in the bowl, then he stuck in the points of these arrows because this
oil was poisonous too. This oil was made from the dogfish liver
and it was mixed with the human body. It had been there for one
year where the body was. They used to be able to get that because
they buried the bodies on trees. They fixed it and figured that the
oil mixed with human bodies would be poisonous. You see, the
chief learned from his father how to fix those arrowheads. And
these arrows, the heads to them are fixed so that just as soon as it
was used and went into the body, whenever they pulled the arrow,
then the head would be left in the body just like a bullet. The
poisonous parts stay. The arrowheads were made out of this kind
of rock. [He produced a black stone.] It's so hard you can't work
it. They used to work it in the darkness of the moon, because they
claim that that is the only time it is soft. They used to soak that
in water for five days. They had medicine mixed in with the water.
Then there was a different kind of arrowhead. These weren't supposed to go in the flesh. They were just supposed to stun. Well,
this chief came round the point.'

And so after this long digression into what he regarded as necessary explanatory matter, Boone returned to the incident he had
started to relate. The same thing happened with the other
storytellers.

Sometimes the tale requires little explanation to make its
point. George Fisher told me one of the favourite Makah
legends, which is usually told as ' history, not story like Kwấlti
and those others you've been hearing '.

' This happened in Ozette. This chief fixed up his son to catch
a whale. He built a canoe for him, make harpoon, and blow up
the hair seal for floater. About dozen of them. So when he got
everything, he told his son, " You must bathe every night. You
must bathe every night if you want to be clean, if you want to catch
a whale. Go in the salt water and bathe every night and pray.
Ask for a whale." So this young man went off every night. And
he didn't go bathe at all. He went round look for sweetheart.
Well, about a month, pretty soon this young man brought his sweetheart home to his father's house. Well, this old man got up. They
used to have a flat roof, all flat roof, loose cedar timber on top. So

this old man shoved that board. one side. " You always sleep late in the morning ! " And he goes with the light in the house to his son's bed. And two heads laying there. One woman head and one man. He went to his wife and said, " That young man ! After I had hard time making things, he spoil the things. He got a woman now instead of a whale." He go around, go around. They used to have five, six family in the house, big house. He went around there pouring out all the slops, put them in his square bucket made out of cedar. He open his son's face and throw that on his son's head. He said, " I didn't want you to catch woman ! I want you to catch whale, not woman. You spoil yourself ! " '

Now these details which are presented through the folk tales may not be true descriptions of what the Makah once had and did. But the point is that they are being presented as the culture of their immediate forebears to the children and the young, who cannot check these accounts by their own experience. The accounts have a wide circulation throughout the group, and thus help to keep alive a feeling of belonging to a tradition other than the American; since the accounts presented to them are pictures of a way of life alien to any they find represented among the whites or which they can learn about from books. A knowledge of the incidents also reinforces their sense of belonging to a particular group of people, the Makah ; for though it is recognized that similar characters and incidents occur in the tales of the surrounding tribes, the older people are careful to distinguish the tales they regard as importations from those which they regard as Makah versions.

Outside the context of the folk tales, there are other more direct means of keeping the tradition alive. Some younger people who came too late to see a particular technique or custom will seek an opportunity to ask an older person about things which arouse their interest. They do not expect to incorporate the knowledge into their present lives in any fashion, but they wonder, ' How did the old people do this before the whites came ? ' A woman in her early fifties said that for some time she had been trying to discover how the old people made blankets of dog hair. She asked all the old women in the tribe, but no one was able to explain the technique though several could remember having seen blankets made of dog hair when they were children. Others had similar interests, but each person seemed to seek knowledge on a different point. Winona Clarke interrupted an interview with her grandmother to ask how they made fire before they had matches and said she had been wondering about it recently. Louise Armstrong asked an older relative how many people usually lived in one of the large smokehouses and how they were related to each other. Mrs. Denison, some fifty years old, said that the women of the tribe became curious a few years before about the techniques involved in making clothing from birdskins, and finally they found an old woman who made a small blanket to show them how such things looked. Often, someone would comment, 'I never knew this until recently, but my old cousin has been telling me how it went.'

Older people who wish to learn something which they think is known to some still older person outside their immediate family group usually go through a somewhat more formal procedure. They invite a number of old men and women to dinner and after the dinner they question the guests. During 1942, the Phillip Grays gave a party so that they could ask an old woman how the land used to be owned by the different families at the village of Ozette. Ozette has long been abandoned, and the tiny reservation created about its village has been sold and the money distributed. But Mr. and Mrs. Gray who are descended from former inhabitants of the village, were interested in the subject for some reason. Again, Mrs. Sharpe suggested that we join forces to give a party for the old men so that we could ask them the Makah names of the months. She said that her husband when he was alive customarily invited the old people in order to learn from them about the past. Grace Sterne said that she knew many folk tales because she used to go out to the rocks to gather sea food so that she could invite the old people to come and tell her stories.

Sometimes though a party is not given for the purpose of obtaining information, it develops into a questioning of the old people or a general discussion in an attempt to straighten out the differing accounts that prevail about their ancestors' customs. Sterne once reported such an evening :

'Someone invited us last week sometime, I think. And Val Clement said to Lydia, "I'd like to talk to you tonight while nobody is talking about this Christian business." He said that the Apostolics want him to join, and he told them, "I'd join you people if I didn't

have any Christian talk from my old people. All Indians in Neah
Bay, each family, used to pray. Not inside the house like this Shakers
and Apostolics do. They go out, way out, and pray for the family.
And I been believe in that all my life." Well, Lydia said, " Well,
Val, I want to ask you a question. What did you say when you
prayed ? Some of the white people think that we ain't pray to Jesus.
And I want to hear you, what you used to say when you prayed."
" Well," Val said, " I never used to mention. That's all I used to
say : Great Daylight and Heaven." Lydia said, " Well, I heard one
of the preachers say we talked to the moon." Val said, " No, that's
a mistake right there. Indians never talked to the moon. They
talk to something somewhere. In my early days I used to hear this
old people. Some of them used to cry when they pray. And
anything they ask for, they don't go out and ask once. They used
to have so many days to go out and ask for what they wanted."
Well, I didn't say anything because Val is right. And he said something we don't know. I was sitting next to Warren Grove, and
I said I don't know what it meant. And he said his father used to
tell him to say that word first when he was going to pray. So that's
all we talked about when we was at the party that night.'

Lydia Morris gave a slightly different version of this incident
when she asked me what I had been able to learn about their
old religion :

' The other night I was at a party, and the people there got into
a little argument about the old religion. They all said that the old
people never prayed to the sun or moon, that it was something else.
I said I'd heard some of the old people get up in church and say they
used to pray to the sun. The others said it wasn't true, that they
never did pray to the sun or moon. They used to pray to " Light ".
Val Clement said he could remember some of his old people saying
they didn't pray to the sun but to something that caused the light,
something up above such things as sun and moon. I think that
must be true because I think the Indians always knew there was one
god and prayed to him. I remember when I was pregnant the first
time, my old grandmother was still alive. She would tell me, " Get
up ! Don't lie there in bed, you lazy thing. Get up real early and
go out where you can breathe the freshness and stand there and pray
for your blessing." That real early meant when the sun was just
beginning to brighten the sky, when it was first beginning to get
light.'

The people who had this discussion represent the oldest group
now living with the exception of perhaps three people who

antedate them by only ten years at the most. In spite of this, the questions were phrased not as, 'What do we do?', but as, 'What do you remember hearing that your old people did?' Such incidents as they accumulate drive home the fact that the Makah today do not think of themselves as continuing the customs of their ancestors in most respects, though they are still anxious to remember what happened and what their ancestors did and thought. In a sense, they are amateur ethnographers specializing in Makah culture.

The Latent Culture in Relation to Makah Life

This knowledge of a former way of life, the tradition that they still possess certain skills learned before the old conditions of life were outmoded, in short the possession of this latent culture, gives a superficial wash of alien flavour to the life of the Makah in their village. If the observer concentrates upon the reconstruction of such materials into a coherent pattern to represent the culture of the Makah, it will seem that the group has little in common with other Americans and that they retain much of their old culture. They have retained a good deal of tradition, but it has passed from a living reality about them into the realm of 'story' and memory. A check on the way the people live and on what they do and talk about shows this pretty clearly. If you could not talk with people, there is nothing in what you could see of the village life that would lead you to suspect that the Makah were once whalers, except for the designs of whales on the baskets in the trading store, and these are outnumbered by black duck designs which are easier to make and sell as well. Nothing in the life of the village would give a clue to the former existence of *kloqwali*, *c'áyIkˣ*, and *dóX̌ub* societies, save for a few dances and costumes displayed only on Makah Day.

To take the background material of this latent culture as the more important element in the life of the Makah would be comparable to assuming that because Americans know that some years ago horses were a common means of transportation and because many older people know from actual experience how to care for and drive horses that the horse is more important than the automobile in American life. Today, in a small American town, everyone uses automobiles and no one owns a horse, but the older people brag about their ability as horsemen and tell stories about horses, and perhaps compare the present custom with the past to the former's disadvantage. The Makah too look back to a former period when the things which occupy their thoughts and lives at present did not exist; but their reminiscences cannot be regarded as the most important element in their present lives. The Makah have too much vitality for that. The fact that they were great whale hunters fifty years ago is of less importance than that they are now commercial fishermen who operate with power boats and commercial fishing tackle. The fact that fifty years ago they were organized into ceremonial secret societies is of less importance than that now they are members of church groups : Presbyterian, Shaker, and Apostolic. The fact that fifty years ago and more they lived in smokehouses that housed a number of related family groups is now of less importance than that they live in ' white-style ' houses whose occupants are usually members of the same immediate family group. Undoubtedly the former life has left traces in the thinking of the Makah which are of major importance in determining their present behaviour, as we shall see in the next section, but the customs themselves have vanished. Only 30 people, or slightly over 8 per cent of the tribal members, ever lived a life in which the former conditions were realities which they saw and experienced. Ninety-two per cent of the people, all those under sixty, either witnessed the old life not at all or saw it only as small children.

Yet these things have far more importance than providing material for the storytellers who help people to pass the time at parties or providing the subject of conversation when visitors drop in for the evening—when old tales are told and minor wrangles develop over details where each is sure that he received the correct information from his parents and grandparents. Every social group tries to thrust its roots into the past. The Makah do so through their tradition. It enters into the concept of the Makah as a people with a common background distinct from all other groups. And for those to whom the tradition has a reality based on experience, it gives a perspective on life not shared with the whites, or indeed today with many younger members of the tribe.

There is no reason to expect the tradition to meet with sudden death. Some of it undoubtedly is being passed on to children now growing up. Some will be passed on to their children. Probably, however, this generation will transfer less than in the past. While children are still exposed to the recital of the tales and to descriptions of the old culture, many other activities compete for their attention. With films, the radio, books, and magazines, people are no longer dependent upon their own efforts for entertainment. Children are not at home to listen to the older people every evening. Instead they may be wandering about the village or at the cinema or at some school activity. If they are home, the adults may be out at similar entertainments or away at a drinking party. Men are likely to be employed during the day at the lumber camp or elsewhere, and the boys are not working beside them learning the crafts their fathers transmitted to them. The boys themselves are drifting back and forth on their bicycles along the roads of the reservation or are in school. Not all children have much opportunity to listen to grandparents and great-grandparents who may lecture them about the old life. Few live in the same household with any old person regarded as either knowing much of the tradition or being interested in transmitting it. Only one-fourth of the Makah children, a total of forty-two, live in households containing three or more generations. In some of these households, the grandparents are relatively young people, perhaps fifty years old. Only twenty-six children live in households with grandparents over sixty, and even people of sixty and seventy spent their childhood in the boarding school away from the village and are unsure of their own knowledge. Between the very old who know most and the young there is now also a language barrier.

The tribe as a body makes an attempt to perpetuate a part of the tradition through the Makah Day ceremonies in which the older people perform dances and songs regarded as part of the tribal tradition. But this occurs only once a year, and at the present time is controlled by young people who are turning it into a tourist attraction rather than attempting to use it as a medium for perpetuating the past. The real teaching of the tradition is carried on informally by those older members of each family who feel so inclined. For much of it, there is no strong emotion involved in whether the young learn or not. The older people would like to have the tradition remembered, and they are eager and pleased if the young show an interest. They will say, 'It's a pity that our young people don't know more about our old ways. Most of them don't even speak their own language any more.' At the same time, the young are allowed to slide away from learning about unimportant matters with few reprimands. Perhaps this is because the old feel guilty about their own failure to follow in the footsteps of their elders. Any attempt they may make to force their children to learn the traditional ways points out clearly how little they themselves did when those who were better able to instruct were living. Emily Lester, in her fifties, once stopped to laugh at something her old parents were recounting, and said she imagined that their parents would have been angry with *them* if they had seen how her parents had stopped practising the old ways.

I also received the impression that while I coming from the outside and knowing nothing of their old life save what I could learn from them or from books was struck constantly by how much they remember, they are more impressed with how much they have forgotten. In comparison with all they think they have lost, what they can remember seems hardly worth perpetuating.

THE MANIFEST TRADITIONAL CULTURE

The effect of the tradition is seen most clearly in the view which the Makah take of their relationships with each other and of their relationships with the supernatural. In these aspects of life, the tradition is manifest through the effect which it has on the adjustment of the Makah to each other and to what we might term the unseen powers about them. In explaining what is happening today in these spheres, they refer constantly to the customs of the past as providing them with standards which they still follow.

In this section, we shall deal with the effect of the tradition upon their adjustment to each other. The following chapter will deal with the tradition as it affects relationships with the supernatural.

How they view Each Other

Social relationships within the Makah group can be understood in terms of two theories of expected behaviour which regulate almost every situation within which one Makah deals with another. One theory calls for the solidarity of all kin, of even remote degree, for mutual assistance and defence. The other theory encourages cut-throat competition for social position with other members of the group. This competition, in conflict with the theory of kinship solidarity, may enter even within family lines when brother competes against brother, or it may be reduced by close friendship existing between two individuals who would normally compete.

These theories are a part of the manifest traditional culture, for behaviour in conformity with either one is usually justified by a description of the former life of the Makah, and the speaker explains that this behaviour is characteristic both of the present Makah and of their ancestors.

The Obligations of Kinship

Informants say that Makah villages were formerly composed of a number of large houses, each one occupied by a number of related small families. Each household (or sometimes two or more related households) acted as a unit, its members co-operating in economic undertakings and also in defence measures against the aggression of neighbouring family groups within the same village. Ownership of fishing grounds, berry patches, and stretches of coastline was vested in the kinship group rather than in the individual or in the whole village. Theoretically control of this property was in the hands of the male head of the house, but all members of the group had access to its resources. The group also owned ceremonial privileges, or *túpat*ʰ, in the form of personal names, dances, costumes, games, songs, and rôles in the secret societies. These *túpat*ʰ could be used only by its members, though in practice the head of the household through whose hands the accumulated wealth of the group passed controlled the uses to which they were put. Before privileges could be displayed to the people or their possession announced, the owners had to distribute property to the assembled guests. The head of the household or his heir, was the one in whose name these assemblages or potlatches were held, and therefore he monopolized the privileges of his family.[1]

---

[1] The ownership of the economic resources, house sites, etc., were also said to be *túpat*ʰ.

Membership in the household could be derived through either maternal or paternal descent, though, with village exogamy and patrilocal residence common, there was a strong tendency for most male members of a household to be related through paternal lines. Each individual, however, had inherited rights to *túpat^h* from descent lines not shared with other members of his household group. If at any time he acquired enough property to give a potlatch, he might use these other *túpat^h*. In such a project, his relatives were expected to aid him with contributions of property and labour so that the occasion might be fittingly impressive.

The position of family or household head was a permanent one which ordinarily devolved upon the eldest son of the last incumbent. However, such was the respect for primogeniture, if the oldest child was a daughter, she and her children took precedence of her brother and his family, though she could never become the head of the household, and was usually married and lived in another village. Within the extended family, moreover, there was no simple division into 'leader' and 'followers'. Instead, there was a constant gradation in rank, with the oldest child at the summit with his children, then the next oldest, and so on down, until the youngest child was subordinated to all older siblings, and his children were subordinated to all their children. This gradation in precedence theoretically continued through all time, determined forever by the original birth order of the siblings from whom all descended. This relative position was indicated by the use of two kinship terms, *babíIk^x s* and *yúq^wiIk^x s*. The former was used with reference to an older sibling or a relative descended from a senior line ; the latter referred to a younger sibling or a relative descended from a junior line. No matter how distant the original tie, juniors owed obedience and respect to seniors. Rank within the family was thus theoretically largely a matter of ascribed status determined by birth order.

Control of individuals was left to the family group and especially to the authority of the head of the extended family. In all transactions within the village community, the individual acted as a member of a family rather than as a citizen of the village. The village, indeed, was an alliance among a number of family groups each of which preserved its independence to a large extent. Older people who claim to remember seeing the extended families said, ' It was just like a law to those old Indians. It was all in the family, and they took care of everyone.'

Today the large household groups do not exist, nor does joint ownership of family rights in land or other economic resources. In 1942, the largest household contained fifteen members of three generations. All were descendants of the family head and his wife, with the exception of two sons-in-law. Most households consist of but a single immediate family. The median and modal households contained five people. The average number per household was 4·14.[1] The absence of large units in 1942 is particularly significant since there was considerable pressure for families to live together so that they might rent houses to outsiders who were urgent for a place to live. Yet few were willing to do so. The accepted standard today is for each ' family ' to have its own house. This applies to childless young couples and to old people whose children have all married as well as to couples with children. The introduction of milled lumber which made it possible for every man to build his own house and thus realize an ambition to become a household head along with the pressure of Indian agents who considered the old expanded family dwellings and units to be ' uncivilized ' have probably been the effective forces which have brought about this result.

Despite the disappearance of the large household groups, the feeling that there are bodies of kin who should co-operate does exist, though the kinship groups are no longer clearly defined, Their outlines are blurred because marriages within the village now subject individuals to the conflicting claims of maternal and paternal lines for their allegiance. Where this occurred in the past, residence in a particular household determined the primary allegiance, but this no longer exists to give the individual a guide in sorting out his obligations to his many kinsmen, some of whom are in direct conflict with each other.

The existence of the feeling that organization within the village is still on the basis of large kinship groups is shown by the common tendency of informants to explain former conditions by reference to present-day line-ups. Sterne said, when he

[1] About 1866, the four Makah villages then in existence contained 47 houses, which means that on an average each house contained about 14 people. See Swan, 1869, p. 6.

explained how they formerly mobilized a large group for some undertaking : ' Well, it's like this, you see. I've got cousins, the two Denisons and Arnold Black.[1]   I decide to do something and I call them together and tell them what I want. Then they help me out. That's the way it is with us Indians.' Another informant, Sally Grove, said : ' Now speaking of relations, I don't know how we are related to the Allans, but seems like we are closely related. It always seems like that even if they were third and fourth cousins. It always seems like that because the relations used to stick together. Now like you were another family here. They used to want to have a big family in case they should get in trouble right here in the tribe.'

The demand for kinship solidarity also exists. There is an expectation that all kinsmen will aid each other and will protect each other's interests against outsiders. This expectation is so strong that people are criticized harshly for a failure to live up to their kinship obligations though these are in conflict with the interests of the larger group, the tribe, to which they also belong. Even those outside their immediate kinship group express their disapproval of transgressions in this respect.

The strength of the expectation that kinship obligations override all other duties is demonstrated most clearly when it is necessary for someone to make a choice between behaviour in co-operation with his kin or in co-operation with some larger group to which he also belongs and which is not primarily organized on kinship lines. Then he is censored strongly no matter what course he follows, but in general the strongest censure is reserved for those who violate kinship obligations even in line with their duties towards the larger group.

For this reason the Makah are perpetually at odds with whoever holds the office of tribal policeman. One man who held the office was accused of theft, murder, and rape. But the final disapproval of the group was expressed over the fact that he was prone to arrest certain of his relatives for drunkenness and other misdemeanours. The Makah admit freely that the people were

---

[1] The Denisons are sons of his mother's sister ; Black's father was a brother of Sterne's paternal grandmother. Sterne feels that he, the Denisons, and the Blacks form a kinship group that should co-operate, though neither the Denisons nor the Blacks would consider themselves to be members of a common group save in relation to Sterne.

guilty, but their guilt did not justify to the Makah the action of the policeman in arresting relatives. Members of the tribe, as unrelated to the aggrieved people as it is possible for a Makah to be to another Makah, complained to me, 'That's a fine way to treat relatives!' The man's first cousin said that she would no longer visit him, ' because of the way he treats his relatives. I never thought he would turn out to be so mean.' During the tenure in office of another man, his first cousin ran for the tribal council, basing his campaign on one issue—the promise to have the man removed from the police force. I joked about it to a Makah woman and said, ' Is that a way to treat a relative?' She sniffed loudly and replied, ' Well, the police is always putting him and his boys in jail. That's no way to treat a relative either.'

The Makah also accuse their policemen of favouring relatives over other members of the tribe, and failing to arrest them for offences such as drunkenness and bigamy which arouse the law against other Makah. This course, however, is regarded as a more normal state of affairs. Warren Grove, who was once on the police force, said that the job of being policeman was a headache for him and for others who had held the office because it conflicted with the claims of kinship. It is impossible to do one's duty as a policeman and also to fulfil properly one's kinship obligations. He said : ' I used to just hate that job. I'd see these boys, lots of them my relatives, doing things, and I just couldn't arrest them. So I used to look the other way and pretend not to see anything.'

The dangers of kinship solidarity to the proper functioning of the legal system of the tribe are thoroughly recognized by the Makah. Precautions to minimize the danger are incorporated into the court system. There is one chief judge who tries cases in the extremely unlikely event that none of his close relatives are involved. If he is disqualified, the three associate judges have jurisdiction. The Makah explain that this rather complicated system is necessary because no judge can be expected to try fairly a case involving a close relative.[1] ' I know it sounds awkward, but that's the way it has to be here because of the relationships.' Even these precautions, however, do not prevent accusations that

[1] This is certainly not a trait restricted to the Makah. But the Makah explain their system by reference to their own peculiar standards rather than to general human conduct.

the judges decide cases not on their merits but in terms of the kinship relationships involved.　When Dave Boone and his son's widow contested the ownership of some property, Boone's daughter complained that her sister-in-law won the case ' because she's related to the judge '.　When witnesses appear, the testimony of those related to the persons involved is discounted in the expectation that the witnesses will side with their relatives regardless of the facts of the case.　Some Makah even maintain that relatives are unable to accept facts which undermine the position of their kin.　A number of the more intelligent assured me on numerous occasions, ' I don't really know how this goes, and there are lots of different stories about it.　But this is the way I heard it from my relative, so naturally I believe it was this way. That's the way we people are here.'

Kinship solidarity is thus a factor that interferes with the functioning of the tribe as a unit.　Any organization within the Makah group is faced with this same obstacle to the development of full participation and co-operation of all members.　Kinship solidarity usually proves a stumbling-block over which all organizations topple.

One of the clubs, which a few years ago had a membership including most adult members of the tribe, was so moribund during 1942 that it could hardly be said to exist.　When meetings were called, only a few members appeared, and these were close relatives of the president.　Other members claimed that the club was now controlled by one family in its own interests, and they therefore refused to support it.　Sterne criticized the club strongly on this ground, and his views though more articulately expressed, correspond to those given by others :

' I got a good one to tell you.　These boys, they start up a club. Well, it cost two bits to join and ten cents a month.　Everybody started joining it, young fellows and old fellows.　Well, everything was good, was pretty strong club.　Anything they want, they do it. Anybody got sick, member of that club, they give him wood, they give him grub, help him out.　It was that way for two years.　So they elect a new president, and some of them didn't like the new president.　And it didn't run so good like the first president.　Look like it was kind of select.　Well, this president pick out his family— look like it was club run by a family, just a family, never have a meeting.　Well, another year, third year, they had elections again and we elect another fellow. That's Andy Grove. When Andy Grove got in, it's only ten members left out of seventy members. And that same outfit start to make another club.'

This seems to be the common fate of clubs at Neah Bay.

The Sewing Room, built by the Indian Service as a centre for the women of the village, ran reasonably smoothly under the direction of a white employee of the Indian Service, though there were cries of favouritism hurled at her. When she was transferred and a Makah woman was placed in charge of the building by the Tribal Council, the rumours increased in number and bitterness. Women who were not related to her declared on all sides, ' Well, it's supposed to be for the tribe, but now it looks like it's just for one family. She gives everything to her own relatives, and we don't get anything out of it. The tribe should close it up.'

Kinship solidarity is thus a hindrance to the development of organized group activity on a larger scale than that possible along kinship lines. It is also a liability to those who wish to operate some business enterprise, for a plea of kinship is used to underline a demand for credit and gifts which is ruinous to the small business man. Restaurants and tourist cabins which cater for strangers have some chance of succeeding in Makah hands. Stores or other enterprises which serve the local community are a bad gamble, for it is difficult (or impossible) to combine the rôles of a good kinsman who helps his relatives and a good business man who profits from his customers in a small community where these are one and the same.

In other fields, however, kinship solidarity is still a positive good to the Makah. It has an important rôle in the mobilization of a number of individuals for various activities. When someone embarks upon an undertaking which demands resources or labour outside the scope of his immediate family group, he is assured —at least theoretically—of the support of his kin. When a fishing boat must be brought up on the beach for repair, the owner calls upon his kinsmen to help him. They are expected to respond, though it may mean the sacrifice of their own plans for that period. When a house is to be repaired, if the job is beyond the skill or strength of the owner, he feels most ill treated if his relatives do not volunteer their services. It is his right to expect help from his close relatives.

The largest undertakings today are probably the wedding parties. Sometime within the first few years of marriage, a couple is chivareed and greeted with a formal demand that all members of the tribe be entertained with a large party. Since from three to four hundred people may appear for the dinner which is a necessary part of the occasion, this is a major effort which requires the co-operation of more than a small group. For the occasion, the extended family mobilizes its resources. Some donate food for the dinner. Others help to prepare the hall where the feast is held. They help to cook the stews, cakes, and pies which crowd the tables, and also act as waiters and waitresses to serve the assembled crowd. Before the party, relatives meet to plan the undertaking and to practice the family dances and songs if these are to be part of the entertainment. In an interrelated community such as the Makah, it is difficult to discover how remote the connection must be before the relatives cease to participate in the undertaking. No particular rule regulates this. Before the wedding party in honour of one couple, where the man derives his Makah status through his mother, the relatives who discussed the undertaking included his mother's mother, her siblings, and their descendants. There was unfavourable comment because another family was not called to take part. The Carletons, to whose line the husband belongs, tried to justify their failure to invite the other family to participate on the grounds that they could not remember whether or not the families were closely related. This to the genealogy-conscious older Makah only aggravated the mistake, for according to them the head of the aggrieved family is the son of the first cousin of the husband's great-grandmother, and therefore the two lines are still too closely related to have their relationship ignored in this manner.[1] Commonly first, second, and third cousins co-operate in the giving of a wedding party for any member of the group. When Arnold Black gave a party for his daughter who married a man of another tribe, he borrowed the *túpat*ʰ games owned by his second cousin, Sterne. When the Jack Grays gave wedding parties for their sons, they were assured of the co-operation of the Foote-Fisher group to which Mrs. Gray belongs, and of the

---

[1] The relationship is, the aggrieved family head is the mother's mother's mother's mother's sister's son's son of the man in whose honour the party was being given.

Gray-Sharpe-Thorne group to which Jack Gray belongs. Both groups contributed money, supplies, and service, and the Grays were permitted to use *túpat*[h] held by Peter Fisher, the great-uncle of the two boys. A few years before, Mason Denison had the responsibility of arranging a wedding party for his son. As a firm member of the Presbyterian Church, he felt that he himself could not participate in the affair since the church was opposed to the use of Makah dances, songs, and games. At the same time the convention governing wedding parties is sufficiently strong for him to have recognized that one must be given. Denison was able to meet his obligations without being personally involved by turning the management of the party over to his first cousin.

Occasionally individuals violate the expectations of kinship solidarity by refusing to participate in wedding parties involving their close kin. The strong reaction aroused by this is another indication of the sensitivity of the Makah to such behaviour. Ruby Hare's aunt and cousins were strongly criticized for their failure to appear at her party. When Valery Thorne gave her party, some of her relatives quarrelled over details and withdrew from the affair entirely. Others in the village made a special effort to show their disapproval of this behaviour. Sally Grove pulled herself from a sick bed and went to the dinner ' to show the people that we weren't against Valery too '. In the fall the whole Thorne family threatened to boycott the party given for a Gray who married a Black, because of their feud with the Blacks. Many Makah were scandalized. The Thornes and Grays are considered to form part of the same extended family, and as recently as a hundred years ago they had a common ancestor. Most people would probably say the relationship is remote, and that the Thornes have good cause to dislike the Blacks who refused to let one of their members marry the Thorne girl by whom he had begotten a child. To the Makah, however, the occasion was one that called for family solidarity. Solidarity won, and the Thornes appeared at the party.

Though kinship solidarity appears most obviously in connection with these large social undertakings, it is also effective in organizing activity in ordinary daily life. Relationship ties bring with them the responsibility to visit close kin frequently. Brothers and sisters visit each other each day and bring gifts of food or clothing at frequent intervals. When a fisherman is lucky, he is likely to retain a part of his catch for the households of his relatives. In an emergency, relatives are expected to help with gifts of money or supplies, though complaints and the efforts to organize clubs for mutual assistance indicate that expectations are not always met. Whenever any difficulty arises, relatives are apt to gather for informal conferences, even when the person immediately concerned has no desire for outside interference. Older members of the group are called in to lecture growing children on their family histories, and on their obligations to their relatives and the conduct expected of them as upper class Makah. At times, the family group arranges the marriage alliances of its young people. The pressure upon the young is usually more successful in preventing marriages of which the older people disapprove than it is in forwarding the marriages they desire, but still a number of recent marriages have been arranged. In one case, the father of the girl objected to the match, but his objections were overruled by older people distantly related to him who decided that the match was suitable.

Informal visiting and assistance is strongest between immediate collateral and lineal kin, but even those who can no longer trace their exact relationship participate. Sally Grove and Howard Sterne still recognize the obligation of visiting each other periodically, though they do not know quite how they come to be kinsmen. I once asked Mrs. Grove if she visits Sterne's wife. She replied, ' No, I never visit her ! We're not related. I visit her husband. He's the one I'm related to.' Sheila Day and Mary Carleton are equally distant kinsmen, yet I often found Mrs. Day at the Carleton house. Mrs. Carleton explained, ' This woman visits me all the time because we are relatives.'

The old people complain that kinship solidarity along with a knowledge of genealogies is disappearing and that the young neither know their genealogies nor respect their kinship obligations. This may be true, but even among children and young people a feeling exists that kinship, even though it is remote, still creates a special bond. Sylvia Mead said that when her granddaughter began school the children were ' mean ' to her. Mrs. Mead went to see Barbara Thorne, who is a few years older than the Mead grandchild, and told her she must be good to the child ' because you two are close relatives '. Thereafter the

Thorne child constituted herself the protector of the little girl, who is her second cousin. When I questioned the Kellers about whether one might accept food in someone else's house, their great-grandson who was seven interrupted with a laugh at the ignorance that would permit such a question. He assured me that one may eat only where one has relatives. Brenda Sterne, at six, explained her choice of friends among the other children of her age by saying that they were relatives. When Joan Hewitt, about twenty-four, did some job about the village for other people, she frequently commented that she did not want to do the job but had to do it because the person who asked was a relative. When she planned a trip to Seattle, one of the Carletons asked her for a ride. She complained to me afterwards, ' She makes it so hard for me to refuse when she reminds me that we're relatives.' In this case the relationship is so distant that ordinarily the two families ignore its existence and freely express their enmity.

The theory of kinship solidarity is thus of immense importance in the life of the Makah, affecting all age levels from the young to the very old. Their adjustments to each other are affected by the factor of kinship and the expectations regarding appropriate behaviour between kin. Both the ties of kinship and the behaviour connected with them are regarded as firmly based in Makah tradition rather than as recent developments from contacts with the whites or as recent growths in response to the situation in which they now live.

Kinship solidarity functions in relationships between Makah, and does not affect them in relationships with whites who are outside the nexus of kinship ties. Indeed, the Makah sometimes contrast themselves with whites by pointing out that the latter seem to have no feeling for kin beyond the immediate family circle.

Rivalry for Prestige

The other theory which operates in the adjustment of the Makah to each other is that of competition between individuals for the leadership of the group, for prestige, and for social pre-eminence over other Makah. This theory does not affect their adjustment to the whites, who apparently are regarded as beyond the scope of rivalry. Instead, the competition is regarded as a type of relationship which exists only between Makah or between Makah and Indians of neighbouring groups with whom they formerly competed through the potlatch. The struggle for prestige, moreover, is justified as behaviour in accordance with standards recognized by their ancestors and passed on to them.

Here, however, it must be emphasized that there is not necessarily any agreement among the Makah about the details of their tradition wherein they explain the occurrence of rivalry and define prestige. Sometimes, indeed, it seems as though each individual has received a particular revelation with regard to what earlier Makah behaviour and belief were in this respect. They are only agreed that there is and always has been a struggle for social pre-eminence. Some represent the social life of the Makah group today as a mobile society in which people are struggling to improve their social position both through raising their own rank and undermining that of their rivals. Others claim that it is a crystallized class structure in which status is determined by birth and in which rivalry is restricted to those born into relatively equal positions. Each view is said by its upholders to be typical of the social system of the early Makah.

According to some informants, the system of prestige was intimately interlocked with the structure of the large extended families and the existence of a slave class. The society of each of the villages was divided into three classes : the *čábAt*, the *báččIb*, and the *kúXu*. The *kúXu*, at the bottom of the social hierarchy, were slaves captured in war or purchased from other tribes. They were therefore aliens to the villages in which they lived, and their status remained that of aliens. So did that of their children who also continued in the slave class. Slaves were not allowed to intermarry with free-born Makah. Any degree of slave blood was a permanent stigma against a family line, and the word ' slave ' was a stinging insult. While the slaves lived in the same house with their owners and took part in much of the social life of the villages, their position was without honour, As the Makah say, ' The slaves had no standing among the other people.' The *báččIb* were the common people of the village, the descendants of the junior lines of the extended family. People of this class did not control the allegiance of any followers and were not wealthy enough to hold great potlatches in their own names. Their names were not known beyond the boundaries

of their own villages ; and since names themselves were family
heirlooms, the family heads who controlled the family ceremonial privileges refused to allow the commoners to assume the
famous names owned by the family line. As some informants
expressed it, ' They were good honest people, but they were not
wealthy, and they had to work for their living. They were the
younger brothers of the big people, and they worked for them.'
At the top of the social hierarchy were the čábAt. This term is
translated as ' rich man ' or ' chief ' or ' big man '. It is this class
which most interests the Makah, and it is with regard to its composition and rôle that there is most disagreement. They agree
that the ' chiefs ' were wealthy leaders who owned smokehouses,
held potlatches, bore the important names, and were famous
throughout the tribes to which the Makah were known. The
' chiefs ' were related to the ' commoners ', but they attempted
to intermarry with others of the ' chief ' class to preserve the
purity of their lines from contamination with commoner blood.
Here agreement ends.

To some, ' chief ' is coterminous with household or family
head and is purely an ascribed status. They insist that only the
first-born son and daughter of the household head could inherit
his status as ' chief ', and that their position was not dependent
upon individual merit. Others prefer to believe that all members
of the ' chief's ' family inherited his status, and that each child
was therefore beyond the challenge of rivalry from other members of the group. To others, the ' chief ' class is largely an
achieved status, for they insist that the potential ' chief ' had to
justify his position through great deeds, such as becoming a
successful whale or elk hunter, or he dropped back into the class
of commoners to be replaced by a younger brother or cousin
who was more successful and thus was recognized as more
worthy to lead the family. Others say that any person who
could acquire sufficient wealth, by any means, to hold large
potlatches in his own name became a chief.

Between the heads of families, however selected, there was
constant competition through the potlatch system to raise their
relative position in relation to each other in hopes of becoming
the recognized leader of the village. But according to most
informants, no one family ever gained the leadership of any
village. Therefore the ' chiefs ' were the principal men of the

extended families or the men who had prestige because of their accomplishments, but no one family had precedence over the others in its village or over the tribe as a whole. Others claim that each village had its ' chief ' who ranked above the heads of the other families, and that the five Makah villages also recognized one family as having precedence over all the other family or village heads.

The Makah today therefore do not possess a common coherent picture of their former social organization. They are not interested in understanding how this former organization worked or how individuals found their place within it. They are interested in their own status at the present time, and they turn to their traditions as one means of bolstering or ensuring what they believe their present status ought to be.

Some individuals now wish to project the system of class bodily into the present social life of the village, though they admit that there are no slaves now. To their thinking, however, those with slave blood can still be placed in a class subordinate to the others in the village and virtually disfranchised, because to them it is unthinkable that anyone descended from slaves should have a right to a voice in the affairs of the tribe. Others are willing to admit that conditions have changed and that it is no longer possible to carry out the old system as they think it once existed. But any attempt on the part of others to suggest that they or their ancestors held a lower social position than that to which they think themselves entitled still arouses their ire.

The result is that in Neah Bay today a class system theoretically exists, but it is impossible for the observer to place any single person in his proper class because there are no generally accepted standards as to what constitutes a valid claim to class status. Nor is there any generally accepted placing of individuals in various classes recognized by all Makah themselves. Yet, they are conscious of class and it enters into their thinking with reference to other Makah to an extent that is incomprehensible to the new-comer. Each individual claims high-class status for himself and his immediate ancestors ; each usually derides the claims of other Makah unless they happen to be close relatives—and even a close relative is not safe since his claims to status can always be derided on the ground that through some line not shared with you he descends from low-class people, or it may be claimed that he has not achieved enough to justify his equal position with your own.

Hardly had I been in the village a week when I heard from all sides that a class system exists and is highly important. I was told : ' We Indians are just like the whites. We class up. It's been that way from way back. There are high-class people and middle-class people and then real low-class people. Most people here come from the lower class, though they don't like it to be said. You can tell the difference though when you meet people. Only the high-class people know how to act. The others naturally don't know anything about how things should be done. They had no old people to teach them. Just certain families know.' [1] Each person saying this then said, of course, that his family was of upper-class status and had been so from as far back as Makah tradition went, and proceeded to warn me against families which he called low class. People told me that these families were so unprincipled that they would work me bodily harm, and also that they were ' so low class ' that they knew nothing about Makah traditions. It would therefore be useless to work with them in obtaining information about the old times. Soon, however, I met people who warned me in the same terms against contact with those with whom I had been speaking, and added that the first were trying to pervert Makah history into a glorification of their own family lines though they really came from very low-class ancestors indeed. So it went from person to person until I found that everyone in the village accused others of being low-class and not entitled to speak for the Makah or to hold up their heads in front of the really good people.

Some of the most insistent upon their high status assured me that I would see the difference in class status by observing behaviour and by watching for seating arrangements and other forms of precedence at tribal gatherings or other social gatherings. They also said that even today they avoid marriages across class line. When Sheila Day, a woman in her late forties, was telling me of the old system, her young niece was present. Mrs. Day used the opportunity to turn the interview into a lecture to the niece on the subject of class.

[1] This is a paraphrase of a number of statements heard from different people and from members of different and relatively unrelated family groups.

' They just had to get married to the same kind of class they belonged. For one reason, them chiefs wanted to marry the same class of people as they were themselves. So when they got children, they didn't want their children—well, like if I got mad at you and said, " You're low class, part slave ! " you'd be hurt. So they wanted to get married same class generation after generation so all the children were the same class. So if I married a low-class person, then well my niece could call my son a low-class boy. That's what my father used to tell me. That's how I found out. That's why they used to marry the upper class, so all the time they would stay the upper class ; the middle class, the middle class ; the slaves, slaves. Only crazy ones didn't obey orders. Even to my day they used to say that, " Slaves ! " Now [turning to her niece], I know that your family was chiefs, and I tell you this. They didn't want no slaves for their children ! They didn't want anybody to be able to say that to them.'

Others when asked about such matters hooted at the idea of precedence and said that this existed only in the minds of those who want to make themselves big : the really big people who come from important families do not need to use such means to make others aware of who they are and from where they come. Many also said that marriages now inter-relate everyone in the village, and that because of the explicit prohibition of marriages with near kin, they are forced to marry into families which they accuse of low-class blood or to marry outside the tribe entirely. The last is the old solution, but for the past fifty years, at least, marriages within the tribe have been common.[1] Today, again, marriages outside the tribe are the commoner type. Mrs. Lester gave as a reason for this :

' It's pretty bad here now. And everyone wants to think he's a chief. They all speak mean to each other. No one bothers to be polite any more. They all think they're too good for each other. Like it is now with marrying—these boys and girls instead of marrying to the others here at Neah Bay, they don't think that the other

---

[1] Theoretically marriages should not occur between any persons who are known to be related, no matter how distant the tie. In practice, distant relatives do marry, but they are conscious that they are violating Makah custom. I could discover no marriages between first or second cousins. One couple shared a great-great-grandparent, but the relationship was said to be too close. The marriage would not have occurred if the couple had known of the relationship prior to their marriage.

families are good enough. I think some of them really don't know about how things used to be. I guess the old people started to tell them when they were children that they came from good families and chiefs. They were brought up to believe that by their old people who didn't want them to know where they really came from. So now they all think they are the real chiefs here.'

I attempted to see if observation would disclose forms of precedence though some of the Makah might prefer to ignore their implications. As far as I could judge, by observations at six wedding parties as well as numerous smaller gatherings, formal seating arrangements, precedence in service, and special deferential treatment do not occur. There is nothing to indicate how people are regarded by others in the tribe, though there are indications of how they regard themselves. Moreover, an analysis of the marriages which have occurred between members of the tribe indicates that if low-class families do exist, marriage only within one's class is purely mythical ; for marriages have taken place between every two families in the tribe.

Since many Makah insist that inherited status is the real determinant of social position, I attempted to discover if special deference is paid to those descended from people recognized as Makah leaders, and if their position differs from that of the descendants of commoners. This attempt was useless. As I questioned one informant after another, the line up of important men of earlier days changed ; a man would shift from slave to commoner to chief with the particular informant questioned. Sterne, for instance, referred to a man as the last and most famous chief of the Neah Bay Makah but said he had no living descendants. Louis Keller, when questioned about the same man, sneered at the first mention of his name and proceeded to make it clear that the man was a slave purchased by one of his ancestors. From the context of the interviews, it is clear that both informants were referring to the same man. The Carletons and Paulsens always assured me that their ancestors were former chiefs of dí.a^x and blída?. The other Makah refused to countenance this claim, and maintained that the men were commoners of no importance though they tried, unsuccessfully, to raise their status to that of chiefs. Of one they said, ' He was no chief. He just worked for the agency after we had the reservation, and so he started bossing things down here. Now those people want to make him out as chief of the whole tribe. But he was *no chief.*' Some even claimed that the men were part slave, and therefore obviously disqualified from holding any position of importance.

According to the Atkins and their close relatives, the grandfather of the older Atkins was chief of one of the villages at the time Governor Stevens made the treaty with the Makah. Others swear that he was nothing but a slave. Still another man is said by his descendants to have been chief of the blída? group at the time of the treaty. Others in the tribe swore during meetings with government officials over the question of fishing rights at Hoko River that the man was a runaway slave from Canada whom Stevens found hiding at Hoko and therefore his name as chief in the treaty means nothing. They were willing to swear to this though it weakened their case and might lead to the withdrawal of the fishing privileges which the whole tribe enjoyed at Hoko.

There is thus no agreement among Makah about who their former leaders were. This, however, does not prevent their assertion of position based on descent from leaders. A few people do not make such claims. One of the former whale hunters did not, and refused to proclaim that his immediate ancestors were chiefs. But he feels that his position is more assured than that of anyone else now living because he once killed four whales in one year, and to him this exploit places a man in the upper class. Those who cannot boast a similar achievement he considers to be commoners. Almost every other Makah bases his claim to upper-class status on the matter of descent. Warren Grove failed to make such claims for many months after I met him. I was beginning to regard him as an exception to the struggle for position, though his wife made it clear that Grove was a high-class person. Then one night when he had been drinking, he turned to me and said, ' I never told you this before, but I belong to the chiefs. With all these people saying, " I'm chief, I'm chief ! " I don't like to say anything. But I come from a chief line all the way back, and these people here know and respect me.' But when Sterne was explaining the relationship between himself and Grove and mentioned Grove's grandfather, Grace Sterne interrupted in tones of pure spite, ' Warren, did he have a grandfather ! '

The question of hereditary social position is a counter in the game for prestige in which all Makah are involved. Each advances his own claims while at the same time undercutting the position of his rivals by deriding the class status of their ancestors.

The Carletons claim that formerly each village had its head chief and that as descendants of the most important village chief in the tribe they are the ' royal family ' of the Makah. They are not averse to the use of the words ' prince ' and ' princess '. They maintain that the rest of the Makah look up to them and acknowledge their high position. Abraham Carleton quickly shifted the conversation the first time I saw him and said, ' For this Makah Tribe, my family is the head of the tribe that speaks one language.' Asked how they had obtained this position, he said, ' Well, it's just like that Canadian Government, that Queen Victoria family. It's been like that from generation to generation. It comes natural to them from way back. It goes to the son. You see, when I leave, my oldest son will take my place.' He frequently spoke of dealing with the government because of his position as tribal chief.

The rest of the tribe deride his claims. Many murmur that there are slaves among his immediate ancestors ; others say that since neither he nor his father ever achieved deeds great enough to warrant social position he and his family are now on the same level with others in the village. Some argue that he has no right to the names and songs which he claims, and declare roundly that he stole them from families better dowered with hereditary privileges than his own. Hugh Henderson refused to act as an informant on Makah customs, but quickly broke into a tirade on Carleton and his family :

' I can't help you with the old times. It would only cause trouble. I heard you've got some stories, and I think what you got is enough. If I told you something it would only be different and the people won't like it. Each one tells it different now, and I don't want to cause hard feelings. I'm willing to let people say what they want to. Whatever they say is all right. But I and my brother can stand before all the people. We come from a good family, but I don't want to tell about it. All these people now want to make it out that they are from the old times and have good standing in the tribe. I just let them talk. But one thing I will say—beware

P

of Abraham Carleton. He's my cousin, but still Abraham ! Maybe it's wrong for me to say this, but his grandmother came from across. She was a slave. Abraham has no right in with the high-class people. People like that have no standing, but Abraham wants everyone to think that he is a chief. Of course, his father's family took good care of him and raised him, but that ain't nothing for him to feel high about. Whenever we have anything, Abraham always pushes his way in. Even when we try to keep him from talking, he pushes his way forward and speaks when he has no right to be among the people. Even his name—that don't belong to him. That's the name of a chief, and Abraham uses it as his name now. The old chief came over here once and stayed with our old people and taught them some of his songs. Abraham and I were there and listened. Now Abraham claims that the chief gave him the songs and his name too. That's a lie. He stole the songs and the name. He has no right to it.'

Henderson's brother was equally vehement in his warnings against the Carletons. He always implied that his own status is far superior to theirs and that he comes from high-class people without a taint of middle-class or slave blood.

Others declare that the Hendersons are of no real standing in the community because of their descent. Some said that one parent was of high-class status ; the other a commoner. Some said happily that both parents were lowly people. They like to point out that the Hendersons are now trying to declare that they come from a good family and thus make themselves import-ant, but that they never dared to do this while old people in a position to know the truth were still alive. Then no Henderson ever dared to call himself high class. Even Henderson's closest friends make these allegations, though I believe it is always discreetly behind his back.

And those who sneer at the Hendersons as inferiors are in turn accused of coming from slave backgrounds and of attempting to push themselves forward in the affairs of the tribe where they have no right to be. The Blacks are accused of belonging to such a low class that they know nothing and are practically slaves still. Mrs. Sharpe neatly assigned all Groves, McBrides, and Farlows, to a lower class when she said that there were no chiefs at all in the village from which they come, and that formerly they themselves acknowledged this. The Groves, McBrides, and Farlows in their turn regard themselves as of much better blood than any that can be supplied by the village from which Mrs. Sharpe comes. Sally Grove often talked of her chiefly grandfathers and said she once rose in a tribal meeting to defend the nomination to the tribal council of a man whom others said should not belong to the council because of slave descent. She says she told the people, 'I don't think we should consider such things. That's all gone now, and I think we should just consider how good a man he is for the council. I say this because you all know I come from high-class people right back and have no slave blood, so I can speak when those who come from slaves might not like to say this.' Needless to say, other people in the tribe have no hesitation in attacking her grandparents with accusations that they were slaves. Sterne who is a relative admitted her good ancestry but he claimed that neither her father nor her brothers ever performed deeds great enough to justify their position and therefore the family has now returned to the commoners. 'His father was a great chief, but Atkins didn't listen to his father and he never did anything. When he was a man, he tried to be a chief, but nobody would call him a chief. He was just lazy like his son is now, so nobody liked to call him chief.'

Louis Keller and his wife are proud of their ancestry and not at all backward in declaring that they have the right to direct the affairs of the tribe because all the others are of lower status. Sterne sniffed at the Kellers and said, 'Louis may not know I heard about his coming out from slave blood, but my old people told me the story. Now Louis tries to make himself out everything, but I remember what my old people told me.' Mrs. Foote said much the same thing, and relegated the Kellers to the ranks of the commoners when she said that Louis's older brother was able to marry a chief's daughter from another tribe only because one of her relatives whose name *was* known asked for the woman for him.

Mrs. Foote is the sister of Peter Fisher who is another claimant to upper-class status. He has parties where he feeds many people. He has masks, dancing costumes, and games which he displays on family occasions. He is one of the wealthier members of the tribe. Moreover, he claims an unimpeachable descent, and has gone so far as to tell folklore collectors that he is the only surviving descendant of the last chief of the Makah, though he has older siblings still alive. When the Makah read this statement, they were furious. They recognized it as one more attempt to buttress social position by the creation of a fictitious ancestry. Most of them are willing to concede that Fisher's mother belonged to the upper class in a Salish tribe, but they all maintain that his father was a commoner among the Makah, and that it is the rank of Makah ancestors which is of primary importance in determining status in the tribe. Others, not content with this, also attack his maternal ancestry, and say that his mother came to Neah Bay as a slave companion of some high-class woman who married an upper-class Makah. Thus with a commoner father and a slave mother, Fisher is among the lower class. Even those who do not reduce his ancestral status this drastically, look down on Fisher with calm superiority. Sally Grove said that Fisher once accused her of trying to poison him : ' I wanted to go out and ask him what he meant by saying that to all the people ; but my father told me just to ignore it. He said Peter Fisher couldn't hurt me by talking, and his talking just showed what kind of people he was and what low class he came from. My father said to pay no attention to anything like that and to show who I was by ignoring it.' Later she said of Fisher : ' Of course, you have to say that he has worked hard to get up in the world. He's always wanted his things to be better than anyone else's. That's why he's poor and always owes lots of bills. It just shows what kind of person he is. All the Fishers are like that, low class. But Fisher has worked hard to get up. He c'úbaλadth. That means, " he's washing his body to hide where he belongs ".' Mrs. Sharpe has the same attitude towards the Fishers. She declares that Fisher always tries to take precedence of her in tribal gatherings. ' Usually I don't mind. Everyone knows who I am. I don't have to do things the way he does to make my name known.' Sterne said that in the old days, men might have been willing to regard Fisher as among the big men, ' because he's always doing things for the people ', but that people refuse to admit that he is a chief today.

Mrs. Sharpe is a close relative of the Carletons, and married a man who also claimed chiefly status, though the Makah are only too pleased to point out that in truth he had no claim at all. Every derogatory statement made against Carleton is also used against Mrs. Sharpe, though in every interview she told me that the tribe respected and loved her and always consulted her in the choice of tribal officials as a token acknowledgment of her position as head of the tribe. The attitude of the other Makah was summed up by one woman who said : ' That family is always trying to spoil everything for the others. They think they are so much better than the other people, just as if they were royalty. If they came from a really good family, they wouldn't act like that. The people who really come from the best families don't try to make the others act as though they were royalty. One time Mrs. Sharpe told a white family I know that she didn't have to worry about things because her people looked after her, that her tribe kept her supplied with wood and coffee and flour and things like that. She said they would come over and ask her if she needed anything, and she would tell them what she wanted, and they would bring it to her. She wants them to believe that she is a real chief and doesn't have to worry about things like that. She just wants to make the white people believe that.'

From amidst this welter of boasts, insults, charges, and counter-charges, the investigator emerges with an amazement that each family is able to have faith and pride in its own blue blood though no one else in the village may be willing to recognize that the family has any standing in the tribe or possesses a single ancestor of note. The Makah explain the present situation as due to the deliberate distortion of history by the immediately preceding generation, although few of them are willing to face the implications of such an explanation for their own claims to upper-class status. They feel that as the old people who had long memories for genealogies and knew the class system disappeared, each family systematically attempted to raise its social position at the expense of the others in the tribe. Adults would tell the children in the family that they belonged to good lines and omit any mention of the slaves and commoners who might be joined with those ancestors whose names were known throughout the tribe. Since everyone was related eventually, there was always some tenuous claim to noted ancestors, and these were emphasized while less important people vanished from memory. At the same time, the adults indoctrinated their children with the belief that all others who might challenge their position were removed from competition by the blot of slave blood.

What historical information exists indicates that social status was always fairly fluid among the Makah, and much less rigid than among the Nootka tribes further north. In this the Makah show some resemblance to Salish groups to the east. Swan, who was among the Makah in the early 1860's, writes : 'Formerly the tribe had chiefs and head men whose word was law. The strongest man, who had the most friends or relatives, was the head chief, but of late years there has been no head. In every village there are several who claim a descent from chiefs of note and call themselves chiefs and owners of the land, but their claims are seldom recognized, excepting that they are considered as belonging to the aristocracy, and are superior to the . . . common people, or the . . . slaves. They are listened to in counsel, and always invited to feasts ; are sure of a share of all presents, and of their proportion of any whales that are killed ; but no one takes precedence of the rest, although many, if not all, would be very glad to be considered as the head chief provided the rest would consent. The eldest son of a chief succeeds to the title and property of the father . . . The dignity of chief or headman can be attained by any one who possesses personal prowess, and who may be fortunate enough to accumulate property. An instance of this kind is in the case of Sekowt'hl, the head chief of the tribe, who was appointed such by Governor Stevens at the time of making the treaty. Sekowt'hl's mother was a slave, and his father a common person, but he was very brave and very successful in killing whales, and having accumulated much wealth in blankets, canoes, and slaves, was enabled to marry the daughter of a chief, by whom he has a son, who is also celebrated for his strength and bravery, and his success in the whale fishery, and is now considered as one of the principal chiefs of the village at Flattery Rocks, where both father and son reside.'[1]   Paul Kane, who apparently visited the Strait about 1847, records a meeting with Yallakub, who is mentioned as an important chief by a number of early visitors. Kane remarks of Yallakub : 'Independent of his wealth, he possesses vast influence over all the tribe, and has become head chief from his own personal prowess and ability, and not from any hereditary claim to that dignity.'[2]

The old system therefore permitted the rise of new men into

[1] Swan, 1869, p. 52.   [2] Kane, 1859, p. 239.

positions of leadership, but this is a far cry from the present insistence upon claims to high status by all and sundry. My own belief is that the present situation is related first to the increased opportunities for acquiring property and secondly to the ban on potlatches. In pre-white days, it must have been exceptional for someone without the backing of a numerous group of followers to accumulate enough goods to make a distribution to any large number of people. Boasting and the display and assertion of privileges were validated by the distribution of goods. The Makah observed the old maxim, ' Put up or shut up.' Large claims were thus confined to the heads of families through whose hands the accumulated wealth of the family passed, or to the exceptional individuals whose proven abilities, usually in whale hunting, attracted followers willing to assist them. When the whites entered the area and opened new sources of wealth to the Makah, it became possible for men and women to obtain large supplies of goods by their own efforts. They began to hold potlatches, whether or not they had any large numbers of followers to help them, and to demand the right to use family ceremonial prerogatives. The old aristocrats were furious but helpless in this situation, and many people began to compete for status. Then the potlatch and the validation of claims through the distribution of property were banned. There was no longer any traditional way of assessing status or of forcing a man to validate his claims for consideration. People were then free to boast without having to run the gauntlet of public recognition. Others retaliated with home-truths, gossip, and slander.

At the present time, therefore, amidst the conflicting claims, each one is free to present what pretensions he can to upper-class status, and while probably few will acknowledge the justness of the claim, there are none in a position to disavow it effectively. But those who make the claims are also left uncertain of the truth of what they themselves say, for they are certain of the tampering with the true tradition by other family lines in the interest of their own prestige, and they know that their neighbours accuse them of an equal degree of distortion. Young people are ignorant of the genealogies which their elders quote to give force to their own claims or to confound the claims of their opponents, but they are left with the belief that it is important to belong to the upper class and that they have the right to this status. Perhaps Winona

Clarke summed up the situation as well as any when she once commented, ' It's hard to know what's right about the old ways. Everyone here now claims to be chief. They all say that their old people were chiefs, and they're descended from chiefs. There's one thing I'd like to know though, and that's how this Paulsen bunch got to be chiefs. They all hold themselves pretty high and try to lord it over the rest of us. I've never been able to find out where they got it all. Of course, my old people always tell me that we're from chiefs too. I don't really know, but that's what they always tell me—that they were all respected people and rich people right back on both grandmother's and granddad's side with no common people anywhere.'

The importance people attach to hereditary position is also attested by their anxiety to preserve their ancestors' fame from any slurs, whether these be on grounds of low-class origin or of behaviour not sanctioned by Makah custom. When one woman gossiped to me about the long-dead ancestors of some of the Neah Bay people, her husband warned her that if it ever became known in the village she would be beaten. Some saw a written Makah history as dangerous to the prestige of their ancestors unless they themselves controlled the information on which it was based. Lydia Morris helped me to establish contact with older members of her own family, occasionally acted as interpreter, and was very willing to give me information. Nevertheless, she went to other old people whom I used as informants and told them not to give me further data. Those to whom she went seized upon this as an indication that she recognized her family position as insecure and feared that I might learn a different valuation of her ancestors and family than the one she gave me. Louis Keller and his wife were extremely good informants. Nevertheless, they went to other people with whom I was working and ordered them to stop working with me because they were telling me lies about the old times. Again, I was told that this action was based on a fear of what I might discover, and that the ' lies ' of which they spoke was simply a truthful presentation of former Makah life with the rôle of the Keller ancestors reduced to its proper place.

I found that information about former Makah life could not be trusted wherever indications of ancestral status were involved. The childhood residence of older informants is a tender point, difficult to establish. All claim to have lived in houses owned by their own parents, yet each also insists that there were only a few houses in each village and each house contained many people. What they are doing is to affirm that they are hereditary members of the upper class, for the ownership of a house was a sign of upper-class status and the number of people living in the house determined the strength of the following of the household head. It is therefore impossible to work out the household groups as they existed even sixty years ago ; for the houses named for the same village for the same period differ with informants.[1] The ownership of lands and ceremonial privileges is also difficult to investigate. Their possession is also an indication of status, and it is a common practice to accuse others of inserting themselves into *túpat*ʰ groups where they do not belong. Others are said to manufacture false genealogies for recently acquired possessions. Some individuals give long meticulous descriptions of the inheritance of a particular privilege, naming the ancestors through whom it has passed. Other Makah give equally circumstantial accounts of how the people copied the items in recent years, from some other tribe or from museums and elevated them into *túpat*ʰ. The details of potlatch procedure are also greatly disputed. The value of the goods distributed, the way the goods were accumulated, the method of distribution, the number of guests and the tribes from which they were drawn, are subjects for disagreement. Informants describing the same potlatch might be referring to quite different occasions so greatly do their accounts differ. They also disagree about whether there was a system for distributing gifts in order of precedence, whether guests were seated by a particular system, and in other details governing the potlatch.

The history of the tribe itself alters from informant to informant as it is used to highlight the career of a particular family group.

It is therefore possible to say that a good deal of the present-day behaviour of the Makah is in terms of the tradition of what they formerly had, and at the same time the tradition itself is a reflection of the particular struggles of different individuals who repeat the tradition to establish their own position in the social hierarchy. The Makah themselves recognize this. Many

---

[1] For this reason, it is difficult to get any clear picture of the internal structure of the extended family group.

maintained vehemently that I would be unable to find anyone who would give me the true history of the tribe because each one is interested only in his own family glory.

Since hereditary position is largely stalemated by conflicting claims, the Makah might have turned to other means for establishing recognized leaders. In earlier periods occupational status was certainly associated to some extent with social status. Whale hunters (i.e. harpooners) were treated with respect. Doctors, gamblers, and other specialists, whose success was attributed to the possession of powerful guardian spirits, had a status above that of those who only fished, though they might not belong to the highest class. Their success also led to the accumulation of property which enabled them to validate their status through the potlatch system. The old occupational hierarchy has long since vanished, and no new one has emerged. Instead, attention is now centred on the wealth acquired rather than the method of acquisition. This attitude, however, is not a complete departure from tradition, since it appears at the beginning of the agency period. When Makah tell of potlatches given by their parents or other immediate relatives, whom they declare to have been of the highest class, they have no qualms in saying that this one or that accumulated funds for the affair by working as cook, or laundress, or in some other menial capacity, for the agency. They themselves do not feel that they demean themselves or their ancestors by similar work. They reply to any query, 'It's a way of making money, so what's wrong with it?' In their eyes the white collar worker has no more honourable occupation than the fisherman, the lumberjack, or the houseworker. They compare their achievements in terms of results in visible wealth and not by the occupations whereby the wealth is acquired.

Nevertheless, acquisition of wealth does not make the holder secure of social status. Like any other attempt to acquire social standing or to lead the tribe in some enterprise it leads instead to the concerted attacks of rivals who seek to undermine the position of the fortunate one.

The Makah have a word which sums up this attitude. It is *yábacUkX̌*, which means 'jealous. It's a jealous feeling to a man when you want to become a man too.' In this context, ' man ' means an important person. The same word is used to mean

' turn down ', which is the humiliation of a rival by any means at hand, as by insinuations against his ancestors, or by statements that he is poorer or less capable than oneself. Sterne said :

' I know some places they got one chief until this chief die out, and the next generation will take it over, and I think that's why we can't get along any ways. We had too many chiefs, and we had too many minds to think. This place, Neah Bay, if I talk to one of the boys, they don't care what I say. And I kind of think it's what the trouble with us. My grandfather told me, when he wasn't so old—when I was a little boy—he said, " When you become a man, you'll see all your life jealous feeling against each other. I been living long time and I know it. Anything this Indians want to do, they always want to mix it up, somebody mix it up. It cause jealous feeling." But he was right. I found out without anybody told me. That's how we can't get along. I know it's because of laziness. He don't work like the other man, so he has this feeling. Now if I work and make lots of wood and catch lots of fish, well then people will get jealous. That's how they feel now. Anything a man does, seems to me they don't like it because they can't do it. That's how we didn't get this little fish house [the Makah Coopera-tive] going, because they thought the man who ran it was going to get rich on that. And they got some way to try and stop it. It was just jealous feeling. We was pay higher prices for the fish, and the other company was pay two cents less than we were paying, and still Val Clement and Abraham Carleton talk to the boys and telling them we stealing money off them. So the boys went back where they sell fish cheap.'

Any time that it appears that some person is rising into the leadership of the tribe, or is receiving undue attention, or is even showing a greater prosperity, the others ridicule him. One woman said that her husband had always been one of the most prosperous and progressive men in the tribe. He was the first to build a motor-boat and the first to own a car. These signs of prosperity, she said, aroused the hatred of other Makah who jeered at the family. ' When we got our first car everyone was jealous of us. They even said we rode to the toilet in our car.'

Those who obtain positions in any organization, especially in the tribal organization, are accused of stealing tribal money or of being hand-in-glove with the government officials. When Oscar Atkins was on the tribal council and attempting to intro-duce some reforms, the people turned against him and voted him out of office with the accusation that he was trying to run the tribe without any right to do so.   When Cecil Mead as a member of the council represented the tribe at an official celebration, charges were made that he came from slave blood and therefore had no right to represent the tribe.   He retired from the council and from any further attempt at public life.   Peter Fisher ran Makah Day for a number of years, but people complained constantly that he was ruining the celebration by the introduction of foreign costumes and dances.   They said he could not know how to manage things properly since he is not a high-class Makah and has had no opportunity to learn correct ways.   He resigned in disgust.   Some years later, a club of young people took over the programme for Makah Day.   The same situation developed.   One year the chairman was accused not only of ruining the celebration but also of embezzling the funds. Each year, the chairman is the target for numerous charges.

Maude Allan, who is part Makah though she has only lived on the reservation for a few years, said that this is true of everything in the village life.

' I never lived among people until we moved up here, but gradually I've been learning how they are here at the Bay. If one does something, then the rest find out about it and aren't interested to help. They don't care to be mixed up with it at all, but just sit off and laugh at them for doing it. And they don't all get together. It's one little group here and another one there. You never find people all together it seems like. I think they're jealous of each other. It shows up in Makah Day too. That used to be wonderful, I thought. We used to try to come down here every Makah Day, and I thought it was the most wonderful thing I ever saw. But this last year I nearly cried when I saw it. Instead of getting in and helping with it, these people who used to help with Makah Day just sat back and laughed about what the people were doing. They said, " We don't have Makah Day any more. Now it's Jack Gray's Day." And they would say, " Look how Jack Gray does it ! " And they would laugh about it. I don't think that's the way it should be. Maybe they didn't like how it was being done, but they should have gotten in there and tried to make it a good celebration. After all, it's supposed to be a day for the whole tribe. Different old men used to run it. It was pretty good then, I always figured it was the way it should be because they were old-timers and they knew how it should go. But still people would say, " Oh, he's doing it wrong." Of course, people would go and tell the man running it what people were saying. Well, they're old men and naturally they pay more attention to what people say. Finally they all said, " All right ! Let somebody else run Makah Day ! I'll let them see if they can do any better ! " '

Mrs. Allan's statement is a good reflection of the present feeling about Makah Day, but she is probably wrong in her assumption that things went more smoothly in former years. Makah Day has always occasioned jealousy since it was inaugurated about 1920. Even the honour of having initiated the celebration has become a subject of counterclaims. I collected a number of accounts from different people on the origin of the celebration. Each one named a different person as having been responsible for the idea. But in all the accounts one can see the same theme of outraged feeling because some person for the moment was prominent in the affairs of the group. One woman, who has seen every Makah Day, described the first celebration :

' My father was the first one to ask for this Makah Day celebration. He thought they should have it so they wouldn't forget all their old dances and ceremonies, and so the younger people growing up would learn about them. Well, he told one of George Fisher's boys that he should be president of the first celebration. But people started to talk about George's son and to say that he didn't know how things should be done and that he had common blood in him. So he came to my father and said he didn't want to be president because the people talked too much about him. My father said he shouldn't listen but just to do his best. So Joe tried again. Next day he came back and said he just couldn't stand the way people were talking about his people and about him to his face. So he said that my father should be president and he would help him—only my father should be head of it. My father agreed to that, and he started in deciding what should be done. Some of the people were talking just as mean as they could to him too. They didn't like the way things were going, and they talked about him among themselves and to his face too. It made me feel terrible to hear them talk about my father like that. And I was mad. It was the day of the celebration. The agent had given us a steer, and we were cutting it up and the women were cooking it. I was helping roast the meat and bending over the fire feeling bad because of what they were saying about my father and hoping that nobody would speak to me. Because I knew I'd start crying if they did. The old Trader's wife came in and spoke to me then. I just turned my head away. She wanted to know if I was mad at her. I said, " No, but these people say such awful things about my father when he's just trying to do his best to give this for the people." Then I started crying and talking at the same time. I said I was going to tell my father not to have anything to do with it and just let the Makah Day drop so that people wouldn't say such things about him. The Trader's wife said, " You wouldn't want to do that after you've gone to so much work practising the dances and making costumes ! And here you have your meat already cooked. What would you do with that ? " Well, she must have gone off to tell the agent what I said because a man came over and asked me where my father was because the agent wanted to see him. I told him he was over at our house and the man went for him. The agent told him that he would call the people together and scold them and punish them for talking that way to my father. When he told me that, I felt better and wanted to know what he said. My father said he wanted everyone to have a good time that day so he told the agent just to forget about it. I couldn't understand why he should stand for them talking like that about him and then not want to have them punished. He said, " Well, daughter, if they didn't criticize me so much, maybe I'd just let things slide along. It wouldn't matter to me if some things weren't done right. I'd be careless, and the dances and things wouldn't be perfect. But this way, I think about how to get it perfect. It's good for a man to have people criticizing." '

Potlatches, which the Makah say were formerly used as a method of impressing people with the wealth and ceremonial prerogatives of the contestants for prestige, are no longer held today. They have been held, however, in recent years, since the relaxation of the ban against them by the Indian Service, by a number of people who have acquired fairly substantial sums from the sale of timber or from other sources. Each person who has held a potlatch claims that he or she is simply upholding Makah custom and the privileges of his or her particular family, while the others who have also potlatched are upstarts who are trying without success to force an entry into the upper class. Those who have not held potlatches in recent years, and these are the great majority, disclaim any increased respect for those who have, and argue that only those completely lacking in a sense for social niceties would dream of holding a potlatch at the present day. But none had been given for several years prior to 1941, and none were given in 1941–1942 despite the relatively large sums obtained during the year by the men employed on construction jobs.   Those who benefited from the high wages were mostly younger men, and their failure to use their profits for potlatching presumably indicates that the younger members of the tribe no longer are willing to use their funds for this purpose or see in it a method of securing status within the tribe.

The wedding parties are the nearest formal equivalent today to the potlatches.   Through the wedding parties, both hosts and guests may attempt to advance their claims to social preeminence, though others usually find some means to deride their efforts.   The sponsoring of a wedding party devolves upon the family of the husband, unless the man is a foreigner.   In that case, the wife's family sponsors the affair.   The hosts may attempt to outdo others through the abundance of food provided and the display of their hereditary prerogatives.   They make no general distribution of property, and this differentiates the wedding party from the old potlatches.   Instead, the guests bring gifts to the couple for whom the party is held.   Here the guests may indicate their claims to status either by the value of the gift or by the manner in which they present it.   The majority of the guests line up, march past the couple, and deposit packages or money in their laps.   As they march they sing a song which is *túpath* property of one member of the tribe, and he therefore leads the procession and starts the song.   A few families, however, insist upon singing their own potlatch songs.   They then give their gift while its nature is announced to the assembled guests along with the name of the giver.   They, of course, maintain that as members of the upper class it is their privilege to make their presentation individually and with due ceremony.   Those who join the general procession criticize them for attempting to hold themselves above the others in the tribe and hint that they would not need to do this if they were secure in their upper-class status.

Any large social gathering sponsored by an individual or a family may enter into the rivalry.   Each family explains that the parties given by its members have been the best ever given in the tribe.   Others belittle their efforts with statements that the occasions betray that the hosts are of an origin so low that they do not know how to conduct affairs properly.   Though all parties follow much the same pattern, there is still room for criticism and comparisons. The Makah do not seem to recognize a happy medium. If the hosts invite many guests and have more elaborate food than is usually provided, the others accuse them of trying to make themselves out better than they are and of beggaring themselves to impress others with their wealth and position. If they do not invite the people, they are accused of being miserly and unworthy of consideration because they fail to feed the people.

It is generally recognized that if a man wishes to be listened to with respect he ought to feed those he is attempting to influence. However, compliance with this custom does not necessarily lead the Makah to respect his efforts. A good instance of this occurred when Ross North complained to Sterne that nothing was being done to organize festivities in the village and that the old ways were dying out. Sterne told him, ' Well, it's up to you people who're trying to be chiefs to feed the people and get things started.' A few weeks later, Sterne was ridiculing Carleton for serving lunch to a group of Shakers who had come to his house to pray over his sick wife. Sterne said, that other people in the village never did this, and he jeered at Carleton for ' trying to be a big chief'.

The possession of hereditary names, dances, songs, and games, does not secure for the holder any recognized status. At wedding parties, and occasionally at birthday parties, families display their hereditary privileges. Usually a party is the occasion for naming some relative of the hosts or for changing the name of one who already has an Indian name. If the name bestowed is an important one, other families are likely to accuse the bestower of having stolen the name. A few famous names which are much desired are never given now because too great a storm would be aroused among the various contestants for the privilege of holding the name.

The importance attached to the possession of songs is equally great, and the use of another's *túpat*ʰ song is regarded as a great insult. People accuse their relatives of trying to steal their songs, and this gives rise to much hard feeling. Warren Grove and another family are battling over the possession of certain songs which both contend to have the right to control—Grove in the rôle of guardian of his young son who inherits a claim on the songs through his mother. His rival attempted to have his claim to the songs perpetuated by having the songs recorded at a commercial establishment. Even closer relatives are at swords' points over the possession of a song or name which they regard as a particularly valuable prerogative and wish to convert into their exclusive property. Mrs. Sharpe made slighting remarks about her cousin, Abraham Carleton, because he was attempting to claim possession of a family song which she says she controls because she is the oldest in their family. She accuses another relative of attempting to rob her of a song by prompting his dying daughter to ask her to sing it over the deathbed. Such an act means that she was virtually ' throwing away ' the song ; for she can no longer use it in any gathering.

Even bits of family history may be kept from remote relatives to prevent them from using the information for their own prestige. Some Makah prefer to allow this information to vanish from memory rather than share it even with those who are regarded by custom as rightfully entitled to it. Mrs. Louis Keller gave me her genealogy without hesitation, including the name of her grandfather. Sally Grove, who is descended from this man, said that when she and another descendant asked for the name, Mrs. Keller claimed to have forgotten it. Mrs. Grove said, ' Andy told me he didn't believe her. He thought she didn't want us to know. He's going to ask Louis about it. He says he'll believe what Louis says.' Mrs. Keller refused to discuss many subjects through any interpreters save her daughter and granddaughter because, she said, once she was dead the interpreters would attach such information to their own family histories and attribute the deeds of her ancestors to their own. She refuses to provide them with material for fabricating a false greatness.

Manifestations of rivalry are usually confined to sneers, ridicule, and accusations of all types. Occasionally it leads to physical violence, though I heard of none in 1942 which seemed due to quarrels over prestige. Many Makah also believe most firmly that among some families jealousy of position is so great that it leads them to attempt to poison dangerous rivals.[1] This is

[1] I obtained information on poisoning from twelve informants belonging to eight different family groups. All were from older age groups. The youngest were two women in the forties and one woman in the thirties. Only two of the informants were men, and both were old. They gave me data

represented as an old custom, and informants gave long case histories of poisonings committed by one generation after another to eliminate rivals or those who had in some way aroused the hatred of those who controlled the art.[1] I was told, ' These big families, whenever they see anyone getting to be leaders of the tribe, then they poison them or their children, because they don't want anyone else to lead the tribe.'

Emily Lester explained that there were two types of poison : one that kills, and one that destroys the victim's influence over others.

' The way things used to be, the family had some kind of stuff so that if they thought you were getting too big, they could sort of poison you so that after that the people wouldn't like you or listen to you any more. You were sort of condemned like. They would fix something and put it in your food or on your clothes and that would happen. I was talking to old Mrs. Duncan about it, and she said that if she didn't like a person she didn't have to get mad about it and say things. All she had to do was fix this stuff up, and after that no one would pay any more attention to them, and everyone would dislike them. Long ago the best people used to have that done. They wouldn't handle the stuff themselves because a chief wasn't supposed to have anything to do with things like that or touch it. But the chief would have a slave to fix it for him and give it to the people he disliked or that he thought was getting too big. So that's the way it is with people who come from chief families—they know a little about it but not just how it was done. They never handled it themselves.

' That's what was done to the man who started the Shakers down here. He used to be a big man in the Shaker movement, and for a time everything was going good. Everyone went to the Shaker church and got along good together. And the old man would talk to them and tell them how to do. Then some people didn't like him and did that to him. After that he found that people stopped

---

during both formal and informal interviews. Most of the information dealt with the past, but the informants usually maintained that ' those people ' still practised the art.

[1] Poisoning accusations are not confined to situations where rivalry for position exists. Accusations may be made as an aggressive act whenever people are in conflict. One woman said, for instance, that during a protracted quarrel with her husband, he accused her of attempting to poison him. He refused to eat anything she cooked for several weeks.

listening to him. They talked against him and told him to keep
quiet and that he didn't know anything. They would get up and
tell how he had been wild and how he shouldn't be preaching to
them. So they wouldn't listen to him any more. And he was
doing good for them. It would have been better to listen to what
he said because he could help the people. But after someone poisoned
him like that, they all hated him. Finally he gave up going to the
Shaker church at all and started going to the Presbyterian. It's the
same at the meetings here now for the tribe. My father has more
right to talk than anyone else, but someone used that poison on him.
If he gets up to speak, someone will tell him to sit down and not
bother them, that he doesn't know anything. It's getting so that
he is afraid to speak at the meetings at all.'

Poison is thought to be administered usually through food
eaten at tribal gatherings, which thus serve to eliminate rivals in
more ways than one. I was told that some men always enter the
place where a feast is being given through the kitchen so that
they can see who is doing the cooking and so know whether it is
safe to eat or not. Poison may also be given to unsuspecting
children who disobey the injunction against accepting food from
other than relatives. Grace Sterne accuses a woman of deliberately infecting her daughter with a contagious disease, and said
that her children have strict orders never to accept food from
that house or from any other where their parents do not visit.
Peter Fisher and the Carletons accuse members of the Atkins
family of attempting to poison them on a number of occasions.
The Carletons in their turn are regarded askance by others who
accuse them of being especially adept in poisoning arts. Various
other members of the tribe are also accused of having harmed
their rivals in this way.

These accusations in themselves, however, are another means
of humiliating rivals, for it is generally conceded that someone
who is known to dabble in poison can have no standing in the
tribe, though others are afraid to take direct measures against
him or her for fear of retaliation. The logic is evident—the
man or woman who is secure does not need to use these means,
and therefore it is only the person who cannot outdo his rival by
accepted means who must stoop to poisoning. He thus displays
his inferiority. Accusations of poisoning are thus a part of the
morass of gossip and insinuation which quickly engulfs those

who attempt to advance themselves in any way. Whether poisoning actually does occur is a different matter, and one that would be difficult to establish.

The whole picture of rivalry for position gives the impression that the class concepts of the Makah are completely unconstructive and work only to disrupt the smooth functioning of the group. This is not entirely true. The desire for prestige and for social position contributes something to tribal life. Indeed, the incessant gossip and back-biting which goes on can be viewed as an important feature holding Makah in a set of social relationships which is distinctive within wider American society.[1]

[1] A similar situation seems to appear in other Indian groups far removed from the Makah. The description of the Wisconsin Chippewa shows a parallel behaviour. For example, ' Every year . . . the Indians at Lac du Flambeau organize a group project : the tourist " pow-wow ", for which they choose a treasurer, a ticket-collector, and other officials. Financially, the " pow-wow " is usually successful enough. But this does not tell the whole story. There are always quarrels and dissensions about almost every feature of the project. Men who play a prominent part in its organization are criticized for being " bossy " or for pocketing too much money for themselves, and the honesty of the treasurer is usually called into question. A hand-bill is printed to advertise the " pow-wow ". Some of the principal Indian performers are listed. Those not listed may feel angered at the slight and fail to appear at the dance. . . . There is also rivalry about the job of master of ceremonies and much criticism of speeches that are too long or too short. Little of this criticism is of the face-to-face variety ; it circulates in the form of gossip and bickering. In this way, gossip begins to pile up, directed against an unpopular leader, and next year he will be replaced by someone else, who will in turn become a target for criticism. In the summer of 1946, tensions were so strained at a " pow-wow " that a scuffle between two of the dancers broke out in front of the spectators and one of the men (who was intoxicated) was ejected from the arena. The man who ejected him was the leading dancer of the group. He was already unpopular enough among the other Indians for being high-handed and " bossy " ; but this last action was seized upon as an outrageous demonstration of authority, and he was universally condemned.

' The difficulties experienced when engaging in co-operative activities seem to stem, in large measure, from the personality organization of the Chippewa Indians. But Chippewa personality, in turn, is rooted in the non-co-operative atomistic culture. Partly because the individual is not incorporated, early in life, into a rewarding, inter-dependent social world, the average Chippewa presents a picture of considerable isolation. . . .

' The isolated character of Chippewa personality must be traced back to the formative influence of aboriginal social patterns, to the geographic isolation of Chippewa households (particularly in winter time), to the prevailing social

It would be too simple to characterize the bickering and sniping as ' in-group aggression ' and let it go at that. The Makah criticize others in terms of a set of values which operate within the group to govern the behaviour of members of the group. The constant criticism, gossip, and back-biting is a reassertion of these values, which today can be expressed in no other way. If they repressed the gossip and back-biting, the values themselves would disappear, and with them much of the feeling that the Makah are a distinct people.

To some extent the back-biting itself has become an end in itself, a system of behaviour into which the Makah have thrown themselves with a zest and a determination, which have brought the art of verbal denigration to a high peak. Certainly the malicious statements of their fellows give rise to hatred and unhappiness and to a retreat from public view, but from the zest with which they recount their experiences in the field of slander, it is apparent that they have developed this type of behaviour into a game with its own rules and interest.[1] Like all artists, or sportsmen, the Makah delight in playing with their technical

atomism, and to culturally fostered fears of the surrounding world. . . . '— Barnouw, 1950, pp. 17–18.

Similar as the behaviour of Chippewa and Makah may be, I doubt if the conclusions drawn by Barnouw for the Chippewa could be applied to the Makah. Aboriginal Makah social patterns certainly gave enough scope for co-operative behaviour. The people lived in villages, and in large household groups. In whale-hunting, success depended upon perfect co-operation of the crew of the canoe, and sometimes upon co-operation between the crews of several canoes. Numbers of people co-operated in building and using fish traps, and in the building of the large houses. The ceremonies of the secret societies mobilized a large number of people. Potlatches again had their co-operative as well as their competitive elements.

Historical explanations on these lines are therefore dangerous. However, Makah and Chippewa seem to be using similar methods to reinforce different values. The Chippewa criticize those who wield even a transitory authority for being ' bossy '. The Makah criticize them on the grounds that they do not know how to behave properly in positions of authority or that they are attempting to wield an authority which they have no traditional prerogative to use. The Chippewa are thus using gossip and bickering to uphold their values which repudiate the assumption of authority by anyone ; and the Makah to uphold their values which define which people (and in what situations) may appear as leaders of the tribe.

[1] The Makah were experts in ' Lifemanship ' before this art obtained general public recognition.

skill. And only others of their own community have the technical knowledge to compete in the game, or to appreciate the skill with which a point is scored.

An instance shows something of the subtleties involved in the ' turn-down '. The incident was recounted by Howard Sterne, and involves an encounter he had had a few days previously with Ross North :

' Couple days ago I was sitting out front here. And Ross North came along. He told me that he had car trouble and said he didn't know what was wrong with it. And he said, " Howard, you know when a man gets old, he always have a hard time no matter how many children he got. He'll have a hard time all the same. I know a fellow—they said there was a house named the Old House. It was over there, I think." " No, Ross," I said, " you're mistaken. That belong to the first store keeper here years ago." " No, I don't think so. I think you're wrong. The reason I'm talking about this—I heard about a man that got old. He had two sons. They put him there in Old House, and never give him food or water. And he suffering and suffering. Nobody to take care of him. Nobody go near him. And he died in there of starvation. And he got two sons. That was Dent's father." I didn't say anything. I just laughed. That old Dent was my mother's brother, and that old man was my mother's father ! And I said, " Well, Ross, you got the good news." " Well, that's the way it goes, Howard. That's the way it goes. When you get old, no matter how many children you got, you'll get like that." And I didn't say anything—just listen. He was talking about my grandfather ! " All Indians die like that," he said. I never answer him. I just keep my mouth shut and listen to him. And he changes again. " Well, I'm going to cut wood today. And I don't like my son-in-law. He does nothing, and he can't cut wood because he belongs to the church. He just going to lie around all day, and here I'm cutting wood for him, and he stay in my house." That's the time I talk. I said, " Ross, let me tell you something. It ain't your business to take care of that wood for your daughter, because she's married." " No, no, Howard. I love my daughter. That's why I keep them over there." " Well, I think you're mistaken. I have a daughter too. But I had two places to stay. And I told my daughter, ' I think you better stay in this house ', when she married. That's what I did. And I get along with my daughter, and I get along with my son-in-law. We don't have no trouble because we don't live in the same house. Man make mistake to take care of his daughter after

she's married." I got kind of mad at him because he turn my grandfather down. "Well, Howard, I love my children. That's why I
take care of him." And I said, "Well, I let my son-in-law look
after my daughter now. Because I got nothing to do with her."
He said, "Well, Howard, I think I'll go home now."

'That's a man who turn everybody down. Everybody not only
me. But he turn me down this time. And I told Warren, "That
fellow turn me down pretty bad this time." That's why Henderson
came in here when you were here. He heard about it. He said,
"Did he really say that—that your grandfather died without anybody take care of him?" "Yes," I said, "he really say that in
front of my face. And I didn't say anything." "My, my, my.
Look like that man is getting crazy. And he forgot all about your
grandfather and father taking care of your grandmother and great
grandmother. They both used to take care of them. And he got
bad today and turn you down." He was laughing at him. You
see, that's the way it goes from long ago. Man go to man he don't
like and turn him down.'

Here you can see both attack and counter-attack. North scores
against Sterne by turning the conversation into an attack on his
ancestors, by implying that not only were they poverty stricken
but that his own parents were neglectful of their duties to their
relatives. This is about as damaging an accusation as can be
hurled. Sterne makes no attempt to deny the charge itself.
Instead he counters with the statement that he has more than one
house and is therefore in a position to give property to his
daughter, while North is unable to set his children up in separate
households. Thus he is a wealthy man, and the allegation
against his ancestors is obviously false ; while North is a poor
man who does not know how to behave. The score is probably
even, but Sterne attempts to drive home his victory by reporting
that others in the village are laughing at North as crazy and mis-
informed in his original statements.

Only those who are thoroughly aware of Makah values and
who know the ancient gossip can acquit themselves creditably
in these exchanges, which are so important a feature of present-
day Makah life. Bickering and home-truths can be a uniting
bond in a small society, as anyone who has been a member of a
large family probably knows from experience.

To some extent, the Makah feel that bickering is legitimate
only in so far as it is confined within the group, and that

outsiders should not be brought into the matter. It then ceases to be a game. Sally Grove told me once :

'I shouldn't say things about the people here. My father always taught me that. I always remember one time when we were over at Salish. They mentioned some Neah Bay man who was always unfriendly to my father. He was just like a lot of them—he tried to make himself out big to the people in other places and tried to claim he was chief of this whole place. They think they can get away with it with white people and other Indians who don't know how things really are here. But anyway, they mentioned this man at Salish and asked my father about him. My father praised him and said he was a good man and very wealthy. After the Salish men had gone, I said, "How can you do that, Father? Have you forgotten what he tried to do to you just a little while ago? Why didn't you tell them what kind of a man he really is?" My father said, "It's because I think a lot of the Makah people. These people over here look up to the Makah Indians and think they are a brave and good people. I want them always to do that. So when I'm away from Neah Bay, I forget about how they treat me. I just think about the name of the Makah people. It isn't good to say things about them to people from outside." I thought I never would be able to do anything like that, but I used to think about his words. Then—there's a woman here who is Warren's cousin. She got awful mad when Warren married me. I don't know why. I always think if Alice was going to get angry she should have picked out a wife for Warren herself. Once I told Warren that. Anyway, Alice went around saying mean things about me all the time. Then there was a Shaker convention here one time. Some of the delegates stayed with Alice. The next time they had a convention, the same delegates stayed with us. The woman wanted to know where the house was where they had stayed before. I pointed it out to her. Then she said that Alice certainly was a nice woman and that she had been awfully good to them. I thought about what my father said, and I started to praise Alice to the skies. My father was right because it did make me feel better. But Warren's son was home and heard me praising Alice. He wanted to know if I'd forgotten what Alice was saying about me and how she was so mean she didn't even visit me. I told him what my father said. He laughed, but he stood up for me and took my side against his own cousin.'

This feeling, however, is little observed in practice, and most Makah today carry their battles into a wider arena than the battleground provided by their own village. Nevertheless, the feeling is there and emphasizes their unity as a group against the rest of the world.

The values expressed in the system of back-biting also give the tribe some measure of control over its members, for they are fearful of relegating themselves to the lower class if they fail to observe certain standards. It is believed that a well-born person who had high-class parents and grandparents to instruct him will behave in a manner to benefit the people. He should be generous, be willing to co-operate with others, and not be quick to quarrel. Even under severe provocation, he should not react with violence. These are ideals of behaviour which all those aspiring to membership in the upper class must consider. Though the Makah may not be willing to concede that another person is 'high class' because of his behaviour, they are quick to recognize and criticize any manifestation of 'low-class' behaviour. Sheila Day has good reason to hate her husband's relatives, but she visits them often and remains on the friendliest terms with them. Once she told me that others in the tribe wondered how she could behave towards them in the way she did, but that that was the way she had been brought up by her relatives. They taught her to show the kind of people she came from by ignoring whatever evil people did to her and by showing herself kind to everyone. Sally Grove stressed the same point over and over again, and has tried to instil the point of view of passivity in the face of malice into her younger relatives. A 'high-class' person should disregard insults, and never betray the sting before the attacker. Even the young people pay some attention to this code. Winona Clarke told me of how she responded to considerable provocation from Mrs. Porter : the two families have a long-standing feud which goes back for a number of years.

'What really started the trouble was one time when Mrs. Porter got mad at her husband and kicked him out. He was sleeping in a shed with no place to go. So my husband told him he could stay over with us. He moved in. He paid us fifteen dollars a month for room and board, and I don't think that was too much. But Mrs. Porter got mad at us for keeping him. She used to yell at me in the streets. One day I had to go to the store for something. She followed me all the way yelling at me that I didn't have any business looking after her husband. I walked along not looking at her. I just kept singing, " The bear went over the mountain ; the bear went over the mountain ! " The louder she talked, the louder I sang. I didn't want to hear what she was saying, but you could hear her all over town. Someone who saw it told grandmother afterwards she had to laugh it was so funny.'

In this situation, both women knew that one was behaving like a ' low-class ' person, the other like a ' high-class ' person, and the advantage lay with the one who ignored the insults.

The ideals for upper-class behaviour place a high premium on passive rather than aggressive behaviour in a situation which might otherwise lead to serious conflicts between individuals which would disrupt the solidarity of the tribe. The ideal behaviour for a high-class person under attack is summed up in the stereotyped phrase which almost invariably accompanies the description of some unpleasant incident aimed at the narrator : ' They did this (or said this), and I said nothing.' The narrator may then go on to a long account of the nasty things he or she said in reply, but he first bows to convention by uttering this stereotype which expresses the appropriate behaviour under such conditions. And under provocation I have seen many live up to the ideal, aided probably by the recognition that to show anger in these circumstances is to recognize one's opponents as equals who are worthy of anger and attack.

The existence of rivalry, or conflicts arising from other causes, may thus arouse aggression against others in the group. The values attached to status lead in many cases to the suppression of the aggression or to its expression in some indirect fashion which is less likely to lead to open ruptures.

Rivalry affects behaviour in other fields. Since social prestige is thought to be dependent at least in part upon the ability to support one's pretensions through parties and displays of property, the Makah have an active incentive towards improving their economic status. Outstanding success may give rise to gibes and sneers, but these can be the more philosophically accepted by their targets who regard them as the envious expressions of bested rivals. On the other hand, laziness and dependence upon relatives or relief do not produce prestige. When the Makah wish to indicate that a man is unworthy of notice, they are apt to say, ' He never has even had his own house.' This is the mark of the commoner who is dependent upon his relatives for housing, rather than of the upper-class person who is in a position to give shelter to his relatives and entertainment to the tribe.

Men are also led to take responsibility in the affairs of the tribe ; for any position that places them before the public theoretically brings prestige and is an advance over rivals. Thus, though within a few years men in public positions may become weary of the insults hurled at them by others in the group, there is never any lack of candidates for the council, and someone can always be found to shoulder responsibility for tribal celebrations. The insults again are made the easier to bear by the explicit recognition that such expressions are the result of envy rather than of real reason for dissatisfaction.

Summary

Both theories, that of rivalry and that of solidarity, play their rôle in the present life of the Makah. To some extent they offset each other, and allow the Makah to continue to exist as a group. Kinship solidarity which might completely cripple the individual's initiative is kept in check by the existence of rivalry for social preeminence. While a person is assured of his family's support whether or not he himself makes an effort, it is incumbent upon him to achieve something by himself if he wishes to demonstrate the qualities which are regarded as typical of the upper class. On the other hand, rivalry within the group is held somewhat in check by kinship solidarity. It leaves the man who attempts an ambitious project which arouses the envy of others still in a position where he can expect assistance from sufficient people to carry out his undertaking. Rivalry acts as a spur to goad the individual to greater effort ; the solidarity of the kinship group ensures that at least a portion of the tribe can be expected to suppress envy in effective collaboration.

In certain circumstances, however, behaviour in accordance with these theories weakens the development of a tribal unit able to cope effectively with the whites and with organizations which are beyond the operation of either theory. Kinship solidarity is at variance with effective action as members of the tribe since it insists that the first loyalties are owed to kinsmen rather than to the tribe. It also makes it difficult for Makah to build up successful businesses on the reservation in the face of demands by kinsmen for credit and assistance. Rivalry weakens the Makah both in the economic field and in the hindrance it gives to the development of strong political leadership. Since wealth is a factor which can be used in the struggle for prestige, the Makah seem willing to patronize white firms rather than to build up enterprises under Makah control, for these last would contribute to the position of their rivals. Those who give promise of developing into real leaders who might effectively guide the affairs of the tribe are attacked by the others to prevent their consolidation of their position into a permanent status. Many Makah in their statements give the impression that in the final test they prefer being exploited or led by whites to the acceptance of Makah leadership,

It is not necessary to assume that the operation of the theories of kinship solidarity and rivalry acts as a barrier to the continued assimilation of the Makah into American society. They certainly represent a system of values which the Makah hold to differentiate them from the whites, and their behaviour in conformity with these values does differ from their behaviour in relationships with people who are not part of the system. Nevertheless, the theories themselves disrupt relationships within the group, and in the final analysis may be doing their share to disintegrate the Makah as a people forming a distinctive society within the American nation.

CHAPTER VIII

THE MAKAH AND THE SUPERNATURAL

THE official religious life of the Makah seems on the surface to take its departure from the Christian tradition and the organized religious life of the whites, for the majority of the people are Christians, and the only public manifestations of religion are those of the church group. Nevertheless, behind the superstructure of organization lies a body of belief which is related by the Makah to their traditional beliefs in the supernatural.

ORGANIZED RELIGIOUS LIFE

The three churches in Neah Bay—Presbyterian, Apostolic, and Shaker—all show the impress of Protestantism.[1] All hold services on Sunday, and each group also has a meeting in midweek though the day may vary. The meetings take place in buildings set aside for this purpose. One is an old hall. The other two were built as churches. In the buildings are displayed crosses, religious pictures, and Bible texts. During the services of each group, some recognized leader gives a sermon which emphasizes belief in God and the living of a good life. Hymns are sung, and the members join in prayer. All pray in the name of Jesus Christ.

The Presbyterian Church

The Presbyterian church came to Neah Bay in 1903.[2] From the beginning it has been under the supervision of white leaders —either missionaries or ministers—sent by the Presbyterian Board. Its services are of an orthodox nature with nothing to differentiate them from those that might be held in a Presbyterian church in any other area. Before the Sunday morning

---

[1] A few of the alien Indians are Roman Catholics. The wife of one joined the Catholic Church after her marriage. But there is no organized Catholic congregation in the village. A priest occasionally visits the village to hold services.

[2] The Makah had had contact with Christian doctrine and practice prior to that time. At some periods their agents or other employees of the agency were missionaries who tried to Christianize them. However, the Presbyterians were the first to send missionaries whose sole duty was mission work.

service, children and older people gather in the Sunday school, where they study Bible lessons, based on lesson leaflets and Sunday school papers. After the closing hymn, the congregation gathers in the assembly room of the church for the service which winds its orderly way from opening hymn to benediction.

The Apostolic Church

At the Apostolic church, which was introduced in the late 'thirties, a more evangelical type of service occurs. Here the members rise to testify to their faith in God and to relate how their experience as members of the church has helped them to live better lives. Some may confess their sins and promise to amend their ways. Instead of the recitation of a prayer in unison, there is the simultaneous praying of individual utterances, and the prayer position is a kneeling one. But there is the sermon, the prominent use of the Bible, and the singing of hymns from a standard hymnal—though the hymns used are of the Salvation Army type sung with a rhythm and vigour not heard in the Presbyterian church.

The Shaker Church

The Shaker church was introduced about 1903, at much the same time as the Presbyterian. The church in the village has always been controlled by the Makah themselves, since it was first introduced by one of their members. During 1942, however, the Shaker church was in a transition stage during which it was being brought closer to the ritual of the other churches. It was still more divergent from general Protestant practice than the other two groups.

At the first services I attended, people came and went without waiting for the end of the service. They divided into two groups : participants and onlookers. Their hymns were ' Shaker' songs, in which both words and music were ' Indian' though not necessarily Makah. There were no hymn books. Praying was not in unison. Instead it was a simultaneous performance, with each participant voicing his own prayer, a combination of stereotyped phrases common to all though each mixed them in what order he would. A part of the service consisted in the ' shaking' of the participants, who either stood in place shaking violently, or circled the room shaking as they went. During this shaking, several men rang hand-bells. The building rocked with the bells, the stamping of feet, and the voices of the participants who cried out, 'Dear Lord, send us your holy power.' Meanwhile the spectators sat quietly watching.

During the year, as the group came more and more under the influence of the Pentecostal church, the service was modified until it came to resemble more that of the Apostolic church. The 'Shaker' songs vanished, and the congregation used a hymnal of the same type as the Apostolic one. The bells were left untouched on the table. There was little or no shaking. Instead the worshippers knelt for long periods while they prayed in concert though not in unison. The use of the Bible became more and more prominent, with the leader reading long passages from it and using it as a basis for his talks.

Affiliations

These are the visible phenomena of Makah religious life. They are not unique to the group. The Presbyterian church is connected with other Presbyterian churches throughout the country. Its minister, a white man, is responsible to the Presbyterian Board. Its members attend outside church conferences, receive regular church publications, and contribute money to general church funds.

The Apostolic church is closely connected with other Apostolic churches, which are numerous along the West Coast. It has no minister of its own, but relies on the services of the minister in the Port Angeles church. Occasionally it is visited by other ministers and by officials high in the church organization. In 1942, the son of the founder of the church, who is an important figure in the organization, visited Neah Bay and preached to the congregation.[1] Members of the Neah Bay congregation visit the Bible camp held each year at Portland, Oregon, and attend Apostolic services wherever they may happen to be. They

---

[1] According to the account given at different services in the church, the Apostolic church was founded about 1910 by a Scotch woman who had immigrated to the United States. She became dissatisfied with her own church and with others known to her. Finally, she reached the West Coast in her search for health and for a church, and there she had the revelation which led her to found the Apostolics.

receive the monthly newspaper put out by the Apostolic church, which sometimes chronicles their activities.

The Shaker church is a member of the general Shaker organization, which supervises the Shaker churches throughout the West Coast. This, however, is an Indian organization, for the founder of the Shaker church was an Indian who lived in the Puget Sound area and those who have followed him have been Indians.[1] The leader at Neah Bay, though chosen by members of the congregation, is confirmed by the Shaker Bishop. He and other workers attend church conferences where general Shaker policies are discussed. Thus, the association with the Pentecostals was a matter of general Shaker discussion, and, throughout Washington, Shaker churches were modifying their practices in a move to bring the two groups closer together.

Membership

It is difficult to say which church has most members, for while in each there is a small group whose affiliation is well known and who regard themselves as members only of this church, the majority of Makah seem to drift from one church to another. They may attend the services of any, or of all.

In 1942, the Presbyterian church at Neah Bay had 105 enrolled members, including Makah, alien Indians, and whites from Neah Bay and the nearby camps. In 1940, there had been 150 members.[2] Since the white population of the area during this period lost few members, the difference in membership must be due to a shift in the affiliation of Makah and alien Indians. The founding of the Apostolic church may be partially responsible for the shift. In part, however, it may be due to the change in Presbyterian ministers which occurred between the two dates. The whites of Neah Bay said that the former minister persuaded the Shakers that they should join the Presbyterian church so that the tribe might be together in one religious body. However, they said, while the Shakers formally joined the Presbyterians and many were even willing to make offerings to that church, most of them never bothered to attend the services with any

---

[1] For an account of the founding of the Shaker cult, see Mooney, 1896, Chapter 8 ; and Waterman, 1924, pp. 499–507.

[2] *The Presbyterian Church in the United States of America : General Assembly.* 1940. Pt. 1, p. 813 ; 1942, Pt. 1, p. 912.

regularity and they could not be regarded as real members. Instead, they continued in their own Shaker church. The new minister presumably omitted these people from the church list.

Over the year, a fairly large number seem to change from one affiliation to another. For example, in the spring the daughter of Len Carleton was very ill. The Shakers came and shook over her in an attempt to cure her with their power. When she was better, her mother and father asked the Shakers to shake over them to try to give them the power to join that church. Late in the spring, the child's mother was among the participants in the Shaker service. Indeed, she was the only participant who 'shook'; for by that time the rest were emulating the Pentecostals in a less violent form of worship. In the fall, the wife of the new Presbyterian minister started a Ladies' Aid Society. Mrs. Carleton was among the members of this group and also attended the Presbyterian services. During this one year, Mrs. Sterne changed from Presbyterian to Apostolic to Shaker to Apostolic to Shaker-Pentecostal, and by the fall she was regularly attending the Presbyterian Ladies' Aid and sending her youngest child to that Sunday School. During the winter, many people joined the Apostolic church, but soon they started to drop away and were found among the Shakers, the Presbyterians, or the group that call themselves 'heathens' because they belong to no church.

This is a fairly large group. Those who are interested in preserving their Indian games and dances are likely to refuse to join any church because of the common tendency of the churches to look upon these as sinful. Others say they see no reason to join a church. But their claims to the status of 'heathens' does not preclude church attendance. They may go to any one of the churches if for some reason the service interests them. But many are cynical about joining a church. They say that whenever a new church comes in, everyone joins it and for a time it is a strong group. Then it fades away again, and people grow interested in something else.

The shifting from one church to another results in the penetration of knowledge about each throughout the entire community. At some time in their lives, most adults have been both Shaker and Presbyterian. Many have now also belonged to the Apostolic church. Those who have never joined a church are still

R

conversant with the services and with the beliefs of the different groups through attending services and through the proselytizing talks of their friends and relatives.

RELIGIOUS CONCEPTS : POWER

Besides their religious organizations, the Makah also have religious beliefs. Among both church-members and ' heathen ' there is widespread a concept of the supernatural and of the place of religion which is not typical of the beliefs found among the whites. The Makah have a mystical approach to religion based on a view of the universe as filled with supernatural power which can enter human beings.

The Prevalence of the Power Concept

This concept of power is central to both Apostolic and Shaker churches. Though it finds no place in the Presbyterian church as such, members of the Presbyterian church as individuals also believe in the existence of supernatural powers. They will say that the Shakers receive power, that the Apostolics receive power, and that the Indian doctors and others receive power.

Belief in ' power ' is expressed by Christians and ' heathens ' ; by well educated and by poorly educated ; by those who seem most assimilated to American patterns and by those who have been most resistant to assimilation. Information on ninety-four adults indicates that they accept the concept. Thirty-six made some statement on the subject directly to me. Information on the rest either comes at second-hand or is based on their testimonies in Apostolic or Shaker meetings when they spoke about ' the power '. Most of these individuals, however, are in the upper age groups. Young people under twenty-five rarely refer to the subject—only one or two ever brought any reference to religion into their conversation with me. This was in contrast to the older people, who often introduce the subject on their own initiative. The young, drunk or sober, shied clear of the topic.[1]

---

[1] Of the three young women, all in their early twenties, whom I knew best, one said she had no use for Shakers or Apostolics or Indian doctors. Since she was quite open about other subjects, this is probably an accurate indication of her feeling on the subject, especially since she volunteered the information. Another said she did not believe in either Shakers or Apostolics, but once she

The following statement probably reflects the attitude of many Makah on the question of ' power ', though many are less sceptical than the speaker. She is a woman of fifty, whose parents were educated at the Neah Bay boarding school. She went through school at Neah Bay and in Seattle, and is fairly well educated. She has lived much with whites, and is regarded as among the most assimilated of the Makah. She is a member of the Presbyterian church, and is probably one of the most powerful people in the community. Her husband, to whom she refers, is a member of another tribe.

' You know, Indian doctors interest me. My husband is—well, I suppose you could call him an Indian doctor, though I'm not sure that's just right. He was taught this when he was a little boy. Today he can cure people, but he doesn't let the people around here know about it. They don't know about it, and he doesn't do it much. For one thing, he can't mix in much with sick people. He isn't strong himself. But he really can help. When you have a bad headache, he can relieve that. He seems to paralyse your head and back when he's doing it. He told me that I wouldn't believe it, but he can take my breath away from a distance just by using that power that's in him. I don't know whether I believe that or not. I'm the kind that never believes in things until I've seen them for myself. I know that about myself, and I've always been that way.

' One time though I was sick. I sent to this doctor here, but he isn't any good. Then I sent for Dr. ——. He came over and found I had pleurisy and strapped me up. It made me feel worse. I got a bad headache and it felt like my head was breaking open. James said to me, " You're the kind that doesn't believe in things. I can see that in you. You were brought up that way, and you don't believe in the Indian ways. You fight against it." I told him I always had been that way, that was true. Then he came back in a little while and told me that in spite of it he'd try to help and he knew he could do it. I told him I'd like him to try. He started in to wash his hands. Sick as I was, I noticed that. He washed and washed his hands using soap and water. Then he used alcohol and rubbed his hands with that. It was night, and we were alone here. He came over to me and held his hands in front of me—not touching me, but moving them in front of me. It felt hot. Then

said something about Indian doctors which indicated that she believes in their power. A third said she had been a Shaker at one time and had never been so happy. She thought they really have a power that helps them.

he laid his hand on my forehead. I was sitting up. He put his hand on the back of my head, right where my brain sits on the spine, and the other hand right here on my nose. He wasn't pressing heavily but just holding his hands there. Then he said, "You're feeling in great pain, aren't you? I can feel that." I told him it was terrible pain, that I felt sick everywhere from it. He told me that he wasn't going to press hard and that I wasn't to feel frightened but I might begin to feel paralysed. Sure enough, in a little while I began to feel it all through my head and spine. I felt just like I wanted to lie down. Then he was finished. He washed his hands just as carefully as he had before—just as though I were full of germs. Then he went out and started to get supper for me. I don't know what it was, but by the time he finished, I was able to get up and go out there and eat my supper. I felt as well as I ever do.

'Then I began to wonder about it. I told him I thought it was just my imagination—that I thought I was being helped so I really did get better. James told me I could call it what I liked, but he didn't care so long as it helped me. It didn't matter what I called it. James says he can take my breath away too. I told him, "All right! I'd like to see you do it." I think I've got enough will-power so that no one can do that to me. But I'm like that—I've got to find out about a thing before I can believe in it.

'I'm the same way about the Shakers. There was a white man here about four or five years ago—he was a radio repair man. We became good friends, and one time he asked me if I was a Shaker. I told him I wasn't one now but I had been when I was a girl and foolish. He asked if I still went. I told him I liked to go over and sit and watch. He told me he was going to go over that night. He did and sat through till the end. I go and marvel at it. Some of them—it seems like they really do get the power. I wonder if it can be hypnotism—if one person gets it and then his magnetism goes through the rest. I've noticed that people get up and stand there when they're joining and then sometimes they start to shake as though they were catching it from the others. I marvel at their endurance. They can jump and shake for hours at a time. They don't seem to be any stronger than I am, but they can endure to do that. It seems as though they must be getting their endurance from somewhere.

'James is a Shaker too. He doesn't like the way I go and sit and watch. He told me that whenever I go any place, I sit and watch the others and then start to wonder about it instead of believing in it. I don't know if James' doctor power is the same thing as the Shaker. Sometimes I think it can't be. He started to tell me about it once and then stopped. I think he left quite a bit out that he wanted to keep secret.' [1]

As I talked to members of the various churches, I found the same attitude. Whatever church Makah may belong to, they usually show that they believe in 'power' whether found in Indian doctors or in church members. The power of the latter they are likely to call 'the power of Jesus'; but this is not always so. Some of them differentiate between 'good powers' and 'evil powers'. Others seem to believe that 'powers' in themselves have nothing to do with either good or evil. It is the individual who obtains power who determines how it shall be used. The only distinction that these people see is that some experiences or objects are so filled with power that they are only dangerous : the one who experiences them will die because he is not strong enough to endure contact with such powerful forces. Other experiences or objects being less filled with power can benefit human beings. The power once obtained can be used for different purposes, but, in general, power is most prominent in the curing of the sick. This is true whether it is in an Indian doctor, in the Shakers, or in the Apostolics or Pentecostals.

Both Shaker and Apostolic churches were introduced into Neah Bay by persons who had been cured by their power. Joining of either church is usually done after the individual or some member of his family has been cured by the members of the church, who pray over him and attempt to project their power into him. Even those who are cured, however, do not always join the church, unless they have an experience which leads them to think that they have obtained the power pertaining to that particular group. In 1942, Sterne was prayed over by the Shakers. He considered that they helped him to recover from his illness. But, he said, he had experienced nothing when they shook over him, and after a few attempts to receive the Shaker power, he gave up attending the Shaker church. He may have resisted the influence of the group, for he said a number

[1] Further conversations with this woman struck the same note. Her mother and sisters believe in the power of Indian doctors and of the Shakers. They told me numerous incidents they had observed that demonstrated that these powers exist. Her father was said to have been a sceptic who questioned all 'power'.

of times that he was afraid of the Shaker power because those who receive too much are likely to go ' crazy '. He warned his wife against frequently attending their services and tried to persuade her to become an Apostolic or to give up church attendance altogether lest she ' go crazy '.

Many people attend services at any church, but they do not regard themselves as real members even though they take part in the services. They say that this is because they have never experienced the power. Ed Black, a man past sixty, went to all the churches, but he did not regard himself as a Shaker because he had never ' shaken ', nor did he regard himself as a member of the Apostolic church :

' I go to the Apostolics sometimes, but I'm no member. One time I was over there, and when they started to pray at the end, a white friend came over to me and told me I should go forward. I didn't know what it was all about, so I went up. When I got there, the man told me I should kneel down on the bench there and pray. I did it, but I didn't feel anything. Afterwards the white leader came around and asked me if I felt anything. I told him I hadn't. So the man told me to pray some more. I did. Then they wanted to know if I was saved. I told them I didn't know and they shouldn't ask me. If I were saved, I'd have to do something more than just come up there and pray. To be saved takes a long time and you have to feel something. I didn't feel anything, and I wasn't going to say I had just to make them feel good. I'd have to go through a long time before I could get the power and feel saved. When I told him that, the man didn't ask me any more about it. So now I go to the Shakers sometimes and ring the bells for them, and I go to the Apostolics when I feel like it, and sometimes I go to the Presbyterians. But I won't say that I feel things when I don't.' [1]

In the Presbyterian church, nothing is said about ' power ', nor does membership in the church depend upon any power experience. During 1942, I heard of no new people joining the church, nor could I ever learn much about what had led people first to become members. Mrs. McBride said they

[1] Black went through the Neah Bay boarding school and then went for some years to a boarding school away from the reservation. Afterwards he worked in various lumber camps away from the reservation. His first cousin is a pillar of the Presbyterian church.

became interested in the church when her children were small and began to attend the Sunday school. They liked the service and became regular members. Others said they became attached to the church as children when the first missionary came. Healing may once have played its part, for people spoke of how the early missionaries visited and prayed over the sick. But today healing is not considered to be an activity of the Presbyterian group at Neah Bay, nor do its members ever say that they have received ' power ' through their membership in the church. Their references to power are always outside the context of their church experience.

The wife of one of the church elders showed me some small wooden totem poles made by her sons and said that the top figure represented the thunderbird. She added that her grandfather had the thunderbird as his power and that he used to tell them about it : ' You white people say that the thunder is caused when the clouds come together, but the Indians used to believe that a big bird made the thunder. I think it may be somewhat true. My grandfather always said that, and when he died, that day there was no cloud in the sky, but we heard a big clap of thunder. He always said he was close to the thunderbird.' An elder of the church said that his father took him out and started to teach him the prayers and rites for obtaining doctoring power. He said that as he bathed and prayed he saw something that would have given him power if he had gone on with the ritual. He accepts this experience as quite as real as his membership in the church. The power is there, but he no longer seeks it. Sheila Day, in her forties, is a Presbyterian highly regarded by white members of the congregation. One referred to her as one of the finest Christians she has ever known. Unlike the elder, Mrs. Day states her belief in power in Christian terms—but it is no less a belief in the possibility of experiencing power :

' This uncle of mine was out on the ocean. And that's how I found out that Indians really prayed. Of course, there was lots of people, and I think it was only the low kind of people that didn't get that kind of training [to pray]. He was out on the ocean, and they got in a storm. His partner was dying—couldn't paddle any more. And he started to pray. And he saw the light, just like that resurrection picture. It was right in the canoe. And it talked to this uncle of mine. That's how I found out that they really talked to somebody. And he came home alive. And my grandfather was like that too, pray way out in the hills, and he got answer.'

She said that they prayed to 'Light'. The Makah word she gave for this, she then said meant, 'Light. That's Jesus, the Light of the World.'

Mrs. Day has also attempted to join the Shaker church, but has never been able to experience a feeling of ' power ' which would permit it. Her sister-in-law told me : ' They never could make Sheila shake. She tried to become a Shaker because her husband is one, and she thinks they'd get along better if they had the same religion. They shook over her lots of times, but she couldn't shake. While they were shaking over her, all the time she was praying that the bad spirits wouldn't enter her. She prayed for that all the time. They kept trying, but she never shook.' The fact that she failed to join the church is good evidence that a power experience is necessary before one can regard oneself as a good Shaker.

Some people, of course, are sceptical about the existence of power, especially the traditional power of Indian doctors. Sally Grove usually said that she thought Indian doctors and Shakers may be able to kill or help, but this is only because a person thinks they can. Once when she was detailing the long feud between her family and the Carletons, she said that the Carletons once hired a foreign doctor to kill her brother, then a child, with his power. She stared off into space for a moment, and then said with great emphasis, ' But I don't believe he could. I don't believe it. I'll *never* believe it.' She was sceptical on many other subjects as well. Once in describing the *kloqwali* cere-monies, she said, ' And then they pretended that the wolves took the children away.' Her niece interrupted with a laugh, ' Don't say they pretended. Say they did. You never believe. That's why you say that.' At other times, however, she would say that she did not know, that there might be something in power :

' The only thing that I know, they were supposed to kill anybody they wanted to. But I never used to believe in it, and my father didn't either. One time they were talking about it here. Bob Mead is educated. He went to the University. But he was telling one time that he believes in that. He knows of a person in British Columbia. He said this man was sitting in a crowd and someone seemed to hit him with something on his back. He looked back to see who it was, and he said, "I thought somebody hit me with something to make me look !" He looked down and here it was a nail with a human hair. And Mead said he thought that got electricity in it. I don't know. It might be true. But he believed it.'

In another interview, she said, 'My father used to believe in Indian doctors for things like headaches and earaches, but I always used to be ashamed to say that I believed in them until one time I heard the first missionary we had here say that some people do have the power to help headaches and earaches by laying their hands on you. She said that it was electricity in the body and that some people have more than others. After that I didn't mind saying that I believed in it any more.' [1]

Some Makah therefore tend to be sceptical, unless they can base their acceptance of power on some concept derived from the whites. They interpret it in terms of electricity, magnetism, hypnotism, or other similar beliefs. Others have no need to base themselves upon the teaching of the whites and accept the concept of power as originating within their own past.

The Nature of Power

So far we have talked about power, but made no attempt to describe what it is. The Makah, however, seem to have fairly definite notions, about at least certain types of power.

The word they usually translate as ' power ' is *hitÁktÁkˣe*. This they say stands for any type of power that a person receives. However, when they start to explain it, they invariably ignore the Shaker or Apostolic power, and go back to the power experiences which they say were formerly common in their group. They say that boys and men went roaming through the woods seeking for power for different purposes. Some sought for power that would make them whalers ; others sought for gambling power ; others sought for power to help them in war ; still others sought for doctoring power. Sometimes a man received a different type of power from that which he

[1] Mrs. Grove attended both the Neah Bay boarding school and a boarding school away from the reservation. Later she worked as a cook and housemaid for white families in the Sound area. Her father went to the first day-school at Neah Bay. He was reared by a relative who was a noted Indian doctor.

sought, but in general since the Makah used specific ritual and visited spots specific to certain types of power they were likely to receive that which they sought. The ritual and the location of ' power ' spots were treasured family secrets imparted from one generation to the next. Those who had obtained power would take their children to the same spot and instruct them in the ritual, and thus it was passed on from generation to generation. Therefore, the Makah say, it was rare for a person to receive a type of power which his immediate relatives had not obtained. So certain families were whalers ; others were doctors ; others were fishermen. Even if a man found some type of power for which he was not seeking, apparently it was possible for him to ignore it and wait for the power that he wished to manifest itself. When he did experience the power, it entered into him. He received songs and instructions on ritual that had to be observed if he wished the power to remain with him. Usually the experience caused him to become ill for some months, and he only became well again when he finally began to carry out the instructions of the power. He did not reveal to the people or to his own family which power he had received, but by his actions they would know that he had received something. When he began to sing his power songs, they had the clue to the type of power. Then someone who had the same power would be called in to treat him and ' fix ' the power in the proper place in his body. Also, apparently, the power gradually decreased in potency throughout this period until it was weak enough for the recipient to cope with it. His success in the particular field was regarded as a final proof that he had really experienced something. If he failed to carry out instructions, he might die, or the power might leave him at any time.

' Power ' was not one, but many. One man, indeed, might receive several, and it is said that only one power did not make a man very powerful.

This is considered to be the experience common to most of the Makah of older times. However, in rare cases, people received power for which they had never sought. Some power might deliberately seek them out and enter into them. This might happen at night as they slept, or they might stumble across some power-giving phenomenon as they went through the woods or along the beaches. Usually, however, if a person had not received instructions for dealing with a particular power, he would fear to encounter it and try to avoid it lest it prove too strong for him. Any power that came from seeing a strange phenomenon or strange creature while on the ocean or strait always proved too strong for the observer. Usually he was left with only sufficient strength to reach home and relate his experience before he died. Informants are full of tales as to what happened to those unlucky enough to see such beings or to handle some relatively harmless power in the wrong way.

A typical 'power' experience of the traditional type was related by a man who sought power to become a harpooner on whaling expeditions. The man steadfastly refused to generalize his experience and say that others who became whalers had similar experiences, but his account is typical of what others said they thought occurred when a man received whaling power.

'We had a house on the front there at the point. I was walking over to the point there for eight years while I worked for the agency. When I quit working—I resigned—my father came down here a week later. He lives at Waatch. He come to me and ask me if I want to be whale hunter. I said, "Yes." Because I thought it was easy. He was a whale hunter. One week after that they come for me again and want me to go down there. He was going to teach me his prayer. I went down there in afternoon. That night we start in other side of Waatch village. He start in praying, and I listen and listen. But I don't get him. And another night the same thing. But I didn't get it again. And next night. That's third night. I get it a little bit, just a few words. The fifth night we went down again, and I learn his prayer pretty near all of it. That take me six days to learn it. And seven nights, and he told me to pray for myself, and try it. I said, "All right, I'll try it." And I got all that prayer. Because the whale hunters got own prayers. Different prayers. So I prayed for myself. So I take my uncle sometimes to watch if anybody come around, because whale hunter does that way. He's got watch—brother or uncle or father—because he don't want nobody to take his prayer.

'So I learn it. I just do it for myself and go out and pray. Because I don't want to take my father again. He's too old man to go around at night. Take my uncle with me. So I come home here, and I just start praying over here every night. And by the month of December, I was wait. I was wait if everybody was asleep. They had a ditch over here. I went out in the kitchen, front door. We had a porch on the front. That ditch is about three feet from the house. It was dark that night, so I just went out there. And I see something was passing. I look at it. It was a little man. I can see him plain just like daytime. I see his blanket. I jump down and chase him. I wasn't scared. And there was a big stump right on the beach there. It was low tide that night. So I didn't catch him. He just go right in that stump and I can't see him any more. So I come home. I take my blanket and I start. Next day I went down right in Sues point. I start to bathe there that night. Soon as I got in the water, about a minute I guess, and I heard somebody coming. Lot of talk. Lot of people coming. I know he was going to see my blankets on the beach. I stay there and quiet awhile. So I give up. I went down where my clothes is and put my shirt on. And I just start to come home. . . . About five minutes after I got in bed, I was asleep. Soon as I got to sleep, I saw a big house there right on the big rock there at that beach. They had a bay like this bay here. Alongside of the bluff there, there's a house inside. Great big house. And I heard that rattle and thought it was somebody talking and talking. You know they were going to start to singing their whaling song, the little fellows. Everybody getting ready. And some of them have a rattle. But not start to singing yet. But he didn't start to singing when I got up. If I don't left him, I'd got that song. I was sorry I didn't go back again. And I come back again in the morning. I went out again next night. And next night I come home about four o'clock, I guess. Soon as I got in bed, I think, I was half-asleep when the whale was coming in, right in my house. He come in, pass it when I sleep. And I dream it. . . . So my prayers were right, and God give me what I wanted that time.' [1]

Nobody in recent years has received power for whaling, for whale hunting belongs to a vanished way of life. The power-

[1] This man was about seventy, and had attended the boarding school. He was never a fluent informant save on this one subject. This was the longest uninterrupted statement he ever made to me. He told me, however, of another experience when a dog shot its power into him and made him ill. It was removed by a Shaker doctor, who knew through his power what had happened though the man had never told anyone. He also said that his wife had been an Indian doctor. Others confirmed this and said that his sister had had a power experience which killed her because she was not prepared for it. She saw a small man picking up scraps of food around the fire. If she had known what to do, she would have received power to become a doctor, but instead she died.

giving phenomena, however, are thought to still exist though they never manifest themselves today.

The Makah are not certain whether any of their people have received power for doctoring recently, but they think that it may still be possible to gain this power. Sterne related the types of experience that someone wishing to be a doctor would have to undergo :

' It was all kinds of doctors. Some become a doctor by the lizard and some become a doctor by the *haliwa*—it's kind of lizard with eyes in the middle. That will make you a doctor. Some people got doctor from what they call *bacbáiwadiⱯ*. They say it's little man that lives in a cave, but it's spotted all over. Some men when they see that become a big doctor. And sometimes they see this kelp fish in the creek. So they become a doctor when they see that. Now let me see, what else. And this—I think white people call it Jack Lantern—that light in the night time on the ground. They used to tell me if I see that to run full speed and jump over it. When I jump over it, I will catch that juice in there, power, something like that. That's *oštAkˣébos*. That means—well, I don't know how I will make it clear. It means if you discover it you will become a doctor. That's got shorter in Indian, but it's long to explain what it meant. And they claim another thing. They believe Indian way, you see a hand and you'll be a great doctor. You'll see a hand sticking out of the ground. When you see that, you go put your hand close to it so that power will get in your hand. That's the best you can get if you become a doctor, that hand sticking out of the ground. . . . I think Louis's boy found one like that, but he didn't do right what he should do and he died. If you don't do what this tell you— because somebody will tell you just what to do : " You do this, you do this." Like your head is out of order, and your hand will be warm just like a stove when you got that doctor stuff in you. So they talk and talk. Sometimes they run out sometimes. And if you don't obey what he told you—even this kelp fish will tell you what to do—if you don't do right what he said, then you're going to be dead. And sometimes that will leave you if you don't do right what got to be done. It will leave you for good. And that stuff they claim goes in your stomach so that's how you kind of crazy.

' When you become a doctor, you start singing, singing, singing. And you go out night time and go out in the woods. Sometimes they go to the beach. They claim you'll be hot all through your body—you can't wear anything. But they stayed out four days.

After four days, it gets colder, and they come home and start singing. That's where these songs come from. It's almost like this Shaker. That's how they become doctor, Indian doctor.' [1]

Doctors can use their power either for healing, or for injury, since they are thought to be able to throw their power into people and in this way kill them. Power received for doctoring, like any kind of power, sets certain rules for the recipient to observe if he wishes to continue to control the power. If he obeys the rules, the use to which he puts the power is outside any moral concern of whatever sends the power.

Another form of power is distinguished from *hitÁktÁkˣe*. This is called *kˣói*, which is usually translated as ' medicine'. This is inherent in objects which act as luck charms for the finder. Unlike *hitÁktÁkˣe*, *kˣói* can be lost, stolen, or purchased. The person who finds a ' medicine' object receives no songs, has no visions, and does not become ill. He is not thought to have gained any power which inheres in himself. But so long as he remains in possession of the object, he controls something which has power. He usually keeps the object hidden and says nothing to anyone lest the object be stolen from him. The word *kˣói* is also applied to plants which are thought to be useful in healing. Makah refer to them in English as ' medicine', in Makah as ' *kˣói* '. Apparently, plants too have something powerful which is connected with the supernatural. But knowledge of medicine plants is not common property throughout the tribe. Each family is supposed to know certain plants which it uses for treating its own members. They do not give the plants to other families nor do they divulge which plants they use themselves.

Manifestations of Power

Generalizing from the descriptions of *hitÁktÁkˣe* and *kˣói*, it seems clear that any unusual occurrence or object is to be regarded as a manifestation of power and therefore to be treated carefully. Kelp fish, though common enough near the shore, are only

---

[1] Sterne attended the boarding school and then the day-school at Neah Bay. He is a descendant, through both maternal and paternal lines, of a number of powerful doctors. One immediate ancestor is said to have been the most powerful doctor ever known among the Makah. The information he gave checks with that obtained from members of four other families known to have had doctoring power.

ordinary fish. But one found in a pool in the woods gives doctoring power. A china slipper, a small sea animal, found on the rocks is only food. A china slipper seen in the woods is a manifestation of power so great that those who handle it are likely to die from the effects. A crab found on the shore will be taken and eaten ; one seen going into the woods is something to be avoided, though one who handles it properly can obtain a claw which is ' medicine '. Salmonberries are common, and a favourite food. But an unusually large berry or one growing on a double stem is something to be avoided because of power. Anyone incautious enough to eat such a berry is likely to die from the effect of the power. An unusually large devil fish, an elk that is over-sized or oddly marked, or any other animal with marked peculiarities is regarded as a source of power. In addition, there are tiny dwarfs resembling human beings, great giants, and other beings that roam the woods. These also can give power to one who sees them or who comes upon some sign of their presence. To those who do not know how to deal with them, however, they are dangerous.

Recent Experiences with Power

The Makah say that few have had experiences with *hitÁktÁkˣe* in recent years. This may be a defence against the curiosity of the outsider. They are willing enough to talk about power and to express a sincere belief in the experiences of people now long dead whom they knew as children. But one rarely hears that anyone now living has seen or experienced any of these phenomena. A few are said to have done so. Eight individuals told me that they have seen or heard something which comes within the realm of *hitÁktÁkˣe*. Informants attributed power experiences to a few others. In general, however, the Makah either say that they really know nothing about anyone having received power in recent years, or they may refer to someone's claim with a sneer and say that they do not believe the person ever experienced anything.[1]

A few people are said to be ' Indian doctors '. Mrs. Foote, a staunch Apostolic, said that her son is an Indian doctor, but he

[1] I may have been overcautious in my questioning. I asked directly only about one person. Otherwise I asked a blanket question as to whether there were people living in the village who had had power experiences.

only helps members of his own family. Sterne said he had heard that Foote and one of the Fishers might be Indian doctors, but he himself did not know. Apparently there is no way today whereby their claims to power can be tested. Fisher told me of an experience which could well have given him power though he did not claim that it had :

' I've seen a few things that were queer. There were three of us young boys. I was the youngest. These old people used to tell me of a big boot, a china slipper. The bag is just like felt. We was out in the woods running control lines for the main survey of the reservation that time. It was in 1932. There were three of us always used to work together all the time and never work with anybody else. We was running control lines, and about noon when we were having lunch—after we got through, we heard something hitting the tree. A cedar tree. It must have been about nine, ten feet off the ground. It was one of those china slippers. And one of the fellows, the tallest of us, took and pried it off the tree with an axe. And the other fellow got it and sliced it in half. I didn't want to bother it. Just stood and watched. And this didn't look like china slipper. Just all blubber inside, fat. Looked like cream of some kind, but wasn't solid either. And this fellow who pried it off the tree died that same week. I guess he died—he died of pleurisy. And the other fellow who cut it open, he suffered long time before he died. That's all I've seen, and they died pretty close together.' [1]

Neither of these two men is old. Foote is probably about fifty, and has lived away from the reservation a good part of his life. Fisher is a young man about twenty-six or twenty-seven, who has attended Indian boarding schools away from the reservation. He has, however, always been interested in the stories of the old people, and said that he used to visit the old people to hear what they could tell of the old times. One of his close relatives said that at night he is bothered with dreams of monsters such as they used to represent in certain of the masks worn in the *kloqwali* ceremonies—another indication according to some of the possession of power.[2] I never heard, however, of his being called

[1] He also added one or two other incidents which had befallen him, which might have been power experiences, though again he did not say that he had received any power.

[2] There are no such masks in the village today. People say they were all either destroyed or sold long before Fisher was born. He may have seen masks while visiting other tribes, or he may have picked up his ideas about

upon to cure anyone, nor did people commonly refer to him as a man with power.

The only person in the village who openly claims to be a doctor is Ross North. The first time I saw him he dragged out his dancing costumes and also displayed a rattle which he said was of the kind used by doctors. He told of men coming to ask him how he accomplishes the things that he does. His claims are generally derided by the other people in the village. They do not regard him as a doctor nor ask him to treat them. The only people who submit to his ministrations are members of his own family. Others said that he was merely making the claim to power without ever having had a power experience. Sterne sneered at the thought of North acting as doctor, and said :

' He said that one of his grandsons swallowed two bits, and he claimed he got it out. And he claims he can kill a man. And he ask me if I know the vines that will go just like a snake if you cut them. He says you got to put it over your hand and wipe it good and then grab something you want to put into a man. I don't think he'll do it. Yes, if you talk to North, he'll tell you everything. He'd have to stay in bed three or four months if he become a doctor. But he never stay in bed or suffer from that power they get when they become a doctor. That shows when they become a doctor— that power they get in the hands become warm. And they get kind of crazy in the head, got to run out in the woods. They can't stand it in the house, they say.' [1]

Many people said they thought the phenomena that give power

them from some of the ethnographies on Northwest Coast tribes which he has read. He said he obtained his ideas for the totem poles he carves from these books.

[1] This, of course, is an instance of the ' turn down ' referred to in the previous chapter. Sterne lost no opportunity to deride North. Others in the village did the same. North is attempting to make good his claim to high status and to establish his position as a chief. So the Makah laugh at his claims to ancestry, sneer at his hospitality, and deride any statements that he may make which might give him an advantage over others in the group. They generally label him a liar. They frequently warned me against accepting anything he might say.

I found myself, however, having a certain sympathy with their views when North approached me on Makah Day with a headdress modelled on a Plains Indian warbonnet and gave me a long talk on how this was a family heirloom with each feather symbolizing an incident in his family history. North is in his early fifties. Even the young people know that the Makah adopted these headdresses only in the last few years. He may have been speaking in are less frequently encountered now than formerly. They have various explanations as to why this should be so. The Kellers suggested that the cattle grazing through the woods have driven the power phenomena away. Others said that the carrying of guns or metal knives might prevent the seeker from encountering the phenomena—as it were insulating him against the receipt of power. Others had other explanations, and as the men sit along the Front they canvass the question thoroughly.

' We was talking about it a few days ago in that little fish house there—a bunch of us : Val Clement, Jeffry Webb and me, and I think it was Warren Grove. I said, "I think it's the food we eat. It ain't agree with what they used to see." And Val Clement said, " Well, I'll tell you what I think myself. You know this Indians used to be out every night travelling all over. Out of the village, down this way where there is no people stay. That's why this Indians used to get their doctors. But us today—we ain't travelling like them people used to do.' And Jeffry said, ' It's true. They start in different, start in eating different kind of food like the old people used to eat. Here we are eating everything we can see. So I don't think we'll ever get to be doctor, any one of us. Because some of the boys ain't believe in that today." '

Most say that today there are only Shaker doctors, though some believe that the old man who originally introduced the Shaker church to Neah Bay and who once had great power is also an Indian doctor. His daughter said she thinks he is a doctor of the old type. People still send for him occasionally, but since he has grown old and forgetful his services are little sought.

Though the Makah are sceptical of the existence of Indian doctors in their midst, they say that other tribes still possess Indian doctors who have great power which they use both for healing and for killing those who anger them. In their contacts with these people, the Makah are careful to avoid any situation which might expose them to the doctor's power. At Christmas time, in 1941, some Makah went down to the coast to the

derision to mark his displeasure at not being used sufficiently as an informant, but some twenty years earlier he gave another anthropologist elaborate descriptions of certain dances which he said were old Makah dances. No amount of questioning among the old people substantiated this information. As far as they knew, the dances he described were dances which he himself had learned as a boy while staying with another tribe, and in later life he imported them as new dances.

Quinault reservation. Later I was told by Grace Sterne that Ross North had brought back the report that three Indian doctors were present at the gathering. 'They were playing with their tamanamos. *hitÁktÁkˣe*, they call it in Indian. They were playing around with it. That's why Ross North got scared. You know if this *o·štAkˣe* [1] gets in your body, you get sick and die. So you got to be careful when they're playing with it—stay out of their way and not make fun. Because those that have that power, when you make fun of them, they get mad and get even with the one that makes fun of it. That's why Ross North got scared and said he left before twelve o'clock. He said he felt the power before they start. He said he knew that old man was going to do that, so he didn't want to be in the place. Oh, it was a big time that night. Everyone had a power in him. They didn't know which one had the bigger power.'

When people from other tribes visit Neah Bay, the people are apt to be equally wary of them. Mrs. Sterne told about a Bible study meeting in a white man's cabin to which many Shakers went:

'There was a Quileute woman down for it. She'd been feeling bad and she wanted the people here to help her with their power. But everyone was afraid to do anything because the way it is they're afraid that somebody might be there with tamanamos power. People with that power go to Shaker meetings just to catch people and throw their power into them and hurt them. So everybody was just sitting there. Then I got up and started to pray and sing over her. Then I started to shake. When I start to shake, I can't stop. For a long time I was praying over this woman by myself, touching her and trying to put the power into her. . . . I tried to stop shaking, but I couldn't. Then I turned to the others and told them they should come and help me and stop me. They didn't move. So I told them, "Well, it looks like I'll just have to keep on shaking and praying. I can't stop myself, and I'll have to go on till I fall over asleep." So I kept on and on. When I'm like that I can tell what people are thinking. Rose Carleton was sitting there on the side. She began to think, "Grace ought to stop this now. The white people are getting tired of her being like this for so long. It doesn't look right for her to keep it up like this before the white people. They don't know what to think." She didn't say it. She just thought it to herself. Then I turned and came to her. I said,

---

[1] This is specifically doctoring power. The same word is used for doctor.

" We're doing God's work. When we're doing that, we have to keep on doing as God wants us to do. Come and help me ! " She told me afterwards she thought I was right. The others thought so too. So they got up, and after that they shook over the woman and helped her. That's the way with the Shakers. They have to do God's work even if they don't feel like doing it. They have to do it.'

Other people also said that Shaker meetings give an opportunity for doctors from other tribes to attempt to throw their power into one, and that one should be cautious while at the meetings.

The Use of Medicine

The Makah also believe in the present existence of $k^x\acute{o}i$, and a number of families are said to have something that brings them luck. Mrs. Keller said that her husband owns a luck charm, but that he will not talk about it. The Kellers were quite willing to talk about different charms that they thought other families might have, though they always said they really could not know since no one would talk about these things to others in the tribe. It was the same way with other informants—they would say that they themselves knew nothing about the subject, but they thought someone else might have something. The only time I ever received any real information on a charm from a member of the family which owned the charm came when Grace Sterne told me of the ' medicine ' her husband had found :

' One day we took a walk out in the prairie. It was a fine day. On the way back, we saw something. It's just like a small mouse. He said, " It's a mole." Killed it. Put it in his pocket and bring it home. My uncle was down here. He was a medicine man. When my husband got home, he start in using it. He puts it in between that halibut hook. Makes the halibut bite that hook all the time. Oh boy ! He was catching lots of halibut. Then my uncle came down start fishing here. My husband had it hidden in one of his coats hanging up in our bedroom. No one could find it. And through his power, my uncle found it. He took it and start to using it. Then we found out he took it away. That's what this little baby mole is for. Sure crazy that getting them. So every time we see mole, he wants to get it just for that halibut fishing.'

The use of $k^x\acute{o}i$ in the form of herbal medicines is extensive. It is frequently mentioned in conversations. Ross North claimed to have cured his grandson, sent home from the hospital to die, by the use of the medicines he knew. Dorothy Hill's recovery from arthritis was attributed to the use of medicines she inherited from her stepfather. Joan Hewitt said that her father had given her medicines when she was ill, and they had helped her. Mary Paulsen spoke of using her family medicines when she was ill. Specific information, however, is difficult to obtain, for these herbal medicines are family secrets. Informants will say that they have medicines, but that they do not wish to reveal how they are made or how they are used to the outsider.

My own impression, after living a year at Neah Bay, is that the belief in both *hitÁktÁk^xe* and *k^xói* is much more widely spread and important than my notes indicate. When people talked informally to me or to each other, it was usually about the ordinary events of daily life or the latest scandal, or sometimes they would humour my peculiar interests by detailing something they had heard from their grandparents. After the first few months, I had come to the conclusion that almost no one believed in the traditional 'power' experiences, and that the only 'power' received today was that of the Shakers and Apostolics. As the months went on, this impression changed to the belief that this is a closely guarded aspect of Makah life, and that only occasionally is the reserve about it broken. In a situation of this sort, I believe that the fieldworker's impressions are a justifiable part of the record. However, there is some evidence to support it. When I went through recorded and reconstructed interviews and observations on some fifty people, all of them over twenty-five, I found that twenty-eight had given some information that would justify the conclusion that they do believe in *hitÁktÁk^xe* as a factor in their lives. I then classified the fifty people into two groups, on the basis of intimacy. Twenty-one of those who showed a belief in *hitÁktÁk^xe* fell into the group I knew best; seven belonged to the other group. Of those who never referred to the subject in any way or did so only in negative terms, four fell into the group I knew best; eighteen into the other.

The Power of God

The power that is said to be obtained by members of the churches is usually spoken of as 'the power of God'. There is not complete agreement here, however, for at least the Shakers think that numerous powers exist which attempt to enter them. Some are good, and these they think are sent by God. Others are bad, or at least evil in their effect upon the recipient.

The man who introduced the Shaker church to Neah Bay explained the Shaker power as follows : [1]

' When they first start shaking they have rules. They're spiritualists. But they only want to have God's spirit. But the Shakers now don't know that. They think all kinds of spirits come from God. That's why they all start to fall apart and hate each other. . . . That's how I came to leave my people and join the Presbyterian church. I felt ashamed of what had happened to my people. I just left it. But then, after all, I've been following the Shaker religion. I found out that it's very hard to really follow the real religion of the Shakers. That is the real power that belongs to God. Because some evil power can get in any time if one is not careful to follow the rules of the Shakers. Most of them lose the right way of God and start to following anything by a spirit. And then any kind of spirit can come and bother them. Not just the right kind of spirit they're supposed to follow. I found that out too. That's why some of them have got in with the bad spirit. . . . It started getting hard for me because my people started doing wrong things they wouldn't have done if they hadn't been Shakers. If they had their own minds to go by. I tried to tell them at different times how this was and why it should be this way. It's just this evil power, evil spirit get in them so strong they believe in it and won't listen to me. But well, anybody that goes along with the Shaker the right way, they're going to live, and they'll be strong.'

Since the members of his church once turned on him during a meeting and tore out most of his hair, he has some reason to think that they may be possessed by evil spirits as well as good.

Hugh Henderson gave a more orthodox explanation of the Shaker doctrine—or at least one that agreed more with the statements of other informants and seems to reflect the present beliefs of members of the Shaker church. He said that the Shakers believe in the power of Jesus which can enter you and give you power to help others. For this reason, Shakers also speak of themselves as ' The Christians '. They believe that

[1] He spoke through an interpreter. The passage originally therefore stood in the third person, rather than the first. I have shifted it into the first for ease in reading.

reading the Bible is not enough. It is good, but it is only a part of religion. You must also open your heart to receive this power which was found at the time the Bible was written. This you can still receive today because it has never been lost. Henderson said he himself used to be a good Presbyterian, and one who believed in reading his Bible faithfully. Then he was ill, and thought he was going to die. The Shakers came and prayed over him. They sent their power into him. He received the power and recovered. Since then he has known that reading the Bible is not enough and that he himself can receive the spirit of Christ into himself and that this can guide him as well as the Bible. Henderson said that if anyone wishes to join the church, the members come and shake over him. They try to help him receive the spirit of the Lord. All of them are willing to help just as much as possible, but the person must open his heart to the Lord and pray that he be given this power. The others cannot give it to him until he is ready to receive it. Sometimes this takes a long time. Henderson himself was shaken over and began to feel the power sweeping over him. His arms began to shake and he was glad. He could not hold his body still. This is what happens when the power truly enters you.[1]

The power that the Shakers feel manifests itself in different ways, though usually the person possessed by power shakes violently throughout his body. Sally Grove, however, said that she has never shaken, but she has felt as though a cold wind were blowing through her. The Shakers were willing to accept this as a sign that she had received their power. Grace Sterne said that when she has the power she can feel it through her body and that she, and others also, see something but it is not very clear to them. She said that she feels her power ' like heat. My whole body feels hot. When I go near someone we're praying over, I put my hand out close to her body, not touching her, and still I can feel the heat, just like my hands are touching hot steam.'

[1] Henderson told me this the first time he spoke to me. I asked him again about the Shaker religion a few months later when I knew him better. He then denied having ever been a member of the Shaker church, though he repeated the account of how he had been shaken over and received the power. But, he said, his wife had joined the Anglican church when she was in the boarding school, and since the Bible says that husband and wife ' should be of one flesh ', he has not felt that he could join the Shakers. However, he is willing to help them at any time.

Keller also spoke of the heat in his hands during possession. He has also seen a bright light during possession, and on some occasions has had visions of a man clad in metal armour. Various others reported that they felt the power in other ways. The details of the experience show a large range of variations.

Emily Lester's experience with the Shakers indicates that those visited by the power do not always welcome the experience :

' Sometimes the Shakers do cure people. There's a sort of power in them. It feels the way it does when you're very nervous and excited. Sometimes it makes you happy, and sometimes it doesn't. I got to be a Shaker when I was about fourteen. I never joined the church, but I used to go over there to watch the meetings and then I got the power. I still feel it sometimes. I was sitting there looking on when suddenly I felt it. It was like a big light very bright, not very close to me. It was very bright, but I couldn't feel any heat in it. Nobody else seemed to see it. After that I started shaking. I used to see people, faces, or sometimes only eyes. They'd come and look at me. I wouldn't be afraid when I saw those eyes staring at me—I just knew they were there. Then it started to get worse. When I was here alone something would come and knock at the windows, or when I was asleep in bed I felt someone trying to wake me up with a hand on my knee or on my shoulder. My father told me to pray when I felt like that, and it would help. I did that, and it would go away. I think if I'd gone to the Shakers and asked them to shake over me, I might have gotten cured, but I never did. I just went there and watched and helped with the singing. It got so bad I got to be afraid to be alone because I could feel people coming to me all the time. So I quit the Shaker business and didn't think about it any more. I just read my Bible and prayed. Then I seemed to get better. But since I started to drink and smoke, I'm never bothered any more. I never feel it any more, and I'm not afraid to stay alone now. That's why I started to drink—I was afraid of those things.' [1]

The stereotyped phrases uttered by the participants in a Shaker service indicate that they are calling upon the spirit of Christ rather than some other form of spirit. They call out, ' Oh Lord Jesus, send us your holy power.' ' Jesus, let me feel your power !' ' Oh Lord Jesus, help us. Give your power to us.' When the

[1] Mrs. Lester is in her fifties. She went to the day-school at Neah Bay, and also spent several years as a child in white communities near and in Seattle. In recent years, she has lived much in the cities.

power enters into them, they shake. If there is someone to be cured or someone attempting to receive the Shaker power, they approach close to him, running their hands close along his body but apparently not touching him. Sometimes the power gives them songs which are sung at Shaker meetings. I was told that sometimes people in different parts of the state begin to sing the same new song at the same moment. The songs are regarded as gifts from the spirit to the Shaker people, and they spread from one community to another. However, at the present time, in Neah Bay, the principle of the *túpat*ʰ is beginning to be applied to the songs. The first to receive a song is regarded as its owner, and the others will not use it without his permission. Some of the Shakers object to this and claim that the songs are sent to them all though they come through the individual.

The Shaker power is used for purposes other than healing. In 1942, when a Makah was drowned in the Strait, the Shakers met and prayed that his body might be recovered. At his funeral, the Shaker leader announced that it was the power of God that had given them back the body of their 'brother'. The man who introduced the Shaker movement among the Makah claimed that his Shaker power enabled him to discover lost articles and also to prophesy the future. Even his enemies say that all his prophecies save one have come true.

The Apostolics also believe that their members receive the power of Christ and that they can use this in healing. Makah who do not belong to this church still call upon the members to pray over their sick in the hope that the Apostolic power will cure them. On one occasion, the Apostolic leader in Neah Bay was roused in the middle of the night to pray over a man believed to be dying. When he recovered, it was regarded as a demonstration of the efficacy of the Apostolics' power. This curative function, however, is not unique to the Neah Bay branch of the church. Whites who visit the church from outside testify to cures which have been performed through the power of God. In cases of serious illness, the Neah Bay Apostolics send messages to the Port Angeles church to ask for help. Members of the church visit the hospital to pray over the sick, and it was thus that the leaders of the Neah Bay congregation first came in contact with the Apostolic church.

The Apostolics also believe that the possession of their power helps them to lead a good life, though to continue to possess the power they must cut themselves off from all worldly things which might distract them from the spirit. There is no suggestion, however, that the Apostolics are in danger of possession by evil spirits if they fail to follow the rules of the church. The core of the Neah Bay branch moved from the Presbyterian into the Shaker and then into the Apostolic church within a few years. Its members are familiar with Shaker concepts, but the only spirit they mention in connection with the Apostolic church is that of Christ. Yet, there is little room to doubt that it is the power concept which attracted them to the Apostolic church in the first place. Their leader made that clear during a conversation which in substance and even in wording is almost a replica of her formal testimony during church services :

'I was a member of the Presbyterian church. At that time we were prosperous and had everything we wanted. We had a good store. . . . Almost every week we took in two thousand cash to say nothing of credit. We had a good home, and in those days we kept it up. But we thought we deserved these things, that they were the results of our hard work. We thought nothing about God and what he was doing for us, though I was doing church work here and teaching in Sunday School. But I felt I wanted something different though I didn't know what it could be. So I started going to the Shaker church. I'm sure the people here thought it was queer for me to go to the Shakers. But we tried them for six months. There is one thing about the Shaker church. It recognizes the spirit. I had to learn what that was. Nothing in the other church had prepared me for that. Sometimes the spirit the Shakers get is not a good spirit, but then it is a church of confusion. Then the husband of one of the members of our little group was hurt up here at the camp. He was in the hospital at Port Angeles. His wife was worried about him and got in touch with the Apostolic people. They helped him so much that she got interested in it and started to go to Port Angeles to the church there. Then they invited them to come down. They came down several times and met with our group. That's how it got started.' [1]

Others insist that as members of this church they have felt the

[1] The leader is a woman in her forties. She and her husband were employed as teachers by the Indian Service and worked for many years in different schools in the southwestern states. When they retired and returned to Neah Bay, they opened a general store which eventually failed.

power of God and that it has saved them. In their descriptions of possession by the power, however, they do not refer to physical sensations nor do they relate visions. Instead they say only that they feel the power of Jesus within them, and that they hear his voice. Grace Sterne who visited the Apostolic church for a while commented, ' You're supposed to go sort of crazy and start talking with the voice of Jesus, but I never did that there.'

Summary

The statements quoted above make it clear that to the Makah the concept of power is of the utmost importance in their religious life. They see their churches not so much as a passage-way leading them through life into the next world, but as a mechanism for obtaining power which can then be used for imme-diate results in this life. They are likely to compare the churches —the Presbyterian stands outside this general scheme—in terms of power. They are not averse to changing from one church to another because to them the powers of the different churches are not antagonistic. They are either the same or supplementary. A person is fortunate if he receives more power. They regard the rules of the churches more as ritual to secure the acquisition and retention of power than as moral codes which must be observed and which have the sanction of God's displeasure against the errant ones. At the Apostolic and Shaker meetings, theyexpatiate at length on their sins, but I doubt that a sense of sin is of real significance to them.

At least in the Shaker church, the power once obtained need not necessarily be used for a beneficent end. The nuclear group of Apostolics would maintain probably that their power can be used only for good—others who joined talk about the power in terms of ' strength ' rather than of ' beneficence '.

In these respects, the power of the churches is like that of the Indian doctors. They are also alike in that both are used for heal-ing. At the present time, power, save in the form of $k^x\acute{o}i$, has little or no contact with the economic life of the people. The Makah today do not claim either through churches or through other ex-periences to obtain power for success in their daily undertakings.

Today in Neah Bay people are in contact with various organiza-tions and beliefs relating to the supernatural. The concepts of the Presbyterians and the belief in *hitÁktÁk^{x}e* stand at opposite poles.   The Apostolics are the closest to the Presbyterians, save that they demand a literal interpretation of the Bible which is not typical of Presbyterians of today and they admit the experiencing of the spirit of God by the worshippers.   The Shakers come next with their use of the Bible, but they subordinate the authority of the Bible to the manifestations of the spirit, and they admit the experience of other spirits than Christ.   Then comes *hitÅktÅk^xe* which most people do not regard as connected in any way with Christianity.   But at the same time, it must be emphasized that the community is not divided into four different groups each with its own concept of the supernatural.   Instead there are people who can encompass all four beliefs and who do not deny the validity of any ; there are others who accept only one or two ; and perhaps a few who reject all.

Religious Concepts : the World of the Dead

The Makah feel themselves to be surrounded not only by a universe of mysterious powers which they may experience and which are potentially dangerous, but the universe is also inhabited by spirits who were formerly alive on this earth.   These they call ' ghosts '.   Sometimes they refer to them as ' spirituals '. It is not always clear in any given instance whether they are referring to a power phenomenon or a ' ghost ' for both may be called ' spirituals '.   But in theory at least the two are carefully distinguished.

The Life of the Dead

The Makah believe that those who die do not go off to some remote land from whence there is no return.   They think that the spirits stay close around the sites they knew as living people. They roam through the streets of the village, throng into a house that is vacated, and carry on a life much like that lived by the people who survive.   Some say that the dead go to a land beneath the ground, but even so they think that the dead have free access to this earth and come and go when and as they please.

There is not complete agreement on the nature of these spirits. Some feel that when a person dies his spirit becomes completely malevolent, especially to his relatives and those he loved best. These he tries to entice after him so that he may have companionship in the other world.   Others say that the spirits do not realize that they are dead and only wish to be with people whom they love, but that the effect of their presence is evil, despite their good intent. It is generally believed that those who see these spirits have little chance of surviving. Even to be in the presence of a ghost without realizing it, is apt to leave one with a face distorted with paralysis or with some other physical disability. People therefore fear their presence.

Contacts with the Living

Ordinarily, the ' ghosts ' are not seen, though people are certain that they are about the village and along the beach. They do appear in the dreams of the living, and this is regarded as a warning of some impending calamity, for it is thought that the dead have come back to guide some living relative to the land of the dead.

Such beliefs have few outward manifestations. Ordinarily there is little comment upon them by the people of Neah Bay. The Makah go through the regular Christian funeral services, bury their dead in the tribal graveyard overlooking the Strait, and speak of heaven and hell.[1] At the same time, they equally believe that the spirits are around them and may have an effect upon them.

They claim to have evidence that their belief is correct. When they speak of these things they corroborate their statements with tales of ancestors who died, visited the land of the dead and talked with the spirits, and then returned to tell the people what life was like after death. They tell of Indian doctors who followed the soul of a dying man into the spirit world and were able to persuade it to return. They know of people who have glimpsed a dead relative and shortly afterwards died from the effect. Many have seen dead relatives in their dreams or when they were ill, or even when they knew they were awake. They have somehow survived, and can give their experiences as additional evidence that there is no rigid barrier between the living and the dead.

Mrs. Frost said that a former husband had been at a party in

[1] At funerals there are large displays of flowers, and on Memorial Day some families visit the graveyard to place flowers on the family graves. A florist at Port Angeles said that the Makah are among his best customers for funeral pieces.

the village. The steamer came, and all the people ran to the landing. When he had gone a little way, he remembered leaving his cane in the house where the party was being held. He returned, and heard drumming and voices within the building. When he entered, it was quiet and the rooms were empty. He knew that the ghosts had entered the vacant building, as they love to do, and were holding a party there themselves. He lost his voice, but recovered it a few hours later. Mrs. Keller remembered seeing a relative die after an encounter with a ghost. The woman had been weeping for her dead husband. It was the fourth day after the burial. She looked up to see his feet standing beside her. Within a few hours she was dead.

This seeing of the dead is apparently a fairly common occurrence among the Neah Bay people, though one they dread and talk of little. Emily Lester said she saw her husband soon after his death :

'It was four days after he died. I was living in another house then. I was in the kitchen washing clothes. I had the machine by the window with the exhaust pipe sticking out of it, and two big wash tubs on the floor. While I was standing there washing, the engine was making quite a bit of noise. Suddenly the door opened, and my husband walked in. I'd been afraid to look at him when he was in his coffin. I hadn't wanted to go near him then, but now he walked in and I didn't think anything about it. I didn't feel him any different than always. When he died he was working for the agency here, and so they gave him a government coffin—all brown. I didn't like that. And they gave him sort of a black robe to wear in the coffin. They fixed up everything because he was a government employee. Well, when he walked in that time, he had on that robe, black and long. He got up close, and I saw it. That was the first thing that made me remember that he was dead and had been buried four days. I felt my face get hot, and then I must have fainted.'

After this experience she left the house and moved to the city with her children.

These people are older members of the tribe. Younger people seem to have similar experiences. One house in the village had been rented to whites for a number of years. When the owners finally returned to the house, they soon realized that there were spirits about the place. It was a relatively new house, though two people had died in it. They could not decide, however, what caused the manifestations. The owners of the house were not sufficiently afraid of the manifestations to move out of the house, but no member of the family would sleep alone downstairs. Anyone who did so was said to hear footsteps that vanished in the middle of the room or to dream of a huge dark man with great hands outstretched to catch them. A boy of fourteen and a girl of twenty-three were among those who had had such experiences.

A woman in her forties said that she was in Port Angeles the day her brother drowned in the Strait, and she could hear his voice talking to her and calling her to come. She was surprised because she did not know he was coming to Port Angeles that day and she wondered because in spite of hearing his voice she never saw him. When she reached home that night, she first learned that her brother was dead.[1]

Grace Sterne said that she had seen her dead on a number of occasions. Once when she was awake and at work washing clothes, she saw her dead stepfather enter the house and start up the stairs. Another time, when she lay very ill, her dead mother came with two of her dead children and talked to her. Her mother told her that her dead children were being well taken care of and she should stay in this world to care for her living ones.

The Evidence of Dreams

People frequently see the dead in dreams and this is regarded as good evidence for the nature of the life of the dead. Grace Sterne reported a dream in which she saw her dead sister:

' I saw my sister. That's why I don't believe in this white people—I guess the white people got their own heaven but us Indians got our own heaven. We just go back where we're living. It's the

---

[1] She made no mention of the voices at the time, and there was nothing in her behaviour to make one suspect that anything was wrong. She first spoke of hearing her brother's voice about a month after his death. Since the Makah believe that people commonly have a premonition of a death amongst their relatives, she was possibly trying to live up to expected behaviour. On the other hand, she may have had a premonition on that day, and said nothing. Makah frequently announce a premonition of death or disaster, but the disaster usually does not materialize.

same land. I saw it that time I came back from the grave. I was sick that time, and I guess I fell asleep. And she came. Well, Howard's brother was carrying me along on the road. He had a light like this bulb going ahead where we was walking. We walk in the dark and came to the light. I couldn't see what he looked like, but I know it was my husband's brother who died before I was born. And he left me there. " This is as far as I'm going to bring you," he said. In the middle of the graveyard. There's stairs there. I've seen that twice already. That middle of the graveyard opened up, and my sister came up. She said, " This is as far as you're going. You're not going any further. You're just going to see the steps where we go up and down." I peek at the steps. I always say it's just like electric lights in there. " Well," she said, " this is as far as you're coming. I've got a child there left behind. I'm going to leave you there to take care of her even when she's a woman. So I'm letting you go back, and I'm giving you a light. You're going to have light all your life." Because coming, I came the dark way. So my sister was there, and she said she was going to give me the light for all my life. That's the way it goes around. That's what the Indians believe in. . . . I told the people what the preacher lady told us, the one that just came down here with the Pentecostals. She told us not to believe people say the dead people come back because the dead people is just the devil. And the Indian people believe the dead people still among us, but we don't know it, they say. But we just see them in our dreams, they say. That's the way we meet our dead people, when we dream about them.' [1]

Grace Sterne often referred to similar experiences. She said she expected their last car accident because the previous night she dreamed of her first child who died at birth, and this always happens when they are going to have some misfortune. On another occasion, when her husband was making a trip away from the reservation, their son was told to stay home. Mrs. Sterne said that this was because her husband dreamed the previous night about a dead person and thought this might mean they would be killed. ' So he told Louis to stay home and save himself.' [2]

[1] Grace Sterne is about thirty-five. She attended day-school at Neah Bay, but ill health as a child kept her from regular attendance. Her mother was an alien, and had never been to school. Her stepfather attended the boarding school at Neah Bay.

[2] Other types of dreams are also regarded as meaningful. Any dream which shows a person in some misfortune is regarded as a warning. Old

Anyone may have dreams, though certain people are thought to have dreams more generally borne out by future events. Mrs. Foote said :

' My husband was kind of—he could dream things. And his dreams always happen. Like my son-in-law today. He dreams about people and he always say, " Well, you have to be careful. Somebody going to die." That drowning this year. He dreamed about somebody coming, and he said there was going to be a death in the family. A few days later he heard that his cousin was drowned. And then again—about a couple of weeks ago, I happened to go in there and he said, " Well, Mary will never believe my dreams. But she always knows it happens. I dreamed all my folks was there and giving a big meal. I dreamed my dead sister was among them, and she looked real nice. So next day I told Mary to go and ask the Apostolic people to pray over the baby." Mary said, " Well, I had to be home to do some work, and that was the night of that meeting." Then he went out. Soon their daughter came in and said, " Mother, George lost his little girl. She died." Mary said, " You go tell your Dad. He's going out to cut some wood." So she yelled, and he came back. He said, " Well, that's my dream. It's not Lucy's baby after all. It's George's baby ! " He believes in his dreams. That's the way it was with my husband. He sees things in his dreams.' [1]

Again Mrs. Sharpe spoke of another person who saw the dead, but this time it was not a warning of misfortune. ' My sister-in-law was dying. Lydia was there bathing her face and trying to make her comfortable. The doctor had given up, and all the

people said that formerly if anyone had such a dream, the people gathered and acted out the incident which prevented the actual misfortune. This is no longer done, but people worry about the dream. One day Grace Sterne appeared very worried because she had forgotten to warn her small daughter to stay away from the beach. She had dreamed the night before that the child would fall off the jetty and drown.

People frequently relate their dreams and wonder what they mean. If they have persistent bad dreams, they may call in the Shakers or Apostolics to treat them.

[1] Mrs. Foote is past seventy. She and her daughter are Apostolic, but her son-in-law is not. Her husband to whom she refers was an alien Indian whom she said was an Indian doctor. He received his power from an experience in the woods with a power-giving phenomenon, but he failed to do any doctoring until a white ' faith healer ' told him that he must use his power or die.

family were there. Then Mrs. Bone came in the door and stood by the bed and started to shake over her. She kept it up a long, long time. Then Patience sat up and opened her eyes for the first time and asked for water. We saw that ourselves. Before that, she saw her dead children. Maybe she was dreaming, but she saw them ; and she said not to bring her back because she was with the dead, that they should leave her alone.'

Ritual to prevent the Return of the Dead

After a death, the survivors try to minimize the risk of the return of the spirit. Spirits are thought to be particularly attached to any property of which they have not formally divested themselves before death.

In the past, people have taken drastic action if they thought that the spirits of their dead were still haunting their houses. When Sterne's oldest son lay dying, he told his father that they should leave the house because there were too many dead people about and that so long as they lived there they would have misfortune. Sterne ignored the warning, but when other children began to die, he began to heed his son's advice. He finally sold his house and built another. When Carleton's son was on his deathbed, he told his father to burn the house and all the goods because if they continued to live there, the dead would continue to bother them until all the children were dead. Carleton burned the house with all its furnishings. Dave Sharpe suspected that his children died because of the spirits that dwelt with them in the house, so he sold it and built a house away from the centre of the village where nobody had previously lived. It is possible to sell a haunted house, because while ghosts may be dangerous to anyone, they are more apt to injure relatives than complete strangers. Unrelated people can live there without ill results.

Private possessions are usually burned, or broken and thrown out upon the beach immediately after the death of the owner. Some people prefer to invite friends of the dead to take some of the less-personal belongings, for if these objects pass beyond the family, there is little danger of the dead person returning to dispute possession. It is dangerous to keep them within the family. I heard a number of accounts of people who had been incautious enough to retain an article which the dead person had not specifically allotted to them. They were annoyed by spirits until they destroyed the article. But generally the custom of destroying personal property is so taken for granted that it is little questioned. This is indicated by the casual way people speak in conversation, as 'We had a lot of records once, but when my sister died I threw them all down on the beach.' Here, however, I do not know whether the young people approve the custom or if they would follow it if left to their own devices. At the present time, the arrangements are largely in the hands of the older people, who see to it that the custom is observed.

Some families also avoid the names of their dead for some years. Others do not. One family avoids not only the Indian names, which are family *túpat* and therefore their own property, but also the Christian names of their dead. If a surviving member of the family happens to have the same name, this is changed so that the name need never be used. When they speak of an unrelated person who bears the same Christian name, they try to discover some substitute. The substitute may then become general, as other families who themselves do not carry the avoidance to this extreme, adopt the substitute in deference to the family's feelings. However, even this family has begun to relax its avoidance of names in the last few years. Other people feel that both Indian and Christian names should be avoided immediately after the death. I was once asked to write an announcement to be read at a funeral, and Lydia Morris asked me to revise it because I had used the dead man's name. She suggested that we omit any reference to the name because Indians do not like to use the name of the dead.[1] Again, a woman quarrelled with some of her relatives because they named their child for her dead daughter. She did not object to the child's receiving the name, but she grew angry when the parents proceeded to use the name, and said they had no regard for her feelings. Most of the family then began to use a nickname to escape taking sides in the argument.

Others avoid only the use of the Indian name, and this is no hardship to them since Indian names are little used today. Indeed, most people cannot remember what their Indian names are and have to ask other members of the family about the

[1] At the funeral, which was held in the Shaker church and run by Shaker leaders, the man's name was mentioned constantly.

matter.[1] But after a death, if any member does bear the same Indian name as the dead person, his name is changed at the first possible moment. Christian names are used if it is necessary to refer to the dead by name, but even among those who do not avoid names entirely, it is more common to use some descriptive term, such as ' my son who died '. A few families say they make no effort at avoidance at all because they love their dead so much they want to keep their memory alive. This, however, does not seem a common attitude.

The reason for the avoidance is said by some to be due to a fear of attracting the attention of the ghost, who will come when he hears his name. Others say that it is avoided through respect for the feelings of the survivors, who will be hurt if they hear the name. To many, it has become an act of courtesy rather than an avoidance rite based on fear of the dead. They fear only the displeasure of the living, who may overhear and feel that their family is not receiving due respect.

It is not believed that what a person does in this life affects his fate after death—apparently all people become ghosts, no matter how they live.[2] Those who survive can influence the ghosts to some extent, in the sense that they can hold their attachment by the use of their names and by the retention of their personal property. But on the whole, the survivors are at the mercy of those who have gone before. For as the ghosts move about the village, and through its quiet streets, they may attract to themselves the spirits of the living and take them from this life.

The Makah therefore fear the ghosts, from the child who pauses in play to listen wide-eyed to a noise upon the porch and mutter, ' Ghosts coming in ! ' to the old woman who laughs at the sound of a lumber train whistle shrieking through the village and declares, ' That sound will scare all the ghosts away from this village. Now I won't be afraid to go around nights.'

Summary

Though the organized forms of religious life are today in a large measure those found also within purely white communities, through the religious beliefs of the Makah run themes which are

---

[1] See above, Chapter III.

[2] Those who die by drowning are said to turn into white owls.

not typical of orthodox Christian belief. The Makah sees himself surrounded by a world of powerful forces and spirits which can influence his life directly and whose presence he can experience. These spirits or forces are not moral beings, but sources of power which, like electricity, is dangerous to those who do not know how to use it. Harnessed by one who has the proper knowledge and who uses the proper safeguards, it can be turned into a force which may be used by the possessor as he pleases within the limits of the power's potency.

The Makah, therefore, is apt to regard his religious organization or church as a medium for obtaining power, and not as a source of a moral code or a medium for ensuring a happy life after death. For him, with his belief in spirits who live about him in this world irrespective of their actions during their ' mortal ' life, such creeds have little meaning. The Makah does not feel that his actions in this life affect his fate after death. His church becomes then a way of increasing his happiness in this life. This it can do by giving him power to deal with threats to his present existence : power to heal and to foretell the future.

Only in the Presbyterian church is the concept of power outside the creed and activities of the church itself. But the members of this church as individuals hold the concept. They also believe in the immediate presence of the spirits of the dead. Here the formal organization of their church with its official creed reflects only a portion of their own beliefs.

Concepts similar to those which underlie Makah religious belief occur among whites. The power concept has its close parallels in the professions of the faith healers and spiritualistic churches found throughout the country. The belief in the presence of the spirits of the dead is still widespread among the whites. The central position of these concepts in the religious beliefs of the Makah, irrespective of whether or not they belong to a church or what their church is, is not as easily paralleled.

Moreover, the power concept is found as thoroughly embedded in the traditions of the Makah as it is within their expressions of their present beliefs. With respect to religious beliefs, little of the traditional culture can be said to be latent ; for though an individual may maintain that the Makah today do not have power experiences as their ancestors did, his belief in the reality of the ancestral experiences indicates that his concept of the universe is fundamentally the same as that reflected in the tradition which he regards as dead. His traditions assure him that there is power in the universe which can be experienced by man. Details in this tradition that deal with the ritual for obtaining power or with the direction of the power once obtained may well be regarded as part of the latent culture, for there is little evidence that these are manifested now in any form save within the recitation of the tradition. But belief in power is manifest throughout the culture of the Makah.

The effect of this belief is not necessarily to prevent assimilation. The Makah have shown themselves capable of fitting themselves into the structure of religious organizations offered to them by the whites. In one case, they have accepted Presbyterianism, which has no place within it for their concept of power. This presents no particular problem to Makah members of the church, who seem to obtain real satisfaction from their experience within the church while simultaneously they preserve their power concepts outside the context of the church. In another case, they have accepted a church, the Apostolic, which itself professes a concept of power. The Shaker church, founded by Indians and under no direct control from organized Christianity, is still more sympathetic to their concept of power.

The Shaker church might be considered to be an anti-assimilation movement crystallized about the belief in power. In 1942, this was certainly not true, for the entire church was in the process of amalgamating with the Pentecostal church, a Christian group, founded by whites and largely composed of white members, though it proselytizes among all races. Many of the older Shakers object to the innovations in the service and to the projected union with the Pentecostal church, but there is no organized opposition in Neah Bay. Even that remnant of the Makah population which refers to itself as 'Heathen', appears sporadically at the services of the churches and makes no attempt to isolate itself from the whites. Those who belong to this group cannot be regarded as a religious body, in any event, for they are not organized into a definite group in opposition to the churches, nor do they have any public ceremonies. Finally, the beliefs of the 'Heathens' do not differ radically from those held by members of the churches.

No nativistic movement then exists, in the sense of an organized anti-white group which attempts to revive the traditional religious concepts of the people. Instead, the Makah have found their beliefs not incompatible with close association with whites in the same Christian organizations.

CHAPTER IX

CONCLUSION

THE preceding chapters have been devoted to a detailed examination of the way in which the Makah live today : how they view themselves ; how they get along with other Americans ; the beliefs they hold that operate in their relations with each other. Through the discussion has run the theme of assimilation into American society, for during much of the past eighty years the Makah as a people have been subject to measures for promoting this assimilation.

The evidence indicates that the Makah have been assimilated successfully to the extent that the forms of their culture today are largely derived from the whites, and in manipulating these forms they co-operate with the whites in large measure. There has thus developed an interacting society including both Makah and whites, in which either may fulfil certain of the same rôles. But though Makah and whites live together in the same village, work together on the same jobs, trade together at the same establishments, and visit together in each others' homes, the Makah remain a distinct group. There are principles or theories controlling Makah behaviour where it affects other Makah or where it deals with the world of religion which do not underlie the behaviour of whites in comparable situations, and which do not govern the Makah in their relations with whites. There is a body of traditional associations or meanings common to the Makah, but not shared with the whites.[1] Finally, the Makah exist in a political structure which is not shared with the whites, and they continue to think of themselves as a distinctive people in contrast to the whites. All these indicate that the two groups have not merged into one body with a common culture.

---

[1] Linton distinguishes between *form* and *meaning* aspects of trait complexes. His distinction seems useful, though in using these terms I am not following him in applying them specifically to trait complexes. See Linton, 1936, pp. 403-4. The terms 'principles' or 'theories' as I use them refer to phenomena which seem comparable to Kluckhohn's 'idea patterns' or 'sanctioned patterns' rather than to his 'configurations', for they can be given explicit statement by members of the group. See Kluckhohn, 1943, p. 215.

THE SUCCESS OF THE PROGRAMME

For generations the Makah Reservation has been a testing ground in which agents have laboured to mould a people to a pattern imported from beyond the limits of their own society in order to enable them to take their places as members of a larger society than their own group. Similar experiments have been attempted on many other Indian reservations. Yet even a casual acquaintance with the literature suggests that the Makah have been more successfully assimilated than most Indian groups, both with respect to the acceptance of inter-group associations, and with respect to the degree to which cultural differences have been obliterated. This is true even when the comparison is made with tribes which have been an equal length of time under the mandate of the Indian Service.

Such variations in the state of assimilation of people who presumably were subjected to much the same administrative attempts—since agents on all reservations were expected to carry out the broad policies aimed at assimilation—raises the question whether the present condition of a group can throw light upon the efficacy of assimilation programmes. It may well be that the degree of assimilation which a group exhibits is due to some factors inherent within their culture which lead them to take on or reject the culture presented to them, to accept or reject the possibility of associating themselves with those outside their group.[1]

This possibility, however, is an alternative hypothesis which is completely beyond the scope of this study, though I recognize that it is in itself significant. At this late date, it would be fool-hardy to attempt to measure the original resistance of the Makah to culture change ; it would probably be equally difficult to measure that of any group chosen for control. It seems more fruitful to seek an explanation for the relative success of Makah assimilation in the factors which conditioned the impingement of the programme upon them.

Two factors seem to be basic, though one operated to force

[1] See Barnouw, 1950, p. 76 : ' Those differences which we observed in Chippewa and Dakota acculturation were not only the results of contrasting socio-economic conditions ; they reflected as well emotional responses and attitudes characteristic of personality structures which had been moulded by different cultural environments.'

the Makah into conformity with the terms of the policies laid out for them to follow, and the other was more effective in permitting them to make a successful adjustment to the whites who were not fostering the policies among them. The first factor is that of size and concentration of the population : the Makah could be regimented effectively as larger and more scattered tribes could not. The second factor is that of relative economic stability which kept the group from sinking to a lower subsistence level than that which they had when the whites first came. The Indian Service in its work was not faced with the problem of inculcating a people with a standard of living and customs which they had no resources to support, as it was in many areas. The Makah in their contacts with whites were not a pauper group debarred from effective interaction on the ground of poverty.

Economic Stability

With many American Indian groups, the policies of the Indian Service began to operate at a time after the tribes had been broken in warfare with the whites and their original economic adjustments destroyed either by a radical reduction in the area available for their support or because of the exhaustion of their resources. The context within which the Indian agents had to work was not one conducive to great success in establishing a new dispensation, since a life supported by inadequate rations on a restricted reservation was not a satisfying substitute for the old pre-agency days. This was particularly true of the Plains Indians whose subsistence base was wiped out with the vanishing of the buffalo herds. Attempts to introduce a new base in the form of agriculture and stock-raising failed in the ' civilizing ' effect which they were expected to produce and also failed to provide even an adequate living base. This was at least partially due to the unfavourable environment which led to frequent crop failures. The result seems to have been that members of the tribes of this area made few attempts to adjust themselves to ' civilization '. Instead they tended to turn back towards an idealization of the past. There was not enough vitality within their economic life to lead them into new channels of activity.[1]

Groups in the Eastern Woodland, and in the Plains as well,

[1] See Mekeel, 1936 (Dakota) ; Erickson, 1939 (Dakota) ; Goldfrank, 1943 (Blood) ; Elkin, 1940 (Northern Arapaho).

rapidly changed their whole manner of life, under the influence of new stimuli reaching them by way of increased markets for their goods and new material techniques, in the early days of their contact with the whites, without serious disruption to their group life. But this seemed to rest largely upon their possession of adequate resources to allow them to expand their economy and enter into economic relationships with the whites. It was the depletion of their resources to a point where the people could no longer adequately provide for themselves even in terms of their original standards of living, and the concomitant attempt to introduce occupations completely foreign to the groups, which raised barriers to the further inclusion of American standards into their cultures. Once reduced to pauperdom, their poverty was as effective in conditioning the attitude of the whites towards acceptance of them as equals as any other factor in the situation.[1]

The Makah, unlike these other groups, have never had their economy so disrupted that they have been forced to turn to occupations for which they had no previous training. Attempts to introduce agriculture and stock-raising among them met with less success than it did in the Plains, but this did not hinder their making an effective adjustment to the economic systems of the invading whites. At the same time as they came under the authority of the Indian Service, they found themselves in a position where they could exploit more profitably their traditional subsistence resources because the presence of the whites in neighbouring areas made available to them new techniques for application within their usual occupations and also opened to them new markets for disposing of their surpluses. In their own canoes, and later boats, and in the passing steamers, they had transport for their goods to the markets provided by the cities. In their economic enterprises, they learned to co-operate effectively with whites. Indeed, for many years while sealing was the mainstay of tribal existence, many of the seal hunters were in a position to enjoy a higher standard of living than was their Indian agent. One agent commented, 'These Makah Indians are really much better off as a whole than many settlements of white people on the Sound or elsewhere.'[2] Even in more recent years, with the depletion of the fishing banks and the closing of

[1] See Keesing, 1939 ('Menomini Indians of Wisconsin').
[2] See *Report of the Commissioner for Indian Affairs*, 1894, p. 317.

sealing, members of the tribe have not been dependent as a group on rations or government assistance. Wage work for the agency also has played a secondary role—the Makah have either been independent fishermen or have found employment at terms comparable to those which whites receive. Because there has always been the possibility of obtaining at least subsistence from fishing, they have never been forced to receive lower wages than others for comparable work.

The end of their independence therefore did not completely disrupt the old adjustments of the group—their energies could still find outlets through traditional occupations which continued to be rewarding. Though they were dominated by their agents politically, prevented from carrying out many of the forms of their culture, and forced to see their children taken from them with the explicit promise that they were to be trained in such a manner that they would lose their identity with the group, they were actively engaged in reaping the substantial benefits of their economic pursuits and finding themselves in a position to compete effectively with the whites in this field. There was then less need for them to cling to their old customs, and the children who did return to the tribe found themselves able to obtain incomes which assured the living standards acquired in the schools. At the same time, the whites with whom they came in contact— who themselves were economically oriented—recognized their enterprise and gave them some measure of respect for their abilities in this field.

Linton has suggested :

There have been many cases of contact in which [nativistic movements] have not arisen at all. The reasons for this seem to be so variable and in many cases so obscure that nothing like a satisfactory analysis is possible. The most that we can say is that nativistic movements are unlikely to arise in situations where both societies are satisfied with their current relationships, or where societies which find themselves at a disadvantage can see that their condition is improving.[1]

This seems borne out by the evidence supplied by the adjustment of the Makah. Their relations to the whites seem to be largely conditioned by their relative economic security and by their

[1] See Linton, 1943, p. 234.

ability to compete on equal terms with them in occupations which they learn in childhood and which are tied in with their own goals. From the whites they borrow freely to ensure their continued success in this field under changing conditions. To those whites with whom they are thus on a plane of give and take, they make an adjustment with considerable ease ; their frustrations because of cultural and political domination on the other hand have affected primarily their adjustment to the agents of the Indian Service who are the symbols of this domination. To some extent, they have tended to consider the two, agents and economic rivals, in separate categories and to make their adjustments in these terms rather than to a blanket white group.[1]

It is thus obvious that if a programme of assimilation is to be successful, it is of primary importance to provide an economic base which will guarantee a people with a return adequate to place them in a position of equality with those to whom they are to be assimilated. The occupations of the two peoples need not necessarily be similar : comparable rewards rather than comparable occupations seem to be the significant factor. Indeed any attempt to disrupt the traditional occupations or means of exploitation of the environment is likely to produce a sudden social and economic maladjustment, the latter resulting in a lowering of the standard of living of the people to be assimilated. This in turn places them at a disadvantage in relations with the other group and thus hinders their acceptance on terms which are acceptable to them, throwing them back upon their own resources. Such a sequence may well give rise to a conscious rejection of any save minimum contacts with the invaders.

This is an obvious element in any attempt at assimilating a group, yet it seems to have received little attention in the various studies of social change made on Indian groups where the

---

[1] The Makah are not the only group in this area who have been able to exploit a favourable economic situation and to raise their standard of living to that of the whites with whom they associate. See Codere, 1950, for a good account of Kwakiutl economic life. See also Smith, 1940b, on the Puyallup of Washington. By 1872 the Puyallup had become partially assimilated. ' Few of them bothered to collect their annuities which amounted to less than a day's wages. They were self-supporting, all of them speaking some English and a few having absolutely no language difficulty. They dressed and lived like Whites ' (p. 31). The development of the Quileute of the Washington coast is very similar to that of the Makah. See Pettitt, 1950.

emphasis is primarily on cultural determinants rather than the permissive factors of economic opportunity or disability.[1] Yet, since the adjustment of Indian groups in the United States must be made to a wealth-minded people, economic opportunity is of vital importance.

With respect to this factor, in the assimilation of the Makah and any other Indian group, we are dealing, however, not so much with a direct feature of the Indian Service assimilation policies as with a subsidiary factor operating in the relationships of the administered group with the whites and thus incidentally facilitating or hindering the task which the administrators have set before them.

Size of Group as a Factor in Assimilation

It may be that left alone in the above circumstances the Makah would have reached an equally successful adjustment in the same length of time. Still, it seems necessary to assume that their present degree of assimilation is at least partially a function of the thorough Americanization programme to which they have been exposed. Both parties to the programme, the agents and the Makah, consider this to be a major influence in affecting the change from aboriginal culture, and while neither are dispassionate, disinterested observers, their testimony is worthy of consideration. The Makah declare that they lost their old customs because government agents forbade them to practise the customs ; they claim that they were ' civilized ' more rapidly than other Indian groups they know because the ' government ' educated them in the ways of civilization.

The ability of a government to perform this feat seems largely determined by the size of the group with which it is faced and the possibility of easy supervision. Where the group is small and concentrated, as were and are the Makah, it is possible for government employees to supervise personally the daily life of the people and institute an effective ban upon cultural forms which meet their disapproval. Every living Makah, with the exception of those children born within the last ten years, has spent his life

[1] In recent years the Indian Service has recognized the rôle of economic factors and insisted that it is of the utmost importance that Indians should be in a position to acquire adequate incomes if they are to find acceptance in the white world.

in close contact with government agents, teachers, etc., who had a mission to Americanize him and sufficient authority vested in them to exercise sanctions if he refused to accept their terms. This effective control, moreover, was from the first initiated with small children and remained as a factor in their lives up to and in adult life.

Because the group was relatively small and its population concentrated in settled villages, the agents were able to obtain control of almost every child for a greater or lesser period and place it in schools run by the government for the express purpose of teaching it American ways of life and preventing it from learning Makah ways. Every Makah over the age of fifty-five, with but five exceptions, spent some years in the government boarding school ; those under that age had less rigid supervision in a day-school in the village but many also attended boarding schools away from the village where their separation from their own people was even more effective. Thus the formative years of almost every Makah were spent partially under the control of people who were American in culture.[1] All were taught English and forced to use this language in their contacts with each other and the employees of the agency. With a medium of communication established, their chances of penetrating into other portions of American life than its material side increased. They were taught also, through bitter experience, that the way to adjust to the presence of the whites was to hide any nonconformities in their own behaviour under a mask of white culture. What the whites did not know could not become a point for discussion or for pressure to change.

In so far as the school situation could ensure it, therefore, every Makah child learned American culture and obtained some proficiency in practising its outward forms before he returned to his group. In most acculturation studies, it is assumed that the contact between two peoples which leads to the transfer of cultural traits takes place at an adult level on rather remote planes. In a case such as this, the contact was so close and long continued that it resembled more the learning situations whereby the individual takes on the forms of his own culture. These

[1] Makah educated at the boarding school were later teachers in the day-school on a number of occasions, but the school was usually taught by someone brought to the reservation for the purpose.

were children who from their early years were living in intimate
contact with adults who were constantly admonishing them,
teaching them, and endeavouring to mould them into replicas
of other American children. This seems adequate explanation
for the conversance which the Makah show with American
culture, both in its forms and in its meanings.

But it does not necessarily explain the replacement of Makah
culture by American in the context of their own lives. Other
groups of Indians are known where schoolchildren returned to
the tribe and abandoned in so far as they could the behaviour
fostered by their school training while they painfully re-educated
themselves into the life of their own group. Why then did the
Makah so signally fail to do this ?

One explanation must surely include the successful economic
adjustments which the Makah were making at this time, which
placed a premium on acquaintance with white culture and
rewarded the individual for retaining the customs he had learned.
But the size of the group to which he returned is also a factor
which must be considered. With almost every Makah child a
participant in the school experience, those who returned to the
village life found themselves still in contact with others who had
shared this experience. They may have discovered themselves
to be a generation of misfits with a hybrid culture, out of contact
with their relatives of older generations. But in their own
age group, it was the child who had somehow missed the school
experience who found himself a misfit, differing from the
majority of his generation. The reabsorption of the schoolchildren into the tribe was thus made more difficult, for it was not
the re-education of isolated individuals unsupported by any large
group, but the re-education of a whole generation. Nor was it
an effort which had to be made only once ; it had to be made
again and again with each returning group of students.

Perhaps the Makah group could have performed the feat of
reducing each generation of schoolchildren to conformity with
its own standards, with the concomitant inhibition of behaviour
learned in the schools. It was not permitted to attempt the feat.
The agent and his officials were on hand to see that the effects of
the school were not dissipated. Those who had attended school
were kept to the standards of behaviour which they had learned,
even though this kept them from participation in the life of the

rest of their group. In a large group where personal super-vision is impossible because of great distances or scant supervisory personnel, such interdictions are ineffective. Even with a small group, such as the Makah, strict enforcement could not always be obtained, and supervision could on occasion be evaded. But Makah schoolchildren returned to live close by the headquarters of their agent where he might see them daily, where he could hear the sound of drums and voices if any Indian gathering were attempted, where he could interfere in their daily lives and summarily call them to account for behaviour contrary to that with which they were expected to conform.

We know that for many years the Indian Service placed a ban on most of the social activities and religious ceremonies of their Indian charges, including the Makah. Thus as the young people returned to the tribe, they had little opportunity to learn the forms of Makah culture from actual participation. As they lived with the older people, they were instructed in such of the old life as could be transmitted verbally. But the attempt to put this instruction into practice brought them into collision with the agency.

To escape from agency interference, it was necessary to leave the reservation. There were Indian groups within reach of their canoes who were less rigidly supervised than they themselves, but life in these groups could not reinforce that which was specifically Makah in their culture. It was also possible to move out into white settlements, but there the customs and language learned in the schools provided more effective adjustments than did the customs they might learn as Makah. Nowhere did there remain any large body of people relatively untouched by agency influences which could serve as a reservoir of Makah culture from which the formal organizations of their group could be reintro-duced if there should be any relaxation of the pressure for conformity to white standards. Nor was there any literature for the group to use in reconstructing its former life, free from the distortions which time and retrospective falsification play upon verbal tradition.

In the meantime, year by year, a larger proportion of the group had been in the government schools, a larger proportion of the people could speak English, a larger proportion had been kept from effective contact with their own people while they learned

the ways of the whites. Each year the old, who were the con-
servators of Makah traditions, died. With them went the vivid
reality of the old culture, to be replaced by verbal traditions
repeated by those who had never participated in the old ways or
who had but dim and far-off recollections dulled by years of
school and the daily routine of the reservation life.

When the pressure for conformity was finally relaxed, with
the change in Indian Service policy which now encouraged
Indians to incorporate a large measure of their own old customs
into their present life if they desired to do so, they found that those
who knew the old ways were gone. The Makah were now a
hybrid group, both physically and culturally. Those who were
the bearers of Makah culture knew only the verbalization of
most aspects of the tradition ; they had lived most of their lives
in terms of adjustments which included both Makah and whites,
and the majority of their adjustments were recognized as customs
obtained from whites or sufficiently congruent with white
customs to arouse no antagonism in their mentors. These were
now their culture—the other was only tradition, of whose truth
they were often uncertain.

It seems clear then that it is possible to reorganize the life of a
group of people completely under a programme of assimilation,
and bring them to a stage where they willingly incorporate the
formal behaviour of their mentors. In this measure, a programme for enforced assimilation can be said to be successful in
obtaining the results at which it aimed.

The Failures of the Programme

Today the great-grandchildren of the first people to attend
the agency schools are the young citizens of the tribe, just beginning to take control of the tribal organization and of much of
the social life of the village. These same people are the children
and grandchildren of the students of the boarding school where
the agents attempted to institute a complete and radical break
with the past through separating the children from their parents
and from contact with their own people. They themselves
have attended the agency day-school, and more recently the
consolidated local school. In comparison with immigrant
groups from other continents, these people represent fourth- and
fifth-generation Americans, though it was not their ancestors

who came to America, but America which came to their ancestors. And yet, in the Makah group, even today, where there
has been a better adjustment than in many Indian groups subjected to similar measures, and where the situation has been
favourable to the policies used, there has not been complete
assimilation. Cultural differences still persist; and even more
importantly, the people of this generation have not identified
themselves completely with those upon whose behaviour they
have been trained to pattern their lives.

Traditional Culture

The agency programme has been less successful in dealing
with the meaning aspect of culture than it has with the form
aspect. In large areas of behaviour, the life of the Makah today
is oriented by theories or ' sanctioned idea patterns ' which do not
find expression in the same manner or to the same extent in the
life of white groups, and which govern primarily the behaviour
of Makah in their relationships with each other rather than in
interaction with whites.

It would be naïve to regard these theories or meanings which
distinguish the present culture of the Makah as their unchanged
heritage from their ancestors, even though the theories are
congruent with the traditions of old Makah culture which are
recited by members of the group. Culture is responsive to the
situations within which its bearers find themselves ; and though
there is good evidence to support the belief that the different
aspects of culture respond at a differential rate, there is no reason
to expect that the traditional culture of a group can be so resistant
as to survive unchanged the thorough reorganization of the
formal life of the group. It is tempting to regard the theories
of expected behaviour—of kinship solidarity, rivalry, and others
of their ilk—as structures which persist regardless of their content. But very likely the most significant changes in the traditional culture occur with respect to the meaning of the different
customs which are described, just because the meanings are
subjective and find only indirect expression in actual behaviour.
It is possible, therefore, that the traditions reflect the theories
because they have been brought into conformity with the
theories rather than vice versa.

Two forces are at work to bring about the steady revision of the tradition to meet the requirements of the present Makah. Where their behaviour is contrary to the customs of the whites, or where it finds no adequate support from an appeal to white customs, their justification can be derived by an appeal to their own traditions. Tradition then becomes a mythology justifying present behaviour by giving it a basis in established and tested custom rather than a history explaining the origin of this behaviour.

On the other hand, there is also a tendency to revise the tradition to bring it into conformity with the standards of the whites. This may be done purely unconsciously as the group comes to accept these standards as its own and projects them into the past as the only adequate explanations of certain behaviour. If the observer from another culture is prone to misunderstand the implications of a custom he observes or hears described because of the barrier interposed by the unconscious assumptions fostered upon him by his culture, so too is the descendant of the practitioners of customs which have disappeared from all save tradition. He also views the custom in terms of unconscious assumptions, and these are fostered within him by the way he lives at present and not by what his ancestors did in the past. The tendency to distort the tradition may also occur more or less consciously, especially where the group has been made to feel inferior on the grounds of its original culture. The people then tend to protect themselves from such charges of inferiority—and to rehabilitate their ancestors—by equating the customs attacked with those found among the whites, brushing aside the differences in form to point out the similarity in meanings behind the two sets of customs. Some Makah, for instance, maintain steadfastly that their ancestors believed in but one God, and indignantly repudiate the suggestion that they prayed to objects such as sun and moon. I have often been told, ' Before the whites came, the old people had a religion just like the whites, only they didn't have Jesus. That's all we got from the whites. I think the Indians are the true Christians.' The puberty potlatch is equated with a debutante party, potlatches with Christmas giving.

In any group as thoroughly acquainted with all aspects of white culture as the Makah, there is consistent distortion of the tradition to equate the underlying meanings of the two cultures.

There is also, however, the tendency to project differences in behaviour and the underlying codes that govern behaviour back into the tradition to ensure its validation by custom.

Therefore the existence of themes within the present Makah culture which differentiate it from the culture of the surrounding whites is not an indication that the meaning aspect of culture has been left unchanged by the existence of the agency and its attempts to replace Makah culture in all its aspect with that of the whites, and by the contact with the many whites whom the Makah have known more or less intimately. It does seem, however, an indication that those in charge of the Makah were not able to interfere to the same extent in this aspect of culture, nor were they able to insist upon the development of premises similar to those found in white culture. A programme for assimilation can deal directly only with formal behaviour. Banning certain forms, and instituting others, gives no assurance that the underlying assumptions of a people will change directly with the change in the formal aspects of their culture. The premises must change since the life of the people has been drastically affected, but there is a possibility that they will not change to conform with those of the group toward which assimilation is urged. Even if the agents of the programme become aware of the difference in premises, it is difficult to demand conformity in this field since there is no way of judging conformity save by its outward manifestations. You may ban the manifestations, but you cannot directly affect the theories or beliefs or attitudes which underlie the behaviour and which give the behaviour its meaning to those who practise it.

As with the Makah, this aspect of culture may lie impervious to interference from outside agents under the mask of formal conformity in spheres of behaviour where adherence to set patterns can be demanded. This does not mean, however, as already pointed out, that the world of meanings lies impervious to conformity in other spheres, to knowledge of forms and beliefs held by whites and others with whom the people may come in contact, to changes which occur within the life of the group itself in response to changes in its biological, environmental, and social conditions.

With the Makah, it has proved that even eighty years have not been a sufficient length of time to efface the difference in premises, though they have been a small group completely dominated politically by officials of the white world. Eighty years, during which it has been obvious to the Makah that there was no possibility of escape from this domination, have still left them with a residue of behaviour and belief which distinguishes them from white groups in the United States. This has happened though there has been no agency for the perpetuation of their own traditions save in the very people who have been acted upon by the programme—for the Makah have never used their literacy to reduce their traditions to writing and thus ensure their survival.

Behaviour oriented to the System

In the meantime, while the policies for assimilation were being administered to impel the generations toward this goal, systems of behaviour were developing in reaction to the policies themselves. The agency, the reservation, and the status of government wards left their impress upon the people by creating the tribal organization, peculiar forms of land holding, special attitudes toward the government. Furthermore, the position which the programme placed them in with respect to whites seems to have left its impress upon the people in the form of attitudes directed toward the whites. At the end of their period of domination, they emerge with a large portion of their lives oriented to the system in which they have been encased rather than toward taking their places independently of it. They also emerge with some feeling of bitterness toward the group from whence their administrators came and which has been held up to them as a behavioural pattern generation after generation, even though the Makah are a group small enough and in intensive enough contact with whites so that each individual within it has friendships with individual whites which have served to mitigate the bitterness.

Today, there is little reason to expect the end of this type of behaviour differentiating the Makah from the whites. The Makah are capable as individuals of acting within the white world, and do so sporadically as isolated individuals. But further assimilation is checked by the reservation system and the tribal organization, which are now regarded as permanent features by the Indian Service. They place a premium on the continuance of the Makah as a distinctive group. Since we are here evaluating measures for assimilation, rather than the value of assimilation itself, the question of the justification of the new policies of the Indian Service does not enter. It is obvious, however, that the crystallization of a social structure on the basis of hereditary membership is a barrier to assimilation, especially if adherence to membership within the structure is rewarded by special privileges and brings few penalties as over against non-membership, while at the same time the abandonment of membership in order to assimilate completely with the white group is penalized by the withdrawal of these privileges.

Mr. Collier, former Commissioner for Indian Affairs, has declared :

In those cases where geographically, as an existent fact, the Indian is isolated from other races, of course the Reorganization Act does not overcome the isolation. In those cases where, as in at least half of the Indian country, the Indian community is coterminous or intermingled with non-Indian settlement, the Reorganization Act does not stop that mingling. The Reorganization Act 'segregates' exactly as much as, and no more than, a church affiliation or mutual benefit association, cooperative store, garden city suburb, co-partnership enterprise, municipal corporation or in fact almost any organization among whites which commands loyalty.[1]

Perhaps this may be so in some cases, but the fundamental theory of membership and the peculiar status given to members by their relationship to the United States Government make this doubtful. At Neah Bay, it prevents the organization of the joint Indian-white community on a political basis, though today it is difficult to regard the Indians by themselves as representing the significant social unit. The village of Neah Bay seems to be the natural local unit rather than the tribe. Moreover, it leaves some members of the community in a preferred status which they are likely to justify by dwelling upon past wrongs suffered by their group or other groups of Indians at the hands of the whites, some of whom are also their own ancestors. On the other hand, it means that the whites are likely to justify this status on the basis of a congenital inferiority which renders Indians incapable of joining in white society on an equal basis, or to decry it as a prerogative justified by nothing but historical accident.

[1] Collier, 1944, p. 423.

APPENDIX

In 1939, according to the Indian Service records, there were 411 Makah on the tribal roll. The population was composed of 226 males and 185 females. Some 342 Makah were living on their reservation in the village of Neah Bay.[1] No further details on the composition of this population are available from the published records. However, in 1942, I made an informal census of the Makah living at Neah Bay. At that time, 357 were living on the reservation. In the following table I have classified these people into age and sex groups. I have insufficient information to do the same for Makah who were living off the reservation.

TABLE IV

AGE AND SEX DISTRIBUTION

Age Group	M. & F.	% of Total	M.	% of Total M.	F.	% of Total F.
80 years. . .	3	0·8	2	1·0	1	0·5
60–80 ,, . . .	27	7·5	17	9·1	10	5·8
40–60 ,, . . .	48	13·4	30	16·0	18	10·5
25–40 ,, . . .	68	19·0	39	20·8	29	17·0
15–25 ,, . . .	67	18·7	29	15·4	38	22·3
0–15 ,, . . .	144	40·3	70	37·4	74	43·5
Totals . . .	357		187		170	

M. & F., males and females combined ; M., males ; F., females.

Those over 60 years of age rarely know their exact age in years, but I was able to make fairly close estimates by taking certain key persons, fixing their ages on the basis of events which they could remember, and then fitting other people into the series with reference to them, since people knew those older or younger than themselves.

Only one member of the tribe was born before the establishment of the reservation, and he was a tiny child when the agency was first built. Most of those in the group from 60 to 80 years old, spent much of their childhood in the agency boarding school, and

[1] *Statistical Supplement to the Annual Report of the Commissioner of Indian Affairs for 1939*, p. 14. This is the most recent published information for the time when I made the study.

many of them are the children of the first students of the early day-school established at the very beginning of the agency.

The Makah regard themselves as a remnant of a once powerful and numerous group. They have a tradition that in their grand-fathers' days, before the smallpox epidemics swept through the tribe, many thousand people inhabited the Makah villages about the Cape. Old people say that they have heard that once upon a time a single village could muster five hundred warriors. At that time there were so many people living in one village alone that not all knew each other. When the smallpox came and wiped out many of the inhabitants, children were left orphaned whom nobody could identify.

These tales are doubtless exaggerations which help to enhance Makah importance in the eyes of their descendants. They also serve to emphasize the misdeeds of the whites who brought the epidemics and such diseases as tuberculosis which have brought the tribe to its present low ebb. Actually, nothing is known about the former population of the region.[1] In 1861, the Indian Service recorded 654 Makah, and this is the first approximate estimate we have of their number. This was six years after the disastrous 1854 smallpox epidemic when the tribe was much reduced in numbers.[2]

Since 1861, there appears to have been a fairly steady decrease in numbers. I have not been able to obtain population figures for each year, as only 32 out of the 80 years of the agency are represented by published census figures. Table V gives the population for the nearest year in the beginning of each decade to show the decline.[3]

The death rate is undoubtedly still higher than that for the general American population, although the Indian Service in recent years has made a considerable effort to reduce the incidence of tuberculosis

---

[1] Mooney estimated that the Makah villages contained about 2,000 people in 1780 at the time when the whites first appeared in the area. See Mooney, 1928, p. 15. For the havoc wrought by the early smallpox epidemics, see Hancock, 1927, pp. 181–2.

[2] It is not clear whether the 1861 census covered all people then resident in the villages or only those regarded as permanent members of the villages. Moreover, for many years the agency censuses were subject to a number of errors. Some of the agents are accused of padding their census rolls in order to increase the apparent number of their charges. This was offset, however, by the fact that the Makah objected to attempts to enumerate them and when-ever possible hid their children when the census recorder appeared. In later years, the census became more accurate, but for a period the Makah were under the same jurisdiction with a number of other small tribes, and for this period the published population figures are usually for all the people under the agency, and are not broken down by tribe.

[3] Compiled from the *Reports of the Commissioner of Indian Affairs*.

U*

and venereal disease. That the population has remained fairly constant during the past twenty years must be due to a fairly high birth rate, but from the information I have available it is impossible to

TABLE V

Year	Population	Year	Population	Year	Population
1861 654		1890 454		1920 413	
1870 558		1901 413		1932 412	
1883 507		1910 432		1939 411	

compute the fertility rate. The Makah themselves feel that there is no longer a danger of the tribe dying out. They take a lively interest in each new birth, and boast, ' You can't call us vanishing Americans any more.'

BIBLIOGRAPHY

Starred items (*) deal with the Makah and other Nootka-speaking groups.

ABERLE, S. D., 'The Pueblo Indians of New Mexico, Their Land, Economy and Civil Organization', *Memoirs of the American Anthropological Association*, No. 70, 1948.

ANDREWS, C. L., 'The Wreck of the St. Nicholas', *The Washington Historical Quarterly*, **13**, 27–31, 1922.

ANONYMOUS : *A Spanish Voyage to Vancouver and the Northwest Coast of America*. (Translated by CECIL JANE.) London : Argonaut Press, 1930.

* 'Indian Trouble at Neah Bay', *Washington Standard*. April 12, p. 3, col. 1, 1866.

* 'Neah Bay Indians have Commenced War against Whiskey', *Washington Standard*. June 28, p. 2, col. 3, 1873.

* 'Editorial pertaining to the difficulties between H. A. Webster and the Indian Department', *Washington Standard*. January 14, p. 2, col. 1–2, 1873.

* 'The Store of William Gallick at Neah Bay was burned a few days ago', *Washington Standard*. September 15, p. 2, col. 7, 1882.

* 'Allotting Land to the Makah Tribe', *Seattle Post Intelligencer*. July 25, 1907.

ARESTAD, SVERRE, 'The Norwegians in the Pacific Coast Fisheries', *The Pacific Northwest Quarterly*, **34**, 3–17, 1943.

BANCROFT, HUBERT, *The Native Races of the Pacific States*, Vol. I, 208–21. London, Longmans, Green & Company, 1875.

BARNETT, H. G., 'The Coast Salish of Canada', *American Anthropologist*, **40**, 118–41, 1938.

'The Nature of the Potlatch', *American Anthropologist*, **40**, 349–58, 1938.

BARNOUW, VICTOR, 'Acculturation and Personality among the Wisconsin Chippewa', *Memoirs of the American Anthropological Association*, No. 72, 1950.

* BEAN, MARGARET, 'Whale Hunters of the Olympic Peninsula', *Travel*, **57**, 23–25, 1931.

* BRODERSON, PAUL, 'Pelagic Seal Hunting as Carried on by the Makah and Quileute Indians', *Indians at Work*, **6**, 12–16, 1939.

CODERE, HELEN, 'Fighting with Property', *Monographs of the American Ethnological Society*, No. 18, 1950.

COLLIER, JOHN, 'Collier Replies to Mekeel', *American Anthropologist*, **46**, 432, 1944.

* COLSON, ELIZABETH, 'New Customs at Neah Bay', *Radcliffe Quarterly*, **26**, 18–21, 1942.

* 'The Assimilation of an American Indian Group', *Journal of the Rhodes-Livingstone Institute*, **8**, 1–13, 1949.

CURTIS, EDWARD, 'Salish Tribes of the Coast', *The North American Indians*, IX. Norwood, Mass., Plimpton Press, 1910.

★ CURTIS, EDWARD, 'Nootka, Haida', *The North American Indians*, XI. Norwood, Mass., Plimpton Press, 1916.

★ DENSMORE, FRANCES, 'Conscious Effort toward Physical Perfection among the Makah Indians', *American Anthropologist*, **25**, 544–67, 1923.

★ 'Field Studies of Indian Music', *Smithsonian Miscellaneous Collections*, **76**, No. 10, 119–27, 1924 ; **78**, No. 7, 247–54, 1927.

★ 'The Language of the Makah Indians', *American Speech*, **2**, No. 5, 1927.

★ 'The True Story of a Little Stone Image', *American Anthropologist*, **30**, 311–13, 1928.

★ 'Nootka and Quileute Music', *Bulletin of the American Bureau of Ethnology*, **124**, 1939.

★ 'Notes on the Indians' Belief in the Friendliness of Nature', *Southwestern Journal of Anthropology*, **4**, 94–7, 1948.

★ DORSEY, GEORGE, 'Games Played by the Makah Indians of Neah Bay', *American Antiquarian*, **23**, 69–73, 1901.

★ DRUCKER, P., 'The Northern and Central Nootkan Tribes', *Bulletin of the Bureau of American Ethnology*, **144**, 1951.

DUNN, JOHN, *The Oregon Territory*. Philadelphia, Zieber & Co., 1845.

ELKIN, HENRY, 'The Northern Arapaho of Wyoming', pp. 207–55, in R. Linton (ed.), *Acculturation in Seven American Indian Tribes*. New York, Appleton-Century, 1940.

★ ELYEA, WINIFRED, 'The history of Tatoosh Island', *The Washington Historical Quarterly*, **20**, 223–7, 1929.

ERICKSON, ERICK HOMBURGER, 'Observations on Sioux Education', *Journal of Psychology*, **7**, 101–56, 1939.

FORDE, C. DARYLL, *Habitat, Economy, and Society*. London, Methuen, 1948 (6th edition).

FRACHTENBERG, LEO J., 'The Ceremonial Societies of the Quileute Indians', *American Anthropologist*, **23**, 320–52, 1921.

FULLER, GEORGE W., *A History of the Pacific Northwest*. New York, Knopf, 1938 (2nd edition).

★ GIBBS, GEORGE, 'Tribes of Western Washington and Northwestern Oregon', *Contributions to North American Ethnology*, **1**, Pt. 2, 157–361, 1877.

★ GILLIS, ALICE JANE, *History of Neah Bay Agency*. (Unpublished manuscript in the Library of the University of Washington, n.d.)

GOLDFRANK, ESTHER S., 'The Administrative Program and Changes in Blood Society during the Reservation Period', *Applied Anthropology*, **2**, 18–23, 1943.

GREGORY, HOMER E., and BARNES, KATHLEEN, 'North Pacific Fisheries', *American Council of Pacific Relations, Studies of the Pacific*, **3**, 1939.

GUNTHER, ERNA, 'Klallam Ethnography', *University of Washington Publications in Anthropology*, **1**, No. 5, 1927.

★ 'The Modern Basketry of the Makah', *Indians at Work*, **2**, No. 20, 36–40, 1935.

★ 'A Preliminary Report on the Zoological Knowledge of the Makah', pp. 105–18, in R. Lowie (ed.), *Essays in Anthropology Presented to A. L. Kroeber*. Berkeley, University of California Press, 1936.

★ GUNTHER, ERNA, 'Ethnobotany of Western Washington', *University of Washington Publications in Anthropology*, **10**, No. 1, 1945.

HAEBERLIN, HERMANN, and GUNTHER, ERNA, 'The Indians of Puget Sound', *University of Washington Publications in Anthropology*, **4**, 1–83, 1930.

★ HANCOCK, SAMUEL, *The Narrative of Samuel Hancock, 1845–1860*. New York, Robert M. McBride & Co., 1927.

★ IRVINE, ALBERT, 'How the Makah Obtained Possession of Cape Flattery', *Indian Notes and Monographs*, No. 6, 1921.

★ JEWITT, JOHN R., *The Adventures and Sufferings of John R. Jewitt, only survivor of the ship Boston during a captivity of nearly three years among the Savages of Nootka Sound.* Edinburgh (Constable & Co.) and London (Hurst, Robinson & Co.), 1824.

KANE, PAUL, *Wanderings of an Artist among the Indians of North America.* London, Longmans, 1859.

KEESING, F., 'The Menomini Indians of Wisconsin', *Memoirs of the American Philosophical Society*, No. 10. Philadelphia, 1939.

KELLEY, HALL J., *A Geographical Sketch of that Part of North America called Oregon*, pp. 68–71. Boston, J. Howe, 1830.

KLUCKHOHN, CLYDE, 'Covert Culture and Administrative Problems', *American Anthropologist*, **45**, 213–27, 1943.

★ KOPPERT, VINCENT A., 'Contributions to Clayoquet Ethnology', *Catholic University of America, Anthropological Series*, No. 1, 1930.

LANTIS, MARGARET, 'The Alaskan Whale Cult and its Affinities', *American Anthropologist*, **40**, 438–64, 1938.

LAURIDSEN, G. M. and SMITH, A. A., *The Story of Port Angeles and Clallam County, Washington.* Seattle, Lowman & Hanford, 1937.

LEIGHTON, CAROLINE C., *Life at Puget Sound, 1865–1881.* Boston, Lee & Shepard, 1884.

LEWIS, ALBERT B., 'Tribes of the Columbia Valley and the Coast of Washington and Oregon', *Memoirs of the American Anthropological Association*, No. 1, 147–209, 1905–7.

★ LEWIS, LUCIEN M., 'The Last of the Makah Chiefs, Chief Peter'. (Clipping dated November 26, 1905. In C. B. Bagley Scrapbook, No. 5, p. 109, University of Washington Library.)

LINTON, RALPH, *The Study of Man.* New York, Appleton-Century, 1936. *Acculturation in Seven American Indian Tribes.* New York, Appleton-Century, 1940. 'Nativistic Movements', *American Anthropologist*, **45**, 230–40, 1943.

★ MCCURDY, JAMES G., *By Juan de Fuca's Strait.* Portland, Metropolitan Press, 1937.

★ MARCHISTUN, HENRY, 'Whale Hunting with Makah Indians off Cape Flattery', *Seattle Post Intelligencer*, February 18, 1906.

★ MEANY, EDMUND, 'Shaker Church of the Indians', *Seattle Post Intelligencer*, October 22, 1905.

★ 'Story of Quillayutes', *Seattle Post Intelligencer*. (Undated clipping seen in C. B. Bagley Scrapbook, No. 12, p. 100, University of Washington Library.)

MEANY, EDMUND, *History of the State of Washington.* New York, Macmillan, 1924. (Revised edition.)

MEARES, JOHN, *Voyages made in the Years 1788 and 1798, from China to the Northwest Coast of America,* Vols. 1 and 2. London, Logographic Press, n.d.

MEKEEL, H. SCUDDER, ' The Economy of a Modern Teton Dakota Community ', *Yale University Publications in Anthropology,* No. 6, 1936.

DE MOFRAS, DUFLAT, *Travels on the Pacific Coast,* Vol. II (Margarita Eyer Wilbur, ed.). Santa Ana, California, Fine Arts Press, 1937.

MOONEY, JAMES, ' The Ghost Dance Religion ', *Report of the Bureau of American Ethnology,* 14, Pt. 2, Chap. 8, 1896.

' The Aboriginal Population of North America North of Mexico ', *Smithsonian Miscellaneous Collections,* 80, No. 7, 1928.

★ MOSER, CHARLES, *Reminiscences of the West Coast of Vancouver Island.* Victoria, B.C., Acme Press, 1926.

★ NIPPGEN, M. J., ' La Chasse à la baleine chez les Indiens makah ', *L'Ethnographie,* new series, No. 6, 59–64, 1922.

NOON, JOHN A., ' Law and Government of the Grand River Iroquois ', *Viking Fund Publications in Anthropology,* No. 12, 1949.

OLSON, RONALD L., ' The Quinault Indians ', *University of Washington Publications in Anthropology,* 6, No. 1, 1936.

PETTITT, GEORGE A., ' The Quileute of La Push, 1775–1945 ', *Anthropological Records of the University of California,* 14, 1, 1950.

PICKERING, CHARLES, ' The Races of Man ', in *United States Exploring Expedition,* 9, Boston, Little & Brown, 1848.

PRESBYTERIAN CHURCH IN THE UNITED STATES OF AMERICA : General Assembly, Journal and Statistics. (Consulted for period from 1923 to 1944.)

REAGAN, ALBERT, ' Archaeological Notes on Western Washington and Adjacent British Columbia ', *Proceedings, California Academy of Sciences,* 4th series, 7, No. 1, 1917.

★ ' Certain " Writings " of Northwestern Indians ', *American Anthropologist,* 30, 345–7, 1928.

' Some Additional Myths of the Hoh and Quileute Indians ', *Utah Academy of Sciences, Arts and Letters,* 11, 17–37, 1934.

' Some Traditions of the West Coast Indians ', *Utah Academy of Sciences, Arts and Letters,* 11, 73–93, 1934.

★ SAPIR, EDWARD, ' Some Aspects of Nootka Language and Culture ', *American Anthropologist,* 13, 15–28, 1911.

★ ' A girl's puberty feast among the Nootka ', *Transactions of the Royal Society of Canada,* 7, 67–80, 1913.

★ ' Social Organization of the West Coast Tribes ', *Transactions of the Royal Society of Canada,* Series 3, Vol. 9, 1915.

★ and SWADESH, MORRIS, *Nootka Texts.* Philadelphia, Linguistic Society of America, 1939.

SCAMMON, C. M., ' About the Shores of Puget Sound ', *Overland Monthly,* 7, 277–8, 1871.

SCHEFFER, VICTOR B., ' The Sea Otter on the Washington Coast ', *The Pacific Northwest Quarterly,* 31, 371–88, 1940.

SCOULER, JOHN, ' Journal of a Voyage to N.W. America (1824–1826) ', *Quarterly of the Oregon Historical Society*, 6, 195–6, 205, 1905.

SMITH, MARIAN W., ' The Puyallup-Nisqually ', *Columbia University Contributions to Anthropology*, 32, 1940.

' The Puyallup of Washington ', pp. 3–36, in R. Linton (ed.), *Acculturation in Seven American Indian Tribes*. New York, Appleton-Century, 1940.

SPIER, LESLIE, ' The Distribution of Kinship Systems in North America ', *University of Washington Publications in Anthropology*, 1, No. 2, 69–88, 1925.

' The Prophet Dance of the Northwest and its derivatives, the source of the Ghost Dance ', *General Series in Anthropology*, No. 1, 1935.

' Tribal Distributions in Washington ', *General Series in Anthropology*, No. 3, 1936.

★ SPROAT, G. M., *Scenes and Studies of Savage Life*. London, Smith, Elder & Co., 1868.

★ STARLING, E. A., ' Report of E. A. Starling, Agent for Puget Sound ', in Henry R. Schoolcraft, *Information Respecting the History, Condition and Prospects of the Indian Tribes of the United States*, Part IV, 598–602. Philadelphia, Lippincott, Grambo & Co., 1854.

★ SWADESH, MORRIS, ' Motivations in Nootka Warfare ', *Southwestern Journal of Anthropology*, 4, 76–93, 1948.

SWAN, JAMES, *Three Years Residence in Washington Territory*. New York, Harpers, 1857.

★ ' The Indians of Cape Flattery ', *Smithsonian Contributions to Knowledge*, 220, 1869.

★ ' The Indians of Cape Flattery.' (Newspaper clipping dated 1895, in the C. B. Bagley Scrapbook, No. 2, pp. 68–69, University of Washington Library.)

WAGNER, HENRY R., *Spanish Explorations in the Strait of Juan de Fuca*. Santa Ana, Calif., Fine Arts Press, 1933.

WATERMAN, T. T., ' The Shake Religion of Puget Sound ', *Smithsonian Report for 1922*, pp. 499–507, 1924.

★ ' The Whaling Equipment of the Makah Indians ', *University of Washington Publications in Anthropology*, 1, 1–67, 1920.

UNITED STATES GOVERNMENT PUBLICATIONS :

Reports of the Commissioners of Indian Affairs to the Secretary of the Interior. Years 1854–1947.

Constitution and Bylaws of the Makah Indian Tribe of the Makah Indian Reservation, Washington. 1936.

Corporate Charter of the Makah Indian Tribe of the Makah Indian Reservation, Washington. 1937.

INDEX

Printed in Great Britain by Butler & Tanner Ltd., Frome and London